The Method Ringer's Companion

Also by Steve Coleman

The Bellringer's
Early Companion

The Bellringer's
Bedside Companion

The Bob Caller's
Companion

There are more details about all three of these books on pages 435-437

The Method Ringer's Companion

Steve Coleman

SUE COLEMAN PUBLISHING

Much of this book was first published
as articles in The Ringing World

First published 1995
by Sue Coleman
46 Byfords Road, Huntley
Glos. GL19 3EL

This edition – the fourth – April 2008

ISBN 978-0-9523896-8-2

British Library Cataloguing in Publication Data. A catalogue record for this book is available from the British Library.

Printed in Great Britain by
Antony Rowe Ltd, Chippenham, Wilts

To

MY PARENTS

Who

for some inexplicable reason

do not ring

Contents

Ringing Stedman (cont.)

General Matters

Triples and More

Surprise Minor

The Other Surprise

Something Different

A Word Before We Start

Just in case you're not sure, this is a book about ***method ringing***. It's a book of information, advice, diagrams and tips on all the commonly rung methods from Bob Doubles upwards, and it contains the replies to the many and varied method ringing questions I've been asked over the years.

The sections in bold type are readers' letters and the sections in italics are updates from me. The bits in between are my replies. I'm sure you'd have worked that out anyway, but I thought I'd just mention it.

And now that everything's clear, you can either browse through the index for your favourite subjects, or you can turn straight to Chapter 1.

And we'll have a quiet chat about this and that together.

The Very Beginning

1. Getting into Bob Doubles

Starting from Scratch

I ring at a 10cwt suburban ring of six with a small but dedicated band. I have no trouble with plain hunt and I've been hunting the treble to Bob Doubles for more than a year, but I just can't manage to crack Bob Doubles inside. I've learnt the blue line perfectly and I've read the books, but I still can't get it right. Please help.

K.N.
Greater London

Rest assured, you aren't alone. Throughout the length and breadth of Britain, *countless* ringers are struggling to master Bob Doubles inside. *Hundreds* of small but dedicated bands, just like your own, are waging a never ending battle to lift themselves into method ringing via this most popular of all methods. And since most of them have only one or two experienced ringers – if that – it's not surprising they find the going tough.

So don't despair that you're having difficulty. Quite likely your biggest problem is that several of you are all struggling together. But whatever your problem, straightening out one or two points now really is going to help.

The Building Blocks

So let's begin at the very beginning. When you start on Bob Doubles, you might think it should simply be a matter of learning the blue line and getting stuck in. But it's much too hard for that. Instead there are several important skills you need to learn first – several important ***building blocks*** you need to perfect independently and separately before you even attempt your first plain course. Getting them right beforehand will make everything heaps easier, and the more struggling your band is, the more time you need to spend working on them.

Leading

And the first building block is ***leading***. Of course, you've already done plenty of that, but perhaps not on the bell you're going to ring Bob Doubles on. So make sure you know exactly what it feels and sounds like to lead on *that* bell.

Most likely you can already lead well on the treble, but leading just as well on the Two – let alone the Four or Five – could be another matter. It may be odd struck or difficult to handle, or its view may be obstructed. So get some leading practice on your Bob Doubles bell, preferably in some call changes. Note your position relative to the tenor by eye, and then check the effect carefully by ear. This will pay enormous dividends later, and if you can get someone nice to advise you on your striking, so much the better.

The point is that when you start ringing Bob Doubles, there will be times when you haven't a clue who you should be following. That's how life is. And when that happens, you'll need to know how to lead perfectly the moment your conductor or your counting tells you to. You'll need to be able to look at the tenor and lead spot on by eye, no matter how lost you were moments before.

That will give you a quiet place of calm in the maelstrom

of the method, a fixed point to cling on to while you find your bearings, and a foundation of certainty from which to set off into the remainder of the method. In time, of course, you'll be able to lead perfectly in the middle of a method by rhythm alone. But meanwhile, be prepared.

Plain Hunting

Next comes ***plain hunting*** – another skill you've already acquired – but once again, you may not be so sure about it on *all* the bells.

A larger bell than you're used to will be especially difficult. It will be much less inclined to do what you tell it to and much more inclined to act with a will of its own. Changing direction when you lead or lie may be a real problem, as may hunting down fast enough and ringing close enough over the little bells.

So don't give yourself the difficulty of having to cope with all those things at the same time as struggling with the method. Ring several long blocks of plain hunt on your Bob Doubles bell, and really work at getting it right. Concentrate on your handling, and concentrate on your striking as well – preferably with guidance before, during and after from that nice person again. Aim to get everything as smooth and accurate as possible.

Dodging

And then it's time for a *new* skill. ***Dodging***. A dodge is an entirely different action from anything you've ever done before, both physically and mentally, so you need to practise it. And you need to practise it entirely uncluttered by thoughts of Bob Doubles.

The uncluttered point is vital. Learning to ring Bob Doubles should be like learning to drive a car. No one would suggest you tried your first hill start at a busy road junction in the rush hour, yet a great many learners are expected to try their first dodge in the middle of a course of Bob Doubles. Not surprisingly, they don't make a very good job of it because in those circumstances almost no one would.

Of course they get better, but their improvement can only be slow because they only get to do two dodges in each plain course. In a whole month they may get the opportunity to do no more than 25 dodges. Yet they could do 25 dodges in ten minutes *before* their first plain course, and really get the action right. So before you launch into the method, ask your tower captain for some ***dodging practice.***

Dodging Practice

Dodging practice works like this. You take your proposed bell – the Three, say – and you start ringing rounds. When the rounds have settled down, the conductor calls, "Three, Four, Dodge." He calls during one handstroke and the bells dodge at the next handstroke like this.

```
123456 H
123456 B
123456 H "Three, Four
123456 B        Dodge"
124356 H
123456 B
```

How simple that looks, yet how difficult it is to get right. The bells are only out of rounds for one blow, yet it is far more physical than you might suppose, and it requires a complex mixture of firm pulling and precision placing to get it right. The full instructions are:

At the handstroke of the call

Do nothing different but get ready.

At the next backstroke

Pull a little harder so that you can hold up next handstroke.

At the handstroke of the dodge

Hold up and ring perfectly over the Four – but don't pull too hard because you'll need to ring quicker again at the next backstroke.

At the backstroke of the dodge

Pull in sharply to ring spot on after the Two, but pull through firmly enough to ensure you hold your place at the next handstroke and don't end up ringing after the treble instead.

At the handstroke after the dodge

Revert to your even pulling so that you remain in rounds. Don't pull too hard or you will end up clashing with the Four.

Experienced ringers do all that without even thinking about it. But to begin with you'll need to think about it a lot. The aim is to get your bell perfectly positioned throughout the dodge ***and after***. Keep practising until your dodges are the crisp, sharp dodges that are absolutely essential to good Bob Doubles.

More Dodging Practice

123456 H
123456 B
123456 H "Two, Three
123456 B Dodge"
1**32**456 H
123456 B

And once you can dodge perfectly with the Four, your conductor will call you to dodge with the Two. You must then pull ***in*** at handstroke over the treble, but pull through firmly enough to get back ***up*** over the Two again at the following backstroke. Afterwards, you have to stay exactly in thirds place without rising further up and clashing with the Four. This is effectively a ***down dodge*** rather than the ***up dodge*** which you did before.

A ***down dodge*** is a dodge you do in the middle of a piece of hunting down, and an ***up dodge*** is a dodge you do in the middle of a piece of hunting up. The two dodges feel very different and you'll need a lot of practice at both of them.

After that, you can try ***double dodging*** – which is the top picture – and then ***consecutive dodging*** – which is the middle one. Both the double dodging and the consecutive dodging are new and complex skills, and you'll need to work at them hard and repeatedly to get them right. But by the time you can do them, the rest of the band will want to join in too, and you can do a ***rolling dodge*** - which is the picture at the bottom.

When the rounds have completely settled down, the conductor calls, "Commence a rolling dodge," and the treble and Two then dodge at the next handstroke. The Two and Three dodge at the following handstroke, the Three and Four dodge at the handstroke after that, and so

123456 H	"Three, Four
123456 B	Double
12***43***56 H	Dodge"
123456 B	
12***43***56 H	
123456 B	

123456 H	"Three, Four
123456 B	Dodge"
12***43***56 H	"Two, Three
123456 B	Dodge"
1***32***456 H	"Three, Four
123456 B	Dodge"
12***43***56 H	"Two, Three
123456 B	Dodge"
1***32***456 H	"Three, Four
123456 B	Dodge"
and so on	

123456 H	"Commence
123456 B	a Rolling
213456 H	Dodge"
123456 B	
1***32***456 H	
123456 B	
12***43***56 H	
123456 B	
123***54***6 H	
123456 B	
1234***65*** H	
123456 B	

on, all the way to the Five and Six. And when you can all do a rolling dodge, it will be time for a ***rolling double dodge*** – where each pair of bells do ***two*** dodges together instead of one – and a ***double rolling dodge*** where you do two rolling dodges one after another without stopping.

In time you can do a ***double rolling double dodge*** – which speaks for itself – and a ***reverse rolling dodge*** – where the pairs dodge from treble and Two to Five and Six, and then from Five and Six back to treble and Two again. Such things as ***double reverse rolling triple dodges*** go on from there.

Next Time

Dodging practice can be a lot of fun as well as being very pleasant to listen to on a Sunday morning. But much more important, it enables you to perfect an essential skill for Bob Doubles.

You can now lead, you can now hunt and you can now dodge. All your fundamental building blocks are strong, solid and in place, and fully capable of supporting what follows. And what *that* is, is what we shall be looking at next time.

*Not surprisingly, a lot of people ask me about Bob Doubles because it concerns more ringers more deeply than any other method. "**What we want,**" someone once said to me on a ringing course, "**is pages and pages about it.**"*

So I decided to put this series into five chapters and cover all the things I was being asked about. But I was nonetheless a little worried that some Ringing World *readers might think the space better devoted to something more advanced – such as peal reports – so before I got too far, I thought I'd better check with the then Editor, David Thorne.*

"I'm writing a five chapter series on Bob Doubles," I murmured to him casually one Saturday.

"Good," he replied, without turning a hair, showing, as always, how completely in touch he always was with all sections of the ringing community. So with his approval, I sat down that night and started on **A Bit of Theory**.

2. Getting into Bob Doubles

A Bit of Theory

Last time we looked at the ***building blocks*** of Bob Doubles – ***leading***, ***hunting*** and ***dodging*** – but we didn't really talk much about Bob Doubles itself because those building blocks are really the building blocks of ***all*** methods. This time, though, we're going to be quite specific and look at the theory.

Now I expect someone's already told you how Bob Doubles is constructed – or maybe you've read about it in a book – and it *is* interesting if you're interested in that sort of thing. But not everybody is, and in any case it's certainly not needed to ring the method. So it's not *that* sort of theory we're going to look at now. Instead, it's the theory of learning and remembering what to do.

There are many ways of doing that, and you'll probably prefer one of them to all the others, but we're going to look at the two most popular.

The Blue Line

First, the ***Blue Line***. A ***blue line*** is a line drawn through the path of a ***working bell***, and for historical reasons it's always called a ***blue*** line even when it's black like this one.

This is part of the blue line for Bob Doubles starting on the Two. You can see that it's rather like a road map which could exist even without the numbers being written underneath it. Nowadays, the great majority of ringers ring ***by the blue line***, so if you personally feel disinclined to get to grips with it, do at least give it a go.

123456
214356
241536
425136
452316
543216
534126
351426
315246
132546
135246
312546
321456
234156
243516
425316
452136
541236
514326
153426

Most people learn blue lines by looking at them vertically as this one is. But some ringers prefer to turn them on their side so they look more like mountain ranges. If you like, you can turn this book through 90° like this

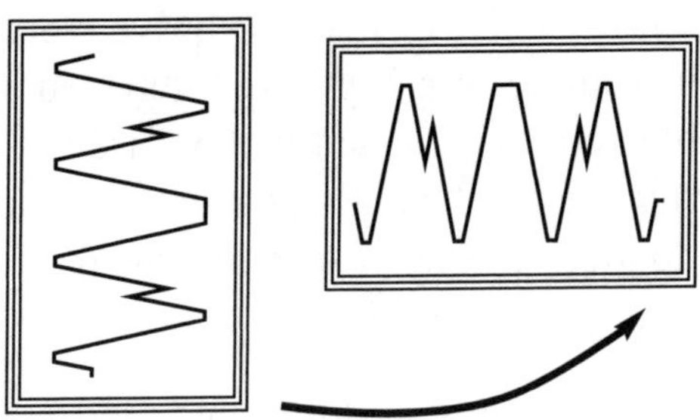

and see what *you* think.

And that was the blue line again, but this time for the whole of the method and *without* the numbers. Once again I started on the Two, and you can see that it's making seconds over the treble at the end. If I'd started on the Three it would look like this, and end in the middle of the 3-4 up dodge.

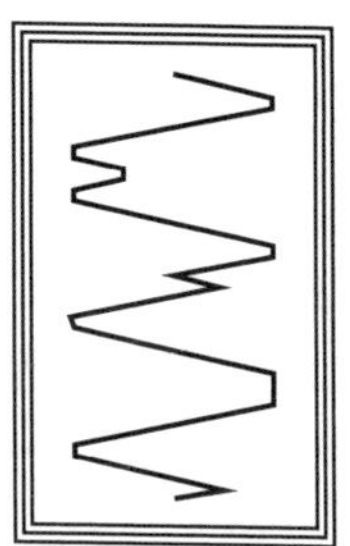

And even if you don't know already, I am sure that with a little study – and possibly a magnifying glass – you'll be able to see that it's exactly the same line except that it starts in a different place. Indeed, ***all*** the ***working bells*** – that's the Two, Three, Four and Five – follow exactly the same line but start in different places. So we often draw one line and then mark on the right hand side of it where each bell starts – as in the picture on the next page.

The four bells are a bit like the four players in a game of *Ludo*. They all start in different places but then all have to go right round the board before they finish where they started.

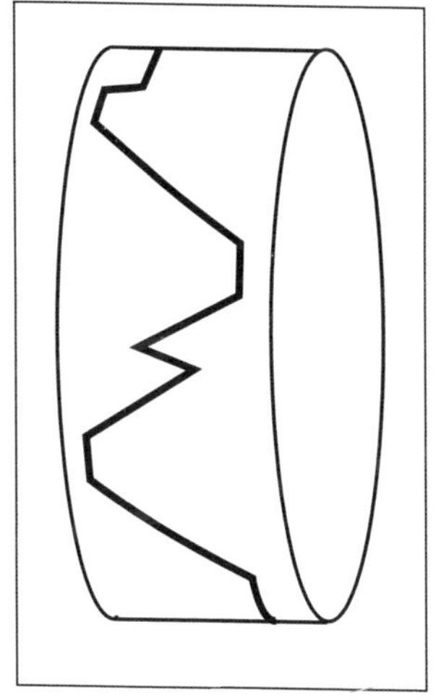

Indeed, you could redraw the blue line I've just drawn, onto a strip of paper, and then bend that strip of paper into a circle before sellotaping the top to the bottom. It would then look like the picture on the right.

And this would make it absolutely clear that Bob Doubles – like all methods – goes round and round, and the blue line is the same for all the working bells.

Of course, the blue line tells you nothing at all about which bells to ring after. You have to work that out by ropesight. Although the blue line is exactly the same for the Two, Three, Four and Five, the bells they ring over are different.

The Order of the Work

And now for something very different. ***The Order of the Work***. Rather than being a ***road map*** of the method – which is what the blue line is – the ***order of the work*** is a verbal expression of it. But it's not a long verbal expression, it's a shorthand one.

If you were going to describe Bob Doubles to someone who had only ever rung plain hunt, you would probably say something like this.

"**Lead,**
hunt out to the back,
hunt down to thirds place,
dodge 3-4 down,
hunt down to lead,
lead,
hunt out to the back,
do four blows in fifths,
hunt down to the front,
lead,
hunt up to fourths place,
dodge 3-4 up,
hunt out to the back,
hunt down to the front,
lead,
make seconds over the treble."

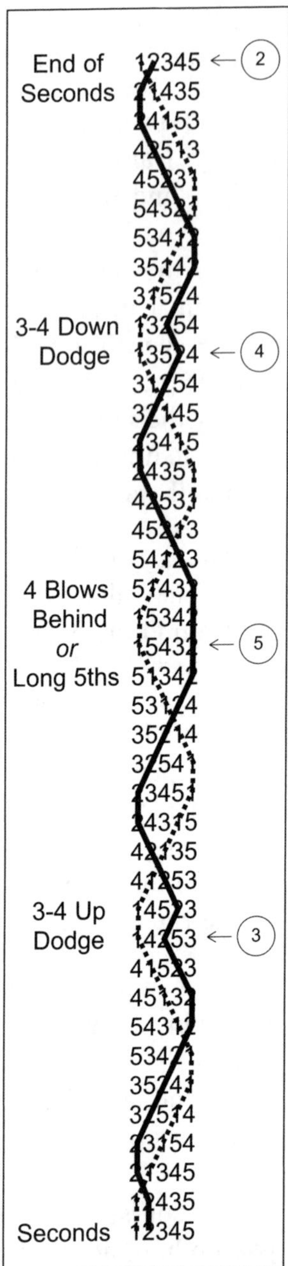

Bob Doubles

Now that's quite a lot to remember, and writing it out took up a good bit of the previous page, so we really need to find a shorter way of thinking of it. And that's where the ***order of the work*** comes in. In the order of the work you miss out the routine parts – like leading and hunting – and you just remember the special bits. So Bob Doubles becomes

3-4 down
Long fifths
3-4 up
Seconds.

That is very brief indeed, but it still fully describes Bob Doubles. It's a good idea to learn it so thoroughly that you can recite it automatically at a moment's notice like your two-times table. You need to know it so well that if someone crept up behind you and shouted, "***Bob Doubles***," you'd have replied, "***3-4 down***, ***long fifths***, ***3-4 up***, ***seconds***," before your feet had even arrived back on the ground.

In your early stages you may need to insert more information into it – such as whether you go up or down after each piece of work – but you must learn the basic skeleton as well.

The Circle of Work

As we noticed earlier, every working bell does the same thing. So the order of the work – like the blue line – is the same for all of them even though each one starts in a different place. It's the *Ludo* effect again, and the chart on the next page may help.

And rather like the paper folding trick on page 15, you can put the order of the work into a circle – although this time you can draw it flat on the page.

Two	Four	Five	Three
3-4 down			
Long fifths	Long fifths		
3-4 up	3-4 up	3-4 up	
Seconds	Seconds	Seconds	Seconds
	3-4 down	3-4 down	3-4 down
		Long fifths	Long fifths
			3-4 up

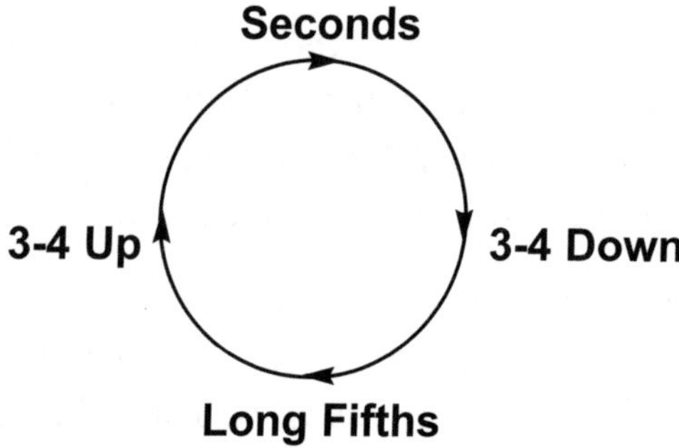

This circle is called ***The Circle of Work***, and some ringers find it very helpful. Some don't, though, so if you personally don't, don't spend too much time studying it.

The Starts

And lastly, important as the order of the work and the blue line are, neither is enough by itself. You also need to know your ***start.***

If you're ringing the Three, for example, you don't just need to know that your next work is seconds. You also need to know that you get there by hunting up and down first. So ringers of all experience learn the blue line and/or the order of the work ***and*** the ***starts*** on all the bells they're likely to ring.

The Extras

And beyond that there's a whole heap of extra things which you *could* learn, and which in time you *should* learn, and which eventually you probably *will* learn. They're all very helpful and we'll look at them in detail later, but you don't need to learn them now. For the moment, you have the basic skills and you have the theory, and that means it's time to get on the end of a bell rope and have a go. And *that* is what we shall be doing next time.

Although this chapter covered the basics of the theory, it didn't include an odd but frequently used meaning of the word, ***lead.*** *Of course,* ***lead*** *has many meanings, but as a noun it's often used to refer to all the changes between the time the treble leads at backstroke and the time it* ***next*** *leads at backstroke. So the changes on the right are a* ***lead*** *of Bob Doubles.*

13524
31254
32145
23415
24351
42531
45213
54123
51432
15342
15432

When you've never come across this meaning before, it seems very peculiar, but it's a good idea to get used to it. Ringers say, "We went wrong after four leads," or, "The rope broke in the last lead of the plain course," and they're always referring to these chunks. Of course, if you're ringing on more than five, a ***lead*** *is longer* *than ten changes because the treble goes up and down through more places.*

A further piece of terminology is that the change when the treble leads at backstroke is sometimes called the ***lead end*** *and sometimes the* ***lead head****, and the* ***two*** *changes when the treble leads at handstroke and backstroke, are sometimes* ***collectively*** *called the* ***lead end****.*

All this can be very confusing, and in addition, the technically minded will tell you forcefully that the most common of these uses is just plain wrong. But, of course, they can't stop a word meaning what it means just because they find it inconvenient, so the technicians will just have to go on grumbling.

Meanwhile, as long as you know that a lead is a lead, you'll have no trouble understanding at least ***one*** *of the terms you are likely to hear while you're* **Putting it all Together**.

3. Getting into Bob Doubles

Putting it all Together

Just to remind you, in Chapter 1 we looked at the basic skills needed to ring Bob Doubles, and in Chapter 2 we looked at learning and remembering the method. This time we're putting it all together.

And as you must certainly know by now, the trouble with all ringing is that everything is much more difficult in practice than it is in theory. You can sit and study for hours and know everything there is to know about what you're going to do, but the moment you get on the end of a bell rope, it is all as nothing.

That doesn't mean that study is unimportant. On the contrary, it's vitally important. It really does help, and the skills practice we looked at in the first chapter really helps too. But this week we're looking at those problems that only assail you during the real thing.

Counting your Place

Now, I expect someone has already told you about ***counting your place***. You probably didn't count your place in call changes, because hardly anyone does, but you were probably encouraged to count it in plain hunt.

And here is the first problem. Although some learners invariably *do* count their place when hunting – and Bob Doubles comes much easier to them as a result – the majority don't.

And this is an interesting point because most of the non-counters nonetheless manage to convince their tower captains that they *are* counters. It seems that their tower captains want to believe that they are, and they, in turn, don't like to disappoint their tower captains. Conversations go like this:

"You ***do*** count your place, don't you?"

"Er ... Ye-e-e-s."

Other learners, of course, don't count their place because they don't know how to.

The point is that most people can hunt perfectly well on five without counting their place at all. They simply ring over each bell in turn to get up to the back, and then they ring over each bell in the same order again to get down to the front. They need ropesight but they don't need to count, so why should they?

But when you ring Bob Doubles you really *do* need to count. You may have managed to plain hunt well enough without counting, but you're most unlikely to be able to ring methods that way. So if you don't count already, now's the time to start.

What it Means

So what does counting your place mean?

Well, in any change – or ***row***, as some people call it –

you're in a particular position. If you're ringing the Three and are in the change 135246, we say you're ***in seconds place*** because you're the second bell to ring. Similarly, if you're ringing the Three in the change 142536, we say you're ***in fifths place.***

So you can keep track of where you are in a method by counting your place to yourself at every blow. For example, when ringing the Three to plain hunt on five you would count,

12345
21435 "Fourths place"
24153 "Fifths place"
42513 "Fifths place"
45231 "Fourths place"
54321 "Thirds place"
53412 "Seconds place"
35142 "Lead"
31524 "Lead"
and so on.

How to do It

That sounds simple enough in theory, but in practice it's nowhere near as simple. When you're struggling with the method, the ropesight and the listening, counting can become very difficult indeed, and you can find yourself counting too early, too late or not at all.

If you count late, you can get confused about which blow your count relates to and then miss out the next one altogether. If you count early, you can end up counting twice for the same blow. Either way, you get one blow out in your counting and things become very confused indeed.

So try and follow these rules.

First, count at exactly the same point in each stroke. Most ringers count at the start of the pull or as their hands come down past their face, but some ringers count a moment later.

Second, always count a number. No matter how doubtful you are that you're still counting correctly, always count *something*. Better to count wrongly than not at all.

Third, don't stop counting when your ropesight fails you. Just keep on counting until it's time to lead. Then, put all your problems behind you and start all over again.

Fourth, count out loud if you have trouble counting in your head. A hint of a whisper is normally enough to make your counting easier, and it shouldn't disturb the others.

And last, if you still have trouble, ask someone to stand with you while you're ringing. You can then count out loud to them and they can tell you what your problems are. Alternatively, you can stand behind someone and count for them while *they're* ringing.

Incidentally, you don't have to say, "Seconds place, thirds place, fourths place ..." etc if you don't want to. Some ringers say, "Seconds, thirds, fourths ..." and others say, "Two, three, four ..."

See which you find easiest. You may find "Two, three, four ..." easiest because it's shorter, but on the other hand you may find it more difficult because you get your place confused with the bell you're ringing over. In that case "Seconds, thirds, fourths ..." might be a good compromise.

Equally, you may find "Seconds place, thirds place, fourths place ..." best because it allows less time for popping in an extra count by mistake. It's entirely up to you.

Finding the Bells

"But what's the good of counting," you ask, "if I can't find the bells to ring after?"

Well, to begin with that may *seem* like a good question, and there are certainly a lot of learners who see it as a reason for not trying to count at all. But the trouble is that it results in them never being able to ring Bob Doubles except by numbers.

Now, I'm not against people ringing Bob Doubles by numbers, and I have considerable admiration for those bands who have managed to master the method without any help or tuition, by doing just that. But there *is* an easier way. So if your ropesight is causing you problems,

> ***Choose the bell with the best view.*** If you can't see all – or most – of the other bells without turning your head right round, you're going to have trouble.
>
> ***Learn where you pass the treble*** – see next – because that decreases the number of bells to worry about and has other benefits as well.
>
> ***Learn which is your after bell*** – that's coming up on page 28 and gives similar benefits.
>
> ***And learn which is your course bell.***

Passing the Treble

And as regards ***passing the treble***, in most towers, when you ring the treble you have a pretty good view of all the other bells, but once you take an inside bell things get more difficult, particularly if you're ringing the Two. You tend to concentrate on all the bells on your left and miss out the treble completely. So to cope with that, you can ***learn when you should ring after the treble.***

And I hasten to reassure you that that's considered absolutely right and proper, and is done in all the very best circles. Indeed, even the most vehement *don't-learn-the-numbers* tower captain, will be perfectly content for you to do it.

The point is that you ring over the treble in exactly the same places in each course ***no matter which bell you're ringing***, so the knowledge you acquire is universal. On the opposite page is a blue line with the places where the treble crosses it added on. The treble is the dotted line.

Learning them all takes a long time, and you probably won't want to start until you've already got a few plain courses under your belt. But when you have, relax in the bath with this chapter and study the picture carefully.

You'll probably have found that there are places where you're particularly inclined to look the wrong way. For example, you might regularly miss ringing over the treble when you're in thirds place after dodging 3-4 down, as lots of ringers do.

So learn the important places first, and then think about the others. You may well find that you need to go back to the bath with this chapter several times.

But watch out, because experienced ringers have a short-hand way of referring to these treble passing places which they'll expect you to learn too. Indeed, this shorthand way is so important that I'm giving it three paragraphs all to itself.

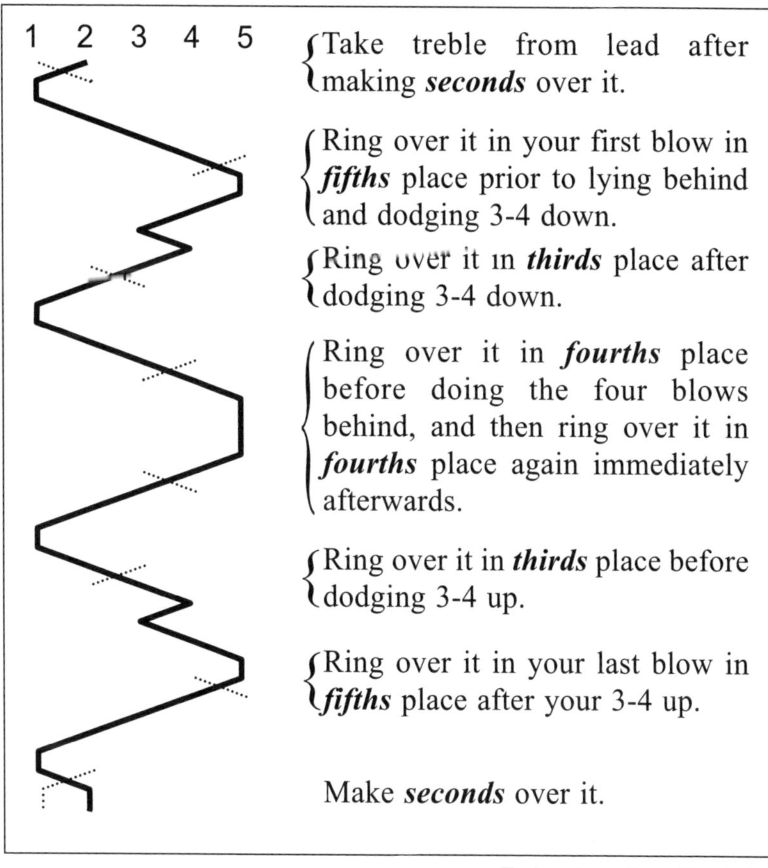

1 2 3 4 5
Take treble from lead after making *seconds* over it.
Ring over it in your first blow in *fifths* place prior to lying behind and dodging 3-4 down.
Ring over it in *thirds* place after dodging 3-4 down.
Ring over it in *fourths* place before doing the four blows behind, and then ring over it in *fourths* place again immediately afterwards.
Ring over it in *thirds* place before dodging 3-4 up.
Ring over it in your last blow in *fifths* place after your 3-4 up.
Make *seconds* over it.

Passing the Treble

If you are in Yths place and the treble is in Xths place. You are said to be ***passing the treble in X-Y***.

If you are hunting up, you are said to be ***passing the treble in X-Y on the way up***.

And,

If you are hunting down, you are said to be ***passing the treble in X-Y on the way down***.

To begin with, that can be very confusing indeed because you don't feel you're ***passing*** the treble at all. You're just ringing after it. But like other odd expressions, the more you say it, the more ordinary it becomes, until in time it sounds quite normal. Indeed, it will become so normal that you'll be able to think of Bob Doubles like this.

Seconds
pass treble 4-5
Dodge 3-4 down
pass treble 2-3
pass treble 3-4
Four blows behind
pass treble 3-4
pass treble 2-3
Dodge 3-4 up
pass treble 4-5
Seconds *over the treble*

Course Bells and After Bells

If you have good or very good ropesight, you won't need to read this section at all, but if you have ropesight problems, knowing about your ***course bells*** and ***after bells*** really will help.

Suppose you're ringing the Two to a plain course. Each time you lead, another bell leads after you. ***It takes you off*** or ***turns you from lead***, as ringers normally put it, and you ring over that bell at your handstroke blow in seconds place after leading.

If you're making seconds, it is of course the treble that takes you off. But ***on all other occasions*** it's the Four.

Now that's very helpful because you always know which bell to ring over in seconds place as you start hunting up.

Since you know that bell – and since you know when to pass the treble – that only leaves two other bells to worry about. And that isn't all that much for your ropesight to cope with.

The Four is called your ***after bell***, and each of the working bells has its own ***after bell*** which you can either learn in advance or quickly look up before you catch hold. They are,

Your Bell	Your After Bell
2	4
3	2
4	5
5	3

Your ***course bell***, on the other hand, is the bell you ring over in seconds place ***before*** you lead. That doesn't aid your ropesight quite as much but it does have other advantages. In particular, if you know your course bell, you may be able to strike much more accurately in seconds place just prior to leading. That will help your rhythm considerably and give you a firm foundation for further progress.

Your Bell	Your Course Bell
2	3
3	5
4	2
5	4

Next Time

And if you can remember all that – or even a little of it – and still ring Bob Doubles at the same time, your ropesight should no longer be much trouble to you. You now have the skills, you now have the theory and you now have the ropesight. Total perfection is almost yours. And it will be, once you can overcome those one or two tricky problems that we'll be looking at next time.

On one occasion I was ringing a plain course of Bob Doubles with a struggling band on their practice night. Not all was going well, and I whispered quietly to the lady on my right that she should be dodging with me in 3-4.

"It's no good telling me where I am," she replied sadly. "I know where I am. It's just that I'm not there."

How well she summed up the endless frustration of it all. And knowing that that is how many people feel, I thought a chapter about ***Those Tricky Problems*** *would definitely help.*

4. Getting into Bob Doubles

Those Tricky Problems

There are one or two posh ringers who seem to think that Bob Doubles isn't very difficult at all and that no one should have any trouble with it. You and I, of course, know better. ***We*** know that there are all sorts of tricky problems that can wrench you suddenly and disastrously into the wrong place, and they can do that no matter how much study and preparation you've done. So while those posh ringers are looking at the peals pages, ***we*** are going to have a quiet chat about those problems together.

Forgetting

We've been six weeks at this now, and I'm sure you can recite a plain course without the slightest difficulty. Most definitely it is at the very forefront of your mind at all possible times.

At all possible times, that is, except when you're actually ringing it. Then, it can drift away behind a kind of hazy and shifting miasma.

Unfortunately, this is an occupational hazard of ringing,

and the great majority of ringers suffer from it from time to time. Fortunately, it does get better, and the more you practise and the more comfortable you get, the less you forget what to do – though by then you're starting Bob Minor and Grandsire and forgetting *those* instead. Meanwhile, the following tips may help.

> ***Always prepare well***. No matter how little use that preparation turns out to be, every little is worthwhile.
>
> ***Try and relax*** before you start. Relaxed concentration always produces the best ringing.
>
> ***Ring with friends*** as much as possible. A warm and supportive atmosphere really helps to keep the memory intact.
>
> ***Concentrate at all times***, and don't stop concentrating in the easy bits. Even while you're hunting and leading, keep reminding yourself what the next piece of work will be.
>
> ***Go back over*** any place where you got lost – after you've stopped ringing. Many ringers get lost in the same place every time because something in the ropesight or sound always puts them off there. If you can get through that point O.K, you may be able to ring the rest of the course perfectly.

Of course, you may not simply forget, you may suffer complete memory melt-down. This is ***ringing panic*** and it's a very real and common problem. You can find a whole chapter on it in *The Bellringer's Bedside Companion*.

Doubting

Doubting is another problem. It's like forgetting but more indecisive. You really *are* sure that you're going to dodge 3-4 down but – then again – *just perhaps* you should be dodging 3-4 up.

So follow the golden rule: ***Do not doubt***. Be like Lord Macaulay and say, "I may be wrong, I sometimes am, but I never doubt."

Doubting is insidiously debilitating and results in half done dodges and sloppy handling. Better by far to be wrong than to doubt. If you're going to dodge 3-4 down, do it positively and crisply come what may.

I add that doubting arises in large measure from traditional ringing teaching. You're never told what you've done ***right***, you're only told what you've done ***wrong***. So you're told that you dodged in the wrong place rather than that you dodged well there.

For my money, it's better by far to do a ***good*** dodge in the ***wrong*** place than a ***bad*** dodge in the ***right*** one. A good dodge is a transferable skill. If you can do it in the wrong place, you can do it just as well in the right place. But a bad dodge is no earthly use to anyone no matter where you put it.

Dodging

And that brings us to dodging. You may have difficulty getting your dodges right, as lots of people do. Quite possibly you count well enough, but you're so busy counting and remembering, that your handling and striking get placed on the sidelines. You know you *should* be ringing the picture at the top left of the next page, but what you *actually* ring is the picture at the top right – and clearly *that's* not right.

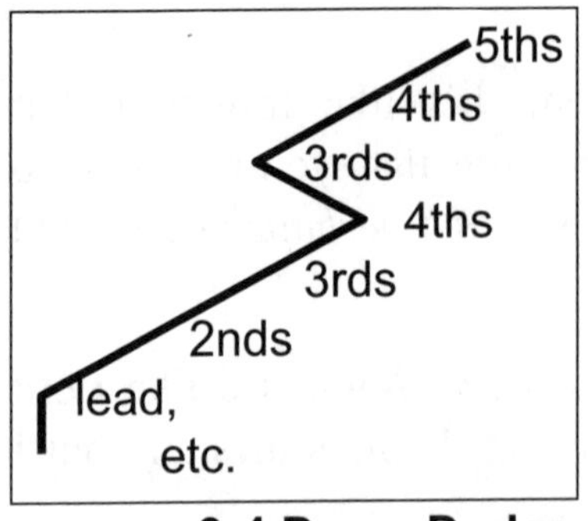

3-4 Down Dodge

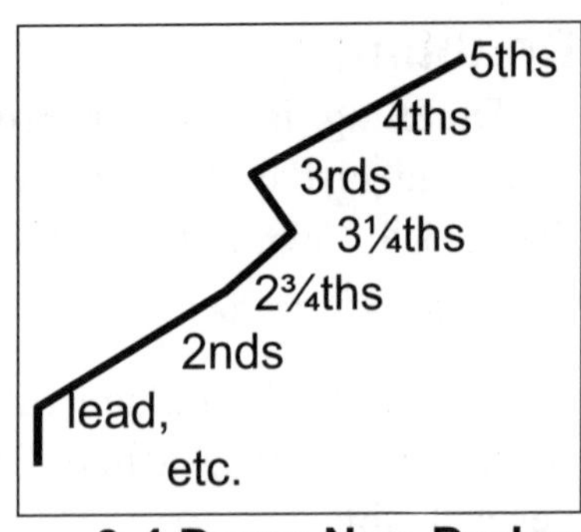

3-4 Down Non-Dodge

Of course, when you start ringing Bob Doubles, it's perfectly reasonable that you don't dodge too well. But obviously you want to improve, so what do you do about it?

First, make sure you have plenty of dodging practice before you start – see Chapter 1 – and go back and do more dodging practice even though you've started ringing the method.

Second, think out in advance how your handling should go. For example, your ***down*** dodge should go something like this.

Fifths place:	Don't pull too hard, as you're about to hunt down.
Fourths place:	Don't pull too hard this time either, but pull ***in*** firmly.
Thirds place:	Pull in firmly again to get down to thirds, but also pull ***through*** firmly so that you can hold up at the next backstroke.

Fourths place:	Hold right up to dodge, but don't pull too hard as you'll need to hunt down again next blow.
Thirds place:	Pull in firmly to get back down, but don't pull ***through*** too firmly as you'll need to get down to seconds place next time.

That's a very physical and complex action, and it's bound to take practice to get it right, but it's essential to know what you *should* be doing.

Third, ask yourself what your dodges *feel* like. Do they feel decidedly physical and definitely different from plain hunting? If they don't, check why they don't.

Fourth, use all your concentration to ensure you know when they're due. If you come upon a dodge like a parked car on a bend, you're bound to have trouble with it.

Fifth, if a sympathetic and experienced ringer is available in your own or a nearby tower, ask him or her to comment on your dodges in detail. There may be just one action at one stroke which needs a little attention, but getting it right could improve your dodging immeasurably.

Going the Right Way

And if you sometimes come out of the dodge unsure about which way to go, it's probably because your dodge wasn't quite crisp enough. The more physical your dodge, the more likely you are to carry on in the right direction afterwards.

But even when you dodge perfectly, you can still get so

involved in your dodge that you lose track of the method and start hunting back the way you came. In effect you do one of these

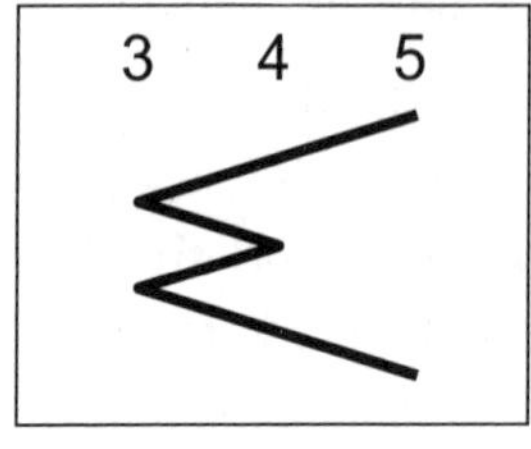

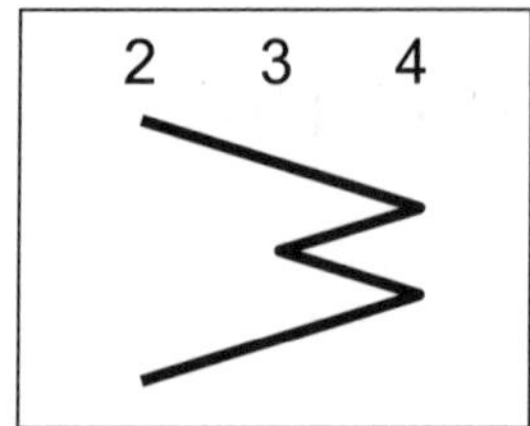

which are commonly known as ***fish tails***.

If that's *your* problem, try remembering that a dodge is really only ***one step back*** as you plain hunt. Think to yourself, "And here is my one step back," as you go back to fourths in your 3-4 down or as you go back to thirds in your 3-4 up. And then carry on positively plain hunting. Many people find this solves the problem.

Seconds

Seconds is the really relaxing part of Bob Doubles. For six blows you're either leading or following the treble. Yet how easy it is to forget to do it because you're worrying so much about those awful dodges.

Partly, the solution is to relax and to practise. But in addition, try really ***looking forward*** to your seconds once the 3-4 up is out of the way, and don't even ***think*** about the 3-4 down until the seconds is past.

Look forward to seconds like you look forward to the weekend on a Friday afternoon. And don't start thinking about Monday morning until Sunday night at the earliest.

Of course, planning your handling will work wonders too.

Beginning and Endings

And now for a major elephant pit that lurks silently and fiendishly to trap the unwary.

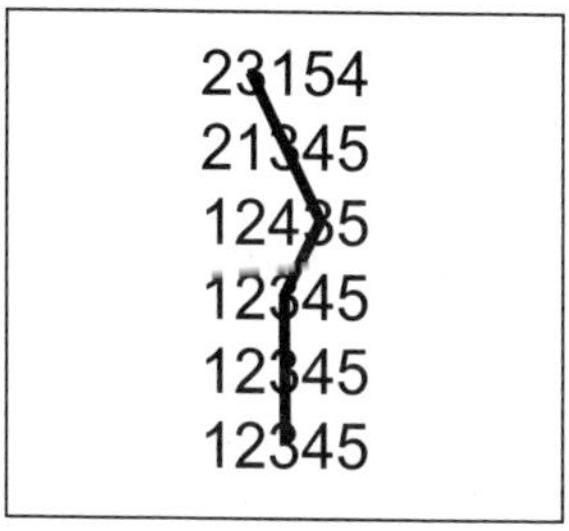

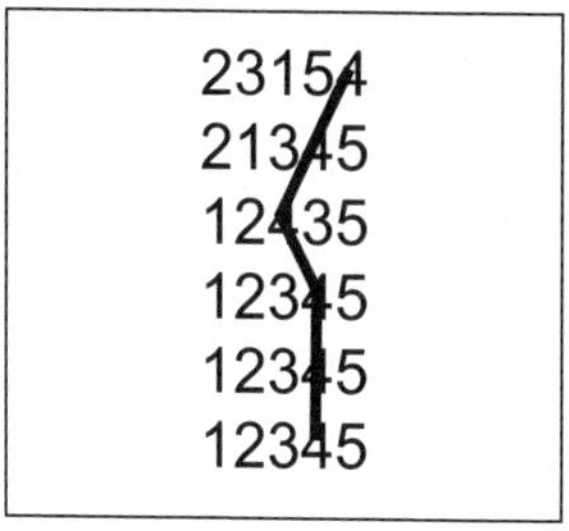

23154
21345
12435
12345
12345
12345

23154
21345
12435
12345
12345
12345

If you always ring the same bell, you'll quickly get used to always ending in the same place. And you'll then develop a handling technique that gets you to do just that. For example, if you always ring the Three, your 3-4 up at the end of a course will look like the top picture, and if you always ring the Four, your 3-4 down will look like the bottom one.

Now, you can easily see that neither of these is anything like a dodge, and indeed, they're known by many as ***bird's beaks***. But you can soon get used to doing one completely automatically if you do it often enough, and then doing the real thing can become very hard indeed.

You might think that you could combine the beginning of the course with the end of the course and so get it right. But you can't. And you can't because you're starting from rounds instead of from the middle of a dodge. It's rather like practising broad jumps and sprinting, and supposing that you could put them together to do the long jump.

So try not to become tied to one bell for too long, or alternatively, always ring more than one course without stopping. Either way, the elephant pit will not catch you.

Next Time

And after all that, you're probably pretty good at plain

courses. So good, indeed, that you're champing at the bit to ring a few bobs. And that's just as well, because *that* is what we shall be looking at next time.

Round about this tricky problems stage, many ringers undergo yet another ***crisis of confidence****. Learning to ring is packed full of them, and almost every learner goes through times of thinking they're the slowest and most incompetent person ever to take up the hobby.*

*Countless times, people have said to me, "****I'm so sorry. I must be the worst person you've ever taught,****" or, "****I'm wasting your time. I'm too slow for you to bother with,****" or, "****I just can't seem to get it. I ought to stop coming.****"*

But, of course, they never are the worst or the slowest, and they definitely ought ***not*** *to stop coming. For most people, learning each new stage is a slow process, and probably that's just as well, because that's one of the things that makes ringing so perennially interesting. Certainly, it never worries me how long anyone takes, and why should it?*

By and large, if you have one good night in four, you're doing well. If you do better than that, you're doing ***very*** *well. So every time you have a really* ***off*** *night and feel despondent, do two things. First, think back to where you were six months ago and prove that in some way or other you're definitely better. And second, turn back to this page and gain strength from the knowledge that tens of thousands of us know just how you're feeling. We're all with you in spirit, and whenever things get tough, think of all us friends standing behind you, willing you on.*

5. Getting into Bob Doubles

Touches

You'll be relieved to know at the outset that we're now on the last chapter. We've spent the previous four perfecting plain courses, so it's time and past to start looking at bobs. Quite likely you've been studying and ringing them for a while now anyway, and that's good. As with all ringing, you're working hard at getting the previous stages better and better while pushing onward at the same time. But whether you've already rung some bobs or not, we're going to spend this chapter looking at them together.

A Bit of History

And if plain courses didn't come easy to you, you were probably a bit dismayed to find there were any bobs at all. Why bother with them, you wondered, when you can just keep repeating the plain course over and over again.

Why indeed?

Well, let's see where the whole idea of touches came from – and a ***touch***, incidentally, is a piece of ringing with bobs and/or singles in.

A little over 400 years ago people started to ring rounds and call changes. They started to ring their bells in an orderly and rhythmical fashion rather than at random. The advances in bell-hanging helped this along, but there were still considerable limitations as to how much the ringers of the time could hold up or pull in to get from one change to the next – far more limitations, indeed, than today. So they normally preferred just to swap over a pair of bells that were sounding consecutively.

Naturally, though, they wanted to create variety. So they tried to find ways of ringing as many different changes as possible simply by swapping over pairs of consecutive sounding bells. They only swapped one pair at time – as most people do in call changes today – so it's not surprising that it was a good while before anyone worked out how to get more than 48 different changes in a single five bell sequence.

Few people, of course, had any kind of schooling, and paper was prohibitively expensive. Indeed, Fabian Stedman noted in 1677 that paper for writing out changes cost five shillings per ream – about a tenth of what it costs today even after more than three centuries of inflation – so a few sheets could cost more than a working man's daily wages.

Not surprisingly, ringers kept searching to find ways of getting more and more changes in the same sequence, first by continuing to swap a single pair at a time, and then by swapping two pairs at a time. Changes where two pairs were swapped were called ***double changes***, and that's where the word ***doubles*** comes from. In methods on five bells, two pairs is the maximum that can be swapped in any one change.

Ultimately, arrangements were found for getting all 120 different changes in the same sequencc, with each change occurring only once.

From a purely theoretically point of view, the composers of the time must have been well pleased with this, and a rule quickly grew up which has been fundamental ever since. When we ring a touch of Doubles we ***never repeat the same change*** and we often try to ring all 120 changes if possible.

The Dogma

And if you haven't been ringing long, you may wonder about this lack of repetition. After all, composers of other music go in for repetition quite a lot. Ravel's *Bolero*, for example, repeats itself over and over again for about twenty minutes and no one minds a bit.

But if a piece of method ringing repeats even a single change, it is said to be ***false***, and experienced ringers get very anxious about it indeed. In fact, if a ***peal*** is found to be false, even though perfectly rung, it is immediately regarded as nothing, and the ringers rip the details from their peal books and expunge them from their records even if the falseness is only discovered years after the event.

As with any piece of dogma, an absence of falseness is of fundamental importance to the majority of ringers even though it is only vaguely rational. Certainly, ringing would be far less interesting without it, and in time you may well feel strongly about it yourself. Meanwhile, if you have any doubts, you'd probably best keep them to yourself.

Bobs

So now we know that we want to ring all the 120 possible changes on five bells and we want to ring them without repetition. A plain course of Bob Doubles is only 40 changes long, so we need to do something about the rest. That's where bobs come in. They are there simply to enable us to ring all the changes. They are no more than little hiccups that send you off into changes you haven't rung before.

And here is another piece of dogma. A bob in any method must normally be no more than the ***slightest possible*** hiccup – the absolute minimum of disruption that's needed to enable you to get out of the plain course and into other changes.

And the third piece of important dogma is that a bob is always a bob. Wherever you encounter it in a touch of Bob Doubles, a bob is always the same. You can't ring one type of bob in one place and another type of bob in another. So only one batch of learning is needed, and from the learner's point of view that must be a good thing.

In other methods there are often things called ***singles*** as well. Singles are very like bobs, but in Bob Doubles only advanced ringers with a taste for the exotic, ring them. If a conductor were to call one without warning you in advance, he would rightly be regarded as a hopeless cad.

What it is

So after all that preamble, what is a bob?

On the left are the changes that occur when the end of one plain course is finishing and another is starting – the little **x**'s and **I**'s show whether the bells are crossing over or lying still. And on the right are the changes that occur when a bob is called at the end of a plain course.

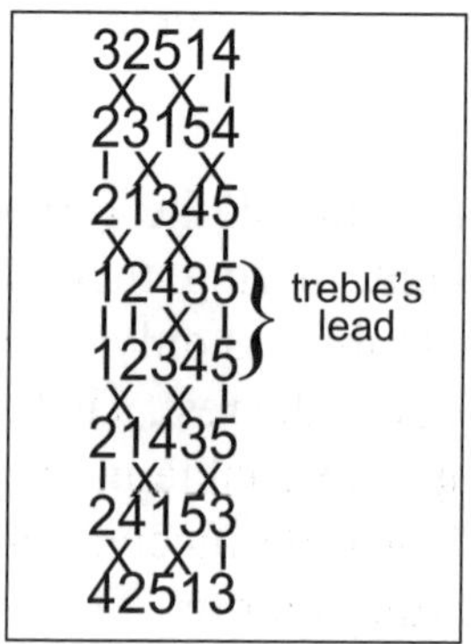

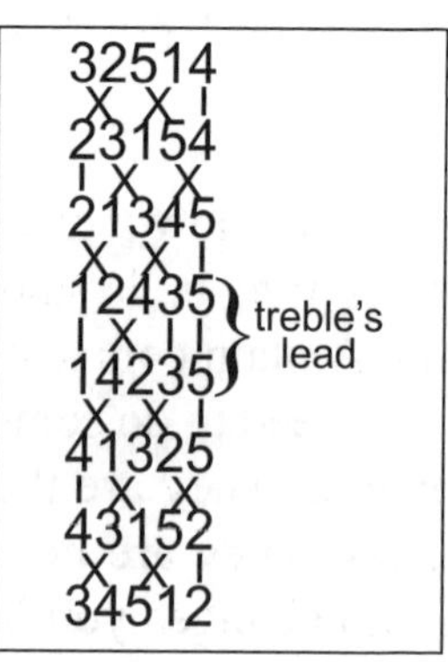

Study the pictures carefully as though you were doing a *spot-the-difference* competition. You'll see that only when the treble leads is there any structural difference at all. Then,

> The bells in seconds and thirds place cross over instead of the bells in thirds and fourths place.

And,

> The bell in fourths place lies still instead of the bell in seconds place.

The bell in fifths place does its four blows behind in both.

That's the theory. It may not help you much to ring bobs, but I thought you'd like to know. The truly important rule is,

> ***Bobs only occur when the treble is leading, and at no other time.***

So if a bob is called when you're going to dodge or make seconds, you'll have to do something else instead. But no one is going to call a bob ***except*** when you're going to dodge, make seconds or do four blows behind.

And if you're rushing through this chapter to get to the meaty bit, go back and read that paragraph again. It's fundamentally important and makes bobs much easier to ring than they otherwise would be.

What to do

There are different ways of remembering what to do at bobs, and the more expert you get, the more ways there are. But for your very first bobs, I recommend that for each possible position you can be in when a bob is called, you learn three things.

1. What work you ***were*** going to do.

2. What work you now do because the bob ***has*** been called.

And,

3. What work you will do next time if no further bob is called.

And since there are only four possible positions you can be in when a bob is called, there are a maximum of four sets of instructions to learn. In fact, though, there are only ***three***, because in one of the four positions the bob doesn't affect you at all. I've put them all in the quick reference table opposite but I'll take you through each one to explain how it works. Note well, though, that the bob is always called ***exactly one whole pull*** before anyone has to do anything different. That's the same length warning as for ***Go*** or ***Stand***.

Running Out

Suppose when a bob is called, you're doing your second blow at lead and about to make seconds. Instead of making seconds immediately, you must plain hunt up to the back, plain hunt down to the front again, and ***then*** make seconds.

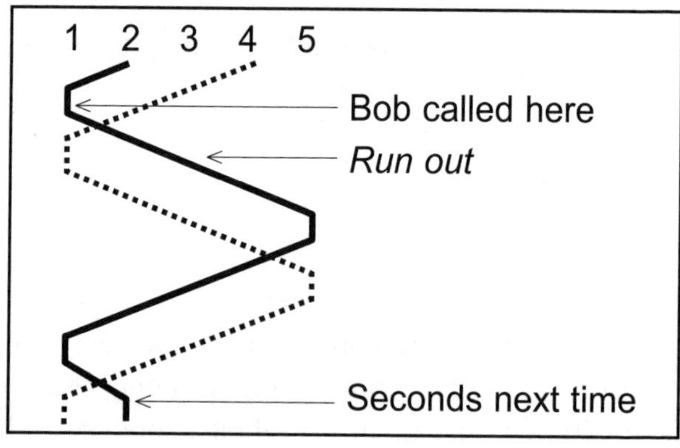

And this hunting up to the back instead of making seconds is known as ***running out***. So your three things to learn are,

Plain Bob Doubles				
What to do at a Bob				
Position when Bob is called	Second blow at lead	Fourths place on the way down	Thirds place on the way up	Fifths place at the start of long fifths
About to	Make seconds	Dodge 3-4 down	Dodge 3-4 up	UNAFFECTED
Do instead	Run out	Run in	Make the bob	
Do next time	Make seconds	Dodge 3-4 down	Make long fifths	

If a bob is called when ***you are about to make seconds,***

Then,

you run out,

And,

make seconds next time.

You need to remember the expression ***running out*** because people use it a lot. If you're lost or confused, someone will say, "**Run out**," and you should instantly know what to do.

Running In

Running in is similar. The rules are,

> If a bob is called when ***you are about to dodge 3-4 down,***

Then,

> ***you hunt straight through to lead,***

And,

> ***dodge 3-4 down next time.***

Once again, if someone shouts, "**Run in**," you must carry on hunting down and ring over the treble in seconds place before leading. Here's the picture.

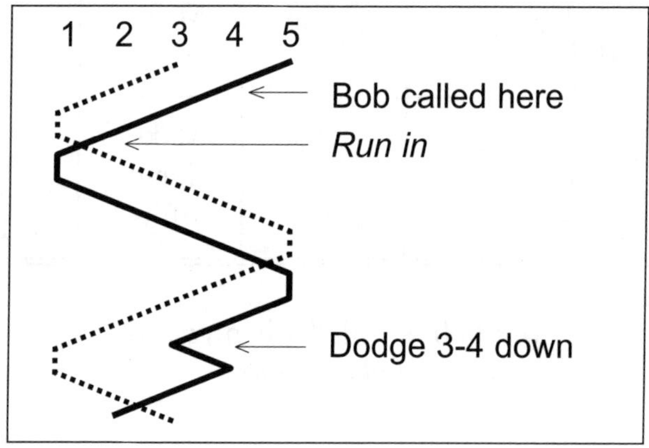

Making the Bob

And the last way of being affected is called ***making the bob.***

> If a bob is called when ***you are about to dodge 3-4 up,***

Then,

> ***you make two blows in fourths***

and go back down to lead,

And,

do long fifths next time.

And the picture looks like this.

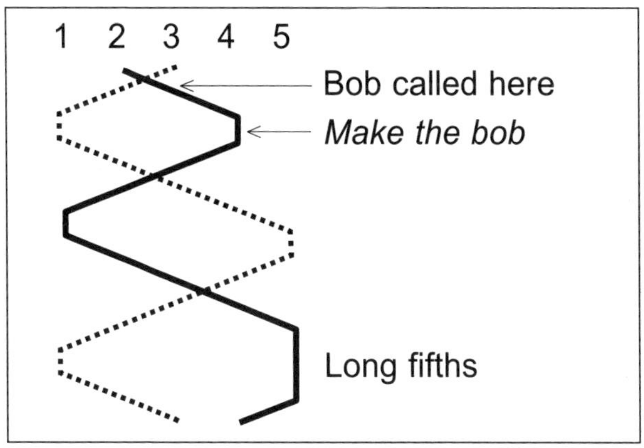

Most people find this the most difficult way of being affected. With the other two you simply postpone what you were going to do and put in some extra plain hunting. But when you ***make the bob***, you have to miss out your dodges and seconds completely and go back to four blows behind next time.

And to add to this, many people find the ropesight tricky too. They get an overpowering urge to ring their second blow in fourths over the bell that's making fifths, and as a result they end up in sixths. So if *you* have that problem, this very simple tip will help.

As you hunt up to make the bob, you'll ring over three bells in the order, **A, treble, B**. You must then come back down again, ringing over the same three bells, in the same order, **A, treble, B**.

Here is an example. Suppose you're on the Three and a bob is called at the end of the plain course. You have hunted up over Two, treble, Four, and you then hunt down over Two, treble, Four. You don't ring over the Five at all.

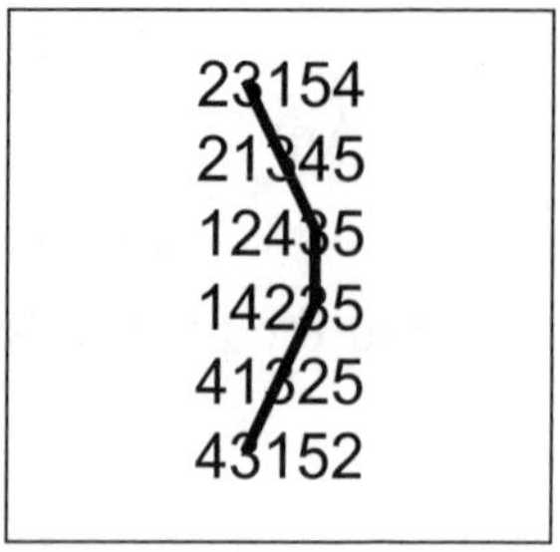

23154
21345
12435
14235
41325
43152

Passing the Treble

And that brings us neatly to thoughts of passing the treble, because somehow, with everything else there is to think about when a bob is called, thoughts of passing the treble seem to take a back seat. And that's a pity because the treble can be a calming anchor in the hectic moments.

Besides, if you try to take the treble in the *wrong* place, you may feel you're getting your bobs wrong even when you're getting them completely right. So the moral is, learn where you pass the treble after each way of being affected by a bob. They are,

Running in At your backstroke blow in seconds place just before you lead.

Running out At your second blow in fifths as you lie behind.

Making the bob At your handstroke blow in thirds place just after making fourths.

A Final Word

And that, at last, is that. Of course, even after reading all these five chapters, you may still not be able to ring Bob Doubles very well. But if so, ***don't worry.*** After all, you could read a whole book about playing Mozart's Horn Concertos and still have trouble getting your embouchure right.

Just keep on putting the practice and study together, and in a few months you'll be scratching your head and saying, "Now, ***why*** did I have trouble with ***that***?"

One Saturday morning as I was mulling over this chapter, I received a most interesting letter from a young ringer from Berkshire. As part of a school project she was researching the origin of certain ringing words and she wondered if I had any ideas about the word **touch**. *As she had already found out, the word has literally dozens of different meanings, and the ringing use might have come from any one of a number of them.*

Well, the most romantic and appealing possibility is that it derives from the word's medieval use as a brief strain of instrumental music. Regrettably, though, that's extremely unlikely. It was only ever a poetical use, and it had virtually died out before method ringing came along. In any event, our use of the word seems to date from rather later than the dawn of method ringing, especially as it didn't appear in print until 1814. Much more likely is that it comes from its meaning as a small quantity of something – a piece or chunk, as it were. Indeed, in East Anglia some ringers still use the word ***piece*** *interchangeably with the word* ***touch***.

What is also interesting, is what it actually means. The Oxford Dictionary defines its ringing meaning as, "a series of changes less than a peal," but, of course, that simply isn't correct. Ringers would not normally call a quarter peal a touch, nor would they use the word for a sequence of call changes. A 120 of Doubles they'd simply call a ***120*** *– normally pronounced* ***one twenty*** *rather than* ***one hundred and twenty*** *– and until recently, older ringers called a 120 of Grandsire a* ***six score***. *Just one of the many idiosyncrasies to puzzle over when you make a start on* **Grandsire Doubles**.

6. Grandsire Doubles

The Shallow End

This is a joint letter from two of us. We're like that person who wrote to you about Bob Doubles except that our trouble is Grandsire. It's not rung a lot in our tower, but the older ringers are fond of it and they normally ring a touch now and again. They keep telling us how easy it is, but we can never understand what they're talking about. What about it?

P.R.S. and J.S.
Staffordshire

Time was, when Grandsire was ***the*** method. For decades it was the only method rung by most towers, and well into recent memory some conductors only said, "Go next hand," or, "Go next," because their bands knew to ring Grandsire and nothing else. Indeed, in quite a lot of towers the conductor only ever called one touch and the band rang it by numbers.

Even when method ringing advanced generally, Grandsire was still the first method taught in most places, so older ringers often have a natural affection for it. And besides, once you get into it, Grandsire is more *enjoyable* than Plain Bob and more musical too.

So what happened to it? Why has Bob Doubles so universally supplanted it as the learner's first method?

The Alternative

Well, there are two reasons. First, a few decades ago many ringing instructors became enthused with the idea of following a rising progression through the various methods. Their goal was Surprise Major or higher, and everything had to lead towards that. Grandsire – and even Stedman – were thought to be dead ends which didn't fit in, and so they were abandoned.

The idea was a product of its time, consistent with the way people looked at things generally. But although it had its merits, the great majority of learners were never going to advance to Surprise Major anyway, and even those that were, would have found a diet of nothing else extremely boring.

But the second reason was far more practical. *Touches of Grandsire are more difficult than touches of Plain Bob.* Bob Doubles may not be so musical and it may not be so challenging, but it *is* easier. So why not, said everyone, learn the easier method first?

Why not indeed? Taking the smallest possible step at each stage is definitely best, and that's why I, too, teach Bob Doubles first. But once you can manage Bob Doubles, it really must be time for the pleasures and pains of Grandsire. And this week we're starting with the pleasures. So take a deep breath and step lightly into the shallow end.

The Plain Course

We learnt all about blue lines and orders of work in Chapter 2, and all that applies as much to Grandsire as it does to Bob Doubles, so if you're at all unsure about them, please go back and have another look. But if you're happy, carry straight on and look at this blue line starting on the Three.

And then have a look at this order of the work.

Thirds
4-5 down
4-5 up.

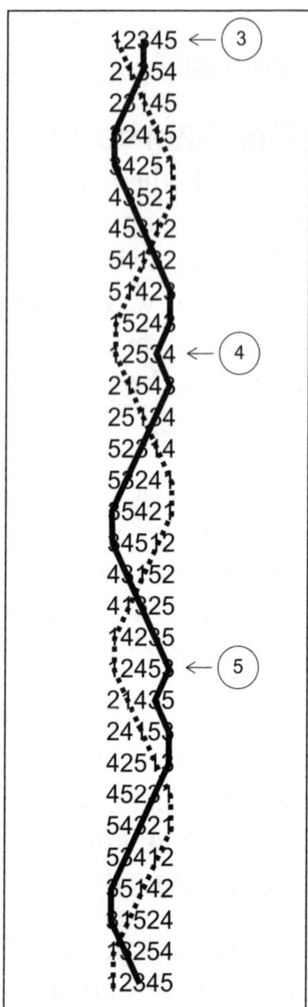

Grandsire Doubles

Ringing It

That doesn't look too difficult. Indeed, it looks easier than Bob Doubles because it's shorter. But how easy you find it when you ring it, will probably depend on how much Bob Doubles you've rung beforehand.

The problem is that the dodges in Grandsire are ***handstroke*** dodges not ***backstroke*** ones. In Bob Doubles when you do a dodge you always step back at ***back-stroke***, so the strokes of each blow of a 3-4 down dodge are these.

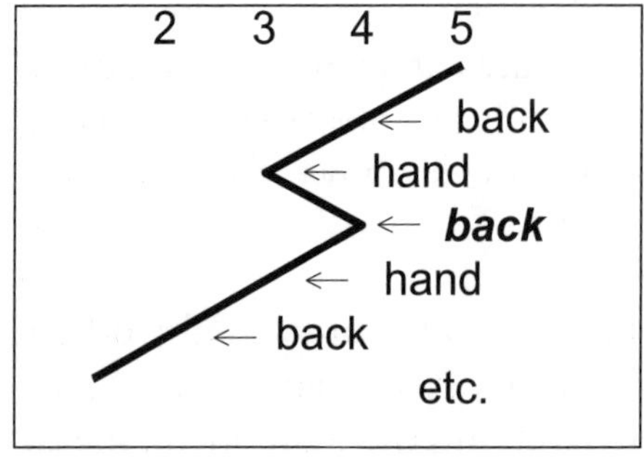

3-4 Down Dodge

But in Grandsire when you do a dodge, you step back at ***handstroke***, so the strokes of each blow of a 4-5 down dodge are as on the next page.

Handstroke Dodges

That may not *sound* much of a problem, but if you don't have it completely clear in your mind before you start, you can find yourself slipping into your Bob Doubles autopilot and trying to dodge at backstroke. Even if you dodge correctly, you can nonetheless have the uncomfortable feeling that you haven't, and then go wrong as a result. And if you *force* yourself to dodge at backstroke, it's even worse. But if you're prepared, you may well find handstroke dodges *easier* than backstroke ones.

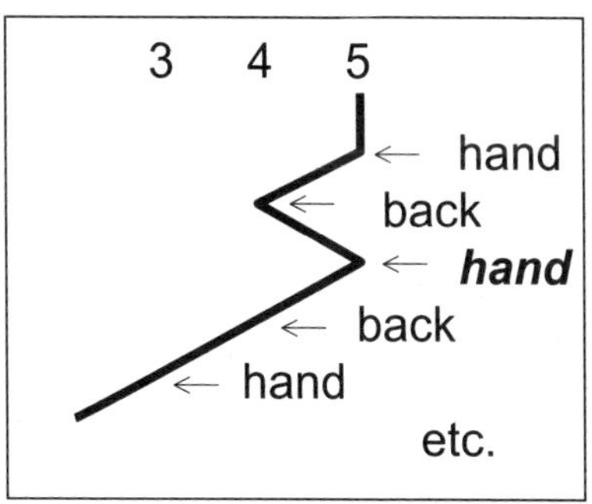

4-5 Down Dodge

The point is that you may well have a good deal more control over your handstrokes than your backstrokes. When you ring a light or medium bell you're normally ringing it more or less to the balance at handstroke, and you can make a last minute decision to pull a little sooner or a little later. But at backstroke you can't. Only rarely are you ringing to the balance at backstroke, and your backstrokes may well follow your handstrokes as night follows day.

So to get your backstrokes in the right place you have to prepare for them properly at the previous handstroke. If you're doing a 3-4 down dodge you have to pull your thirds place handstroke strongly enough to get right up to fourths place at the next backstroke. If you don't, nothing will prevent a clip or a crunch. But in a 4-5 down dodge, a half decent backstroke coupled with a bit of pushing and waiting, may well see you through. Of course, the 4-5 up dodge requires a good pull at handstroke as you dodge back into fourths place, but somehow that comes more naturally as you've been hunting up a moment previously.

Some people even claim that a handstroke dodge is easier because you ring with an open handstroke lead, and in theory it probably should be because the percentage variance when you move up or down one place from back to hand is less than the percentage variance when you move up or down one place from hand to back. But by the time you start ringing methods, the uneven handling that the open handstroke lead requires is so natural to you, that it makes almost no difference.

The Practice

But whether or not you *do* find handstroke dodges easier, you're still going to aim for the best possible handling and striking that you can manage. So share your new found enthusiasm with those long-time Grandsire-philes in your tower, and ring plain course after plain course until every blow is perfect. Then, in two weeks time, you can take an even deeper breath and plunge into **The Deep End**.

The great advantage of writing articles for The Ringing World *is that no one can rush through a whole stack of them. It's like listening to a serial on the radio. No matter how exciting each episode is, you* ***have*** *to wait until next week for the following one. So I could lure people into trying plain courses of Grandsire, and by the time they found out how difficult the bobs were, they were so good at plain courses that the bobs weren't much trouble at all.*

But when all the chapters are together in a book, it's not like that. If you're reading this on a train and you've still got a couple of stations to go – or you're reading it in bed but not feeling sleepy yet – you might rush straight on to the next chapter and then feel discouraged from even **starting** *Grandsire.*

So if you're of a nervous disposition, try turning to one of the general chapters instead, and only coming back to the next one once you've got a few plain courses under your belt. Alternatively, you could even go straight to Chapter 9 and miss out Chapters 7 and 8 completely. But if you're ***absolutely sure*** *you'll be alright, keep straight on, and we'll get this wretched bobs business settled here and now.*

7. Grandsire Doubles

The Deep End

Hopefully, you've been ringing plain courses for a bit now, and equally hopefully, everything is going well. So well, indeed, that you're now feeling pretty good about the whole thing. And that's just as well, because this chapter, I'm sorry to say, is going to be a good bit harder.

A Bit of History

Without doubt ***Grandsire*** is a lovely name for a method. It has a feeling of tradition and timelessness, coupled with a distinctly folksy flavour. You can imagine an ageing country ringer in the distant past, calling Grandsire, ***Grandsire***, because his old grandfather had taught it him when he was just a boy in short trousers.

Indeed, lots of people *do* imagine that, and I have a strong suspicion that Grandsire took such a firm hold on ringers' hearts for exactly that reason. Sadly, though, it is far from the truth.

You will remember that in the last Bob Doubles chapter I explained how the early ringers were continually seeking ways of getting all 120 different five-bell changes into one continuous sequence. One such ringer was "R.R." who was probably Robert Roan, a member of the *Society of College Youths*, and he composed a 120 which we would now recognise as a standard extent of Grandsire Doubles.

We don't know much about Robert Roan, but he was apparently quite well off and for a while was Clerk of the Pantry to Charles I. Somewhere around 1650 he dedicated his new composition to the *College Youths* and accompanied it with a long and particularly awful poem ending with the line,

"***So Grandsire bids you All adieu.***"

Rather engagingly, this was rhymed with "***And drink good sack till sky looks blew,***" and 31 other lines, all with similar endings. Clearly, the poem was meant to be funny.

So it seems that Robert Roan was known to the *College Youths* by the nickname of ***Grandsire***. But was he old?

Well, we don't know, but probably not. The *College Youths* of those days were a group of well-to-do young men getting their fun from dabbling in what was otherwise a common man's duty. Their society had only been in existence for about thirteen years, and although some of them clearly carried on ringing as they got older, in 1650 most of them were genuinely young.

So Robert Roan's nickname, like his poem, was probably a joke too. He only joined the *College Youths* in 1647, was Master in 1652 and composed his extent around that time. He got dismissed from his job as a civil servant at the time of the restoration in 1660, and he was obviously not old then as he petitioned the King several times for a higher redundancy pension. I see him as a youngish man, mixing with a group who were a few years younger still, and being called ***Grandad*** as has no doubt happened since time immemorial.

The Hunt Bell

But even though that's how Grandsire got its name, ***Grandsire***, the man, didn't actually invent ***Grandsire***, the method, at all. He invented a 120 from which the method was obtained a good deal later by a kind of reverse derivation. So it's not surprising that the method is a bit odd, and it's also not surprising, in view of the way the earlier call change compositions had been constructed, that the method was given *two* hunt bells.

Now, I dare say you noticed in the last chapter, that in the plain course there is no start for the Two. Only the Three, Four and Five ring the method, while the Two is left to plain hunt like the treble. It is known as ***the hunt bell***, and we say that it is ***in the hunt***.

And because the Two plain hunts, Grandsire is a particularly good method for the struggling band. If you have only three inside ringers, you can ring a plain course of Grandsire as long as you have two plain hunters. It is also a good method for learning ropesight, because the treble ringer can remember when to pass the Two, and then he only has to find his way through three others.

But, of course, you can't ring all 120 changes if the Two *stays* in the hunt, because you'll never get the changes in which the treble and Two have more than one bell between them. So that alone would make the bobs difficult. But in addition, Robert Roan effectively invented a bob, and we've been using that bob ever since, even though a different one might be easier. And all that together, makes bobs difficult.

Singles

But before we get into bobs in detail, I must also mention ***singles***. A single is much like a bob in that it simply shifts the bells around a bit, but it does that a little differently.

So why do we have singles, particularly as we don't have them in Bob Doubles?

Well, that's a good question, and it will take a page or two to answer. As you well know, there are 120 different changes on five. And if you were ringing any one of them, someone could call you back to rounds by a series of call changes. For example, if you were ringing 43512, the conductor could call,

43512
43152 "5 to 1"
41352 "3 to 1"
14352 "4 to 1"
14325 "5 to 2"
14235 "3 to 2"
12435 "4 to 2"
12345 "4 to 3"

That took seven calls. You could call it in a number of different ways, of course, either with seven calls or with more, but however many calls you used, it would ***have*** to be an odd number. It could ***not*** be an even number.

Now, I could prove this for you if you wanted, but it would take a while, so I hope you're happy to take my word for it – although you can try a few tests if you like.

Odd and Even Changes

Not surprisingly, there are other five bell changes which take an odd number of calls to get back to rounds, and there are also changes which take an even number. In fact there are 60 of the one sort and 60 of the other. The two groups are known as ***odd*** changes and ***even*** changes, or ***out of course*** changes and ***in course*** changes, or sometimes, ***negative*** changes and ***positive*** changes.

Of course, none of this has got anything to do with *ringing* Grandsire, and you can skip it completely if you want. But if you look back for a moment at the plain course of Grandsire Doubles on page 52, you'll see that you get from each change to the next by swapping over exactly ***two*** pairs of bells. So all the changes in a plain course must be ***even*** changes because you could get back to rounds with an even number of calls.

The bob, when we come to it, also swaps exactly two pairs of bells. So even when we put some bobs in, we can still only ring touches with ***even*** changes in. We can never get to ring the ***odd*** changes at all. So we cannot ring all the 120 different ones if we just call bobs.

And that means that we must have a call which swaps just one pair of bells instead of two. We must have a ***single*** swap, and that is where the word ***single*** comes from.

And once we've had ***one*** single, we will keep on ringing ***odd*** changes until another single is called. That's because however many ***even*** numbers you add to an ***odd*** number, you always get another odd number.

I hope that wasn't too confusing. Number theory isn't easy, particularly if you rarely or never come across it. But the result is that singles in Grandsire Doubles are definitely necessary. They aren't necessary in Bob Doubles, though, because there's automatically a *single* swap when the treble leads. The bells in firsts, seconds and fifths place lie still, and only the bells in thirds and fourths swap over.

The Bobs

And having got all that out of the way, you can look at the chart opposite which tells you what to do at bobs. It's just like the Bob Doubles bobs chart in Chapter 5.

Grandsire Doubles

What to do at a Bob

Position when Bob is called	First blow at lead before making thirds	Fourths place over the treble	Seconds place on the way up	Fifths place before hunting down
About to	U N A F F E C T E D	Dodge 4-5 down	Dodge 4-5 up	Carry on being hunt bell
Do instead		Double dodge 4-5 up	Make thirds	Double dodge 4-5 down
Do next time		Make thirds	In the hunt	Dodge 4-5 up

N.B. Grandsire bobs are called at *handstroke*

On the next page there's a similar chart for singles as well. And in case it helps, there are pictures of a bob and single on the page after that. You already know how the charts work, and so all you need to do is learn them both thoroughly. But there, unfortunately, lies the rub, because the learning can be a long and hard grind with your knowledge continually slipping away from you while you're ringing.

Grandsire Doubles				
What to do at a Single				
Position when Single is called	First blow at lead before making thirds	Fourths place over the treble	Seconds place on the way up	Fifths place before hunting down
About to	Make thirds	Dodge 4-5 down	Dodge 4-5 up	Carry on being hunt bell
Do instead	Make seconds	Double dodge 4-5 up	Make *long* thirds	Double dodge 4-5 down
Do next time	In the hunt	Make thirds	Dodge 4-5 down	Dodge 4-5 up
N.B. Grandsire singles are called at *handstroke*				

Indeed, the learning can be such a hard grind, that I recommend you not bothering with it at all, but going straight to the alternative way of ringing calls set out in the next chapter.

A Tip

But whichever method you use, take a firm hold of this fundamentally important tip.

Note well when you go into the hunt.

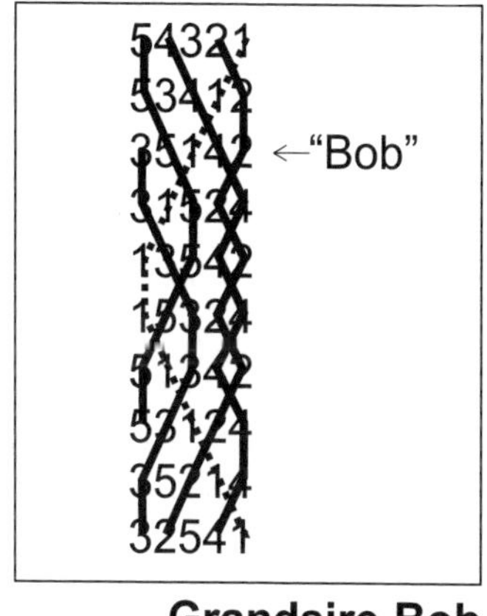

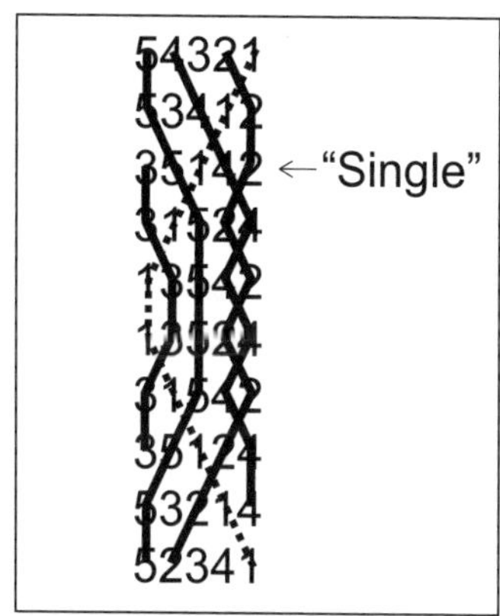

Grandsire Bob **Grandsire Single**

Being in the hunt is something all of its own and very different from either ringing the method or ringing the treble. When you get into the hunt, you must stay in it until there's another call, but it's all too easy to dodge 4-5 down shortly afterwards instead. That is by far and away the commonest mistake in Grandsire, and it's made more often than all the others put together.

So when you go into the hunt, tell yourself clearly and firmly, "***I am the hunt bell***, ***I am in the hunt***, ***and I will not forget it***," and then ***don't*** forget it. In the whole thorny field of Grandsire, ***nothing*** is more important than that.

In an idle moment I once started teaching a budgerigar to say, "Go Grandsire." The budgie – a male – lived with a ringing family, and for some months I persevered tirelessly during coffee breaks in handbell ringing sessions. Eventually I achieved a kind of success – or, at least, I claimed I did – although it never really said, "Go Grandsire," very well. The words came out in a ***Mister Punch*** *voice, accompanied by various clicks, and ending with a soft whistle. It was* *definitely recognisable, though, and a number of ringers stoutly declared that the budgie was a good deal clearer than many of the conductors* ***they*** *knew.*

But the trouble was that I had so often sat by the cage repeating, "Go Grandsire," that it got to be a habit. To my horror, my mind wandered one practice night and I called, "Go - click - click - Grand - click - sire - whooo," Mister Punch-like, completely unconsciously. Two visitors seemed quite disturbed, and I decided that it was definitely time for the bird's conducting career to come to a halt.

So even today he can manage nothing more than plain courses. ***You,*** *though, will want to make doubly sure of touches by reading* **A Tip for Grandsire Bobs**.

8. A Tip for Grandsire Bobs

For the first nine years of my ringing career my tower was a Plain Bob tower. I went from Plain Hunt to Bob Doubles, from Bob Doubles to Bob Minor, and from Bob Minor to Bob Major. That was the extent of our range and we rang little else. Now, though, a new tower captain has taken over and we keep ringing Grandsire. For the past six months we've been practising Grandsire Doubles and Grandsire Triples several times every practice night. I can manage plain courses but bobs and singles seem to be completely beyond me. Can you help?

B.J.W.

I get a lot of cries for help with Grandsire, and that isn't surprising, because bobs and singles are more difficult in Grandsire than in any other method. When a bob is called in Plain Bob only ***some*** of the bells are affected. But in Grandsire they're ***nearly all*** affected.

What's more, if you're affected in Plain Bob, you certainly do something different, but at least you do it where you were going to do something special anyway. At a Grandsire bob, though, you have to start dodging when you would otherwise still be plain hunting.

So there are a lot of ringers who find touches of Grandsire very difficult or impossible. Many struggle for years to master it, and many others just give up and stick to Plain Bob. If you're one of those ringers yourself, this tip is for you.

The Orthodox System

There is, of course, an orthodox system for ringing Grandsire calls, and most people have a go at it first. For each piece of work in the plain course, they learn what they must do instead if a bob or single is called while they're on their way to it. They also learn what they must do next time if no further bob or single is called.

That's probably the most reliable way of ringing Grandsire, but it's also jolly difficult because there's such a lot to learn and remember. Indeed, I strongly suspect that only a small proportion of Grandsire ringers actually ring it that way, with the rest making do with a selection of pointers, tips and hand-to-mouth patent remedies.

My Own System

My own tip is below. And in the best traditions of consumer magazines I can confirm that it has been tried and tested by many Grandsire-phobes over the years, and is generally agreed to be ***Good Value for Money*** and ***Best Buy***. It can be used with equal ease in Grandsire Doubles, Triples, Caters and Cinques.

Let's look at the bob first.

If you're ***above*** thirds place when a bob is called, ***double dodge exactly where you are*** and carry on in the direction you were going anyway.

If you're ***below*** thirds place when a bob is called, ***make thirds*** and go back to lead again.

For example,

> If a bob is called when you're in fourths place on the way up, double dodge 4-5 up.
>
> If a bob is called when you're in sevenths place in Triples and about to hunt down, double dodge 6-7 down.
>
> If you're in seconds place when a bob is called, make thirds and go back to lead.
>
> If you're leading when a bob is called, do the same.

What to do next time

That tells you what to do at the bob. But what do you do next time?

Well, if you double dodge at the bob, note which position you're double dodging in. Then carry on with the method as though you had only done one dodge there instead of two.

For example,

> Suppose you double dodge 4-5 up at a bob. In the plain course 4-5 up is followed by thirds, so ***thirds*** is what you do next time.
>
> Or suppose you double dodge 6-7 down at a bob in Triples. In the plain course 6-7 down is followed by 6-7 up, so ***6-7 up*** is what you do next time.

If you make thirds at the bob, look to see which bell you take off lead. If it's the treble, you've become hunt bell and so must remain in the hunt until there's another call. If you take any other bell off lead, dodge 4-5 down next time.

And at a Single

Of course, in Grandsire there are singles as well as bobs. But fortunately they don't take much extra.

If you're ***above*** thirds place when the single is called, you do exactly the same as if a bob had been called.

If you're ***below*** thirds place when the single is called, then,

> If you're leading, you make seconds and become hunt bell.
>
> If you *aren't* leading, you make ***four blows in thirds***, go back to lead again, and dodge 4-5 down next time.

Learning the Tip

And if we went through that a bit quickly, try reading it again, perhaps with the blue line in front of you. It's far easier to remember than to express, and it has the considerable advantage that you ***never*** have to worry about what you might have done if no bob had been called. At each bob you simply wipe the slate clean and start again.

Spend a while studying it, have a think about it, and then astound your tower captain with your new found expertise.

Rather oddly, this turned out to be one of my most popular articles. It got pinned up in a whole host of ringing chambers, and even now I occasionally come across a semi-legible, mildewed copy, secured by a rusty drawing pin. Indeed, someone once introduced me to a friend, adding, in a hushed whisper, "He wrote ***The Tip for Grandsire Bobs****."*

*"****Oh!****" replied the friend.*

In the weeks after the Tip was published, quite a few people wrote to me about other methods. "I can ring Grandsire now," they said, "but can you help with Stedman?" Or, "The Grandsire's getting on fine, but what should I do about Kent?"

And I was regularly taken privately to one side at District meetings by someone putting their hand over their mouth and hissing, "Have you got a good tip for Little Bob?" as though they were seeking inside information on the 3.30 at Newmarket.

All of which brought home to me that patent ringing tips, like herbal health remedies, have a wide popularity. So although this is the only tip with a chapter to itself, I've included a large selection of them throughout this book. Indeed, you will find several more in **Plain Bob Minor**.

Moving On

9. Plain Bob Minor

Last summer I wished at a wishing well. My wish must stay for ever a secret – or it will not work – and so I cannot tell you what it was. But despite me throwing in £1.50 (in assorted change) there's still no sign of anything happening. Could it be that the well needs help? If I give you the smallest clue that the wish was something to do with ringing Bob Minor by next Easter, could you give the well a hand?

An embarrassed well wisher.

When you set to with a blue line of Bob Minor, you know you're ***moving on***. It's like starting a new course of evening classes or a new term at school. There's the smell of polish, the newly varnished floor, and the quiet confidence that this time everything will be ***alright***. You really *will* study hard, you really *will* do your homework, and all those problems that beset you before, just won't trouble you again.

Hopefully, you're still at that *quietly confident* stage. But even if you're in the *sliding-into-depression* stage or – worse still – the *I'm-never-going-to-make-it* stage, now's the time to rally. Because we're going to go over it all together.

The Method

Bob Minor – as Plain Bob Minor is normally abbreviated to – is, of course, on six. Indeed, although no one knows for certain where the word comes from, ***minor*** means that there are six working bells. So all of the six bells involved have to hunt up and down between lead and sixths place, and all of them but the treble, have to dodge. And it's in exactly *that*, that nearly all the difficulties lie.

But since the easiest thing about Bob Minor is learning it, we'll do that first. The blue line is on the page opposite, and the order of the work, starting on the Two, goes

3-4 down
5-6 down
5-6 up
3-4 up
seconds

And once you've learnt Bob Doubles, it won't take you long to learn Bob Minor as well. There are no long fifths – or indeed, long sixths – but the long fifths in Bob Doubles is replaced by two new pieces of work, 5-6 down and 5-6 up in that order. Mind you, even if it takes you only a few moments to learn, it will still repay long and careful study and revision. The order of the work needs to be absolutely second nature to you by the time you start ringing it, because *that* is when your troubles really begin.

Hunting on Six

Quite possibly, you've never or rarely hunted on six. In the ideal world you would learn plain hunt on five ***and*** six. You would master Bob Doubles inside and at the same time start ringing the treble to Bob Minor. You would be ringing with a strong but friendly and supportive band who would not only guide and advise you, but would provide a solid framework for you to practise your skills in. Moving on to the Two for a course of Bob Minor would then be a relatively small step.

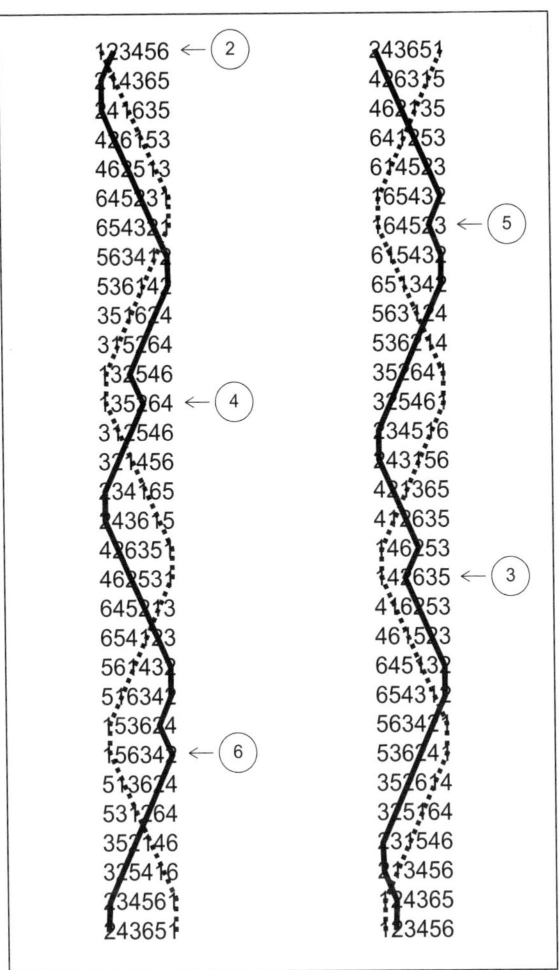

Plain Bob Minor

But the real world is rarely like that, mainly because the majority of teaching bands don't have enough experienced ringers. So what can you do about it?

First, try and get some plain hunting on six *somewhere*. If your own tower isn't strong enough, visit another one or go to a District practice. Tell the tower captain or ringing master that you'd like to ring some plain hunt on six ***and***

nothing more. Don't allow yourself to get pushed into Bob Minor too soon.

Second, really work at the plain hunt. Concentrate on getting your handling and striking as smooth and accurate as possible. Take particular care with your leading because you'll have to do it by rhythm and by ear, rather than by looking at the tenor.

Third, take particular care as you start to hunt down. You've been used to lying behind from backstroke to handstroke and then pulling in at ***backstroke***. You'll now have to lie behind from handstroke to backstroke and then pull in at ***handstroke***. This may sound like only a small change but it definitely isn't. Many ringers never get their Bob Minor right – or, indeed, their Kent or Surprise Minor either – because they don't dig their handstrokes in firmly enough as they start to hunt down. Be very careful about this.

Fourth, in due course if you get the chance, ring the treble to Bob Minor as many times as you can.

The Ropesight

And now for the ropesight. If you have first class ropesight on five, the extra bell may not be much trouble to you. But for most people it's *a lot* of trouble, at least for a short while. So before you go hands-on, stand behind someone for a few courses and follow them carefully.

Learn, too, where you pass the treble. Many of the passing places are the same as Bob Doubles or they're similar, and there are only a few new ones. And consider learning your ***course bells*** and ***after bells*** as well.

Your First Course

And when you're really well prepared, go for your first

plain course. Best of all, it will be with your local band, but quite likely it will have to be at a District practice. You'll go along, full of enthusiasm, and tell the ringing master that you'd like a course of Bob Minor.

"Bob Minor," he'll call, and several people just like yourself will instantly catch hold. You may not get the rope you want, or you may not get a rope at all. Probably, none of you will know how inexperienced you all are, and a distinctly difficult and unsatisfying course – or, indeed, fire-up – will follow. You'll sit down afterwards feeling that Bob Minor is way beyond you.

This happens more with Bob Minor and Bob Major than anything else, and it can be a real problem. Experienced ringers have railed in *The Ringing World* about it, fulminating in a *disgusted-of-Tunbridge-Wells* sort of way about the incompetence of District ringing masters. Their chief complaint being that their own learner didn't get a proper go.

I once saw four *disgusteds-of-Tunbridge-Wells*, all vigorously pushing their own learners into a course of Bob Major, and all being thoroughly annoyed that the other learners weren't being kept out. The moral is that a little give and take makes a big difference. The ringing master will have seen what happened – hopefully – and whilst not saying anything at the time, he'll try and stop it happening again. Make the best of what opportunities you get, keep going to the District practices, and things will surely get better.

Breaking Out

But what if you are a Bob Doubles band determined to break out ***alone*** into Bob Minor? A band all doing it at once, and doing it unsupported?

You are the courageous ones. Solid and determined, you

are taking the big step by yourselves, and I am absolutely with you in spirit. But it certainly won't be easy.

Much of what we discussed earlier applies particularly to you. The plain hunt practice is essential, as is the thorough study of the method. The treble passing places and the *course* and *after* bells are also necessary learning. But in addition, don't be afraid to start somewhere other than the beginning.

The point is that the nearer you are to the start, the less likely you are to go wrong. After all, you get more practice at the first part, and you get more nervous in the uncharted waters. By the time you've done a couple of dodges, you get the uncomfortable feeling that you're boldly ringing where no man has rung before, and your confidence starts slipping.

But you can get over this by starting in the middle and repeating each new bit until you get it right. For example, you can pull off in the change

462135

and when you've all settled down, the conductor can call, "Carry on Bob Minor." You then proceed,

462135
641253
614523
165432
164523
615432
651342

and so on.

It may take you a while but the results will definitely be worth it.

Turning the Tenor In

The break-out band, though, does have one great problem. In Bob Minor the tenor doesn't just ring behind, it moves about. It hunts up, it hunts down and it dodges. Most tenors are significantly heavier than most Fives, and however good a bell yours is, handling it will not be easy.

Ringing the tenor inside to a method, is known as ***turning the tenor in***, and the very existence of the expression points up the problem.

"Have you rung the tenor at Yagton?" one ringer will say to another.

"I've rung it behind to Stedman but I've never turned it in," will be the reply.

Or someone else will say, "You know Fred turned our tenor in to Cambridge last week. And he made a good job of it too."

So don't expect that ringing the tenor to Bob Minor will be anything at all like ringing it behind. You'll need a range and variation of pull, rather than strength, and you're much more likely to overpull than underpull – although you may well do both. You'll also have to pull very soon after the little bells in order to strike in the right place.

Considerable practice, a full awareness of the problems, and the realisation that your early attempts will be nowhere near good enough, are essential if you're going to get it right. There is nothing more disappointing than a male tenor ringer ambling gently down to lead with a supremely macho look on his face and enough space before each blow to accommodate a double-decker bus. Of course, you'll never be like that yourself, but it's best to make absolutely sure.

Bobs

And now for the bobs. Fortunately, they are absolutely no problem, and although I am including a chart here, essentially they're exactly the same as Bob Doubles bobs. You run in, run out, and make the bob, and you're ***unaffected*** in 5-6 down and 5-6 up. The only new thing to remember is that after ***making the bob*** you ***dodge 5-6 down*** next time.

Plain Bob Minor				
What to do at a Bob				
Position when Bob is called	Second blow at lead	Fourths place on the way down	Thirds place on the way up	Fifths or sixths place before 5-6 up or 5-6 down
About to	Make seconds	Dodge 3-4 down	Dodge 3-4 up	UNAFFECTED
Do instead	Run out	Run in	Make the bob	
Do next time	Make seconds	Dodge 3-4 down	Dodge 5-6 down	

Singles

Unlike Bob Doubles, though, Bob Minor also has singles. I explained on page 59 why Grandsire Doubles needs singles, and Bob Minor needs them for a similar reason – although I'm afraid the detailed explanation is even more complicated. Once again, I'm including a chart, and there's a set of rules on the next page.

<table>
<tr><th colspan="5">Plain Bob Minor</th></tr>
<tr><th colspan="5">What to do at a Single</th></tr>
<tr><td>Position when Single is called</td><td>Second blow at lead before making seconds</td><td>Fourths place on the way down</td><td>Thirds place on the way up</td><td>Fifths or sixths place before 5-6 up or 5-6 down</td></tr>
<tr><td>About to</td><td rowspan="3">UNAFFECTED</td><td>Dodge 3-4 down</td><td>Dodge 3-4 up</td><td rowspan="3">UNAFFECTED</td></tr>
<tr><td>Do instead</td><td>Make reverse thirds</td><td>Make the bob</td></tr>
<tr><td>Do next time</td><td>Make seconds</td><td>Dodge 5-6 down</td></tr>
</table>

> If you're about to dodge ***5-6 down*** or ***5-6 up***, or make ***seconds***, you're ***unaffected***.
>
> If you were going to dodge ***3-4 up***, you ***make fourths*** just as though a bob had been called – except that both blows in fourths are over ***the same bell***.

And,

> If you were going to dodge ***3-4 down***, you ***do two blows in thirds*** – over ***the same bell*** – and go back out to the back. You then make seconds next time.

This last way of being affected – known as making ***reverse thirds*** – is by far and away the most difficult, and some ringers ***never*** get the hang of it. The tips for getting it right are,

> Be absolutely determined to do both blows in thirds over the same bell,

And,

> Do not under any circumstances try and ring over the treble until you are right at the back again.

In fact, you ring an astonishing eight blows without ringing over the treble, and most people have great difficulty in bringing themselves to do that. Think of the thirds as a sudden and thrilling handbrake turn, and you can't go wrong.

And After

And after all that fight and effort, will it be worth it?

It certainly will. You are now a six-bell method ringer and nothing will ever be so hard again. You have crossed a major barrier, and stretching before you is a world of fascinating and musical methods just waiting for you to enjoy them; a world packed with fun and opportunity. Ringing may have been fun before, but from now on, things are going to be ***good***.

Some years ago I wrote three articles on learning and practising new methods. They weren't very long and they were very well received, and I was tempted to include them all in this book. But since I had already put them in my first book, ***The Bellringer's Bedside Companion****, I thought that if I included them again here, some people might feel a bit cheated. So I've left them out.*

But I mention them now so that you can get out your ***Bedside Companion*** *and recap on those articles before the next chapter if you want to. Of course, if – speak it only in a whisper – you don't have a copy, don't worry. I think you'll find* **The Best of the Rest** *self-explanatory anyway.*

10. Plain Minor

The Best of the Rest

Time was, when ringers learnt ***the standard methods***. Nobody knew quite what they *were*, but everyone was quite sure what they *weren't*. They certainly included Plain Bob, Grandsire, Stedman, Kent and Oxford, and they certainly did *not* include Reverse Canterbury even though it was widely rung. What else they included changed as time went by and could be a matter of debate.

"Would *you* call Little Bob a standard method?"

"Um ... er ... I *think* I would."

The expression itself dates from the end of the nineteenth century. Academics and teachers were trying to impose many of their personal prejudices on everyone else, and after ***standard*** pronunciation and ***standard*** grammar, what more natural than ***standard*** methods?

In fact, ***Standard Methods*** was the title of a famous book by Jasper Snowdon which came out in two parts – diagrams and letterpress – in 1881. It was undoubtedly a great work and broke entirely new ground, but Snowdon's idea of what was standard then, seems a little odd today. If you can locate an early copy you'll find it contains methods such as Violet and Woodbine which few modern ringers have even heard of, let alone rung.

Nowadays, people don't talk about ***standard methods*** very often – although in Surprise Major they still speak of ***the standard eight*** when referring to the eight methods you can read about in Chapters 42 to 44. But the idea was that the standard methods were the methods that every competent ringer needed to be able to ring in order to fit in with a good ringing practice anywhere.

And that's precisely why the expression has largely died out – because nowadays almost nothing is standard. Although most method ringers can ring Plain Bob, there are plenty of Cambridge ringers who can't ring Kent and plenty of Kent ringers who can't ring Stedman. There are London ringers who don't know Grandsire, and Spliced Surprise ringers who are very shaky in Oxford. Method ringing is more advanced and more widespread than ever before, but it's also far more varied.

So if you were hoping I'd tell you which Plain Minor method to learn after Plain Bob, I am afraid you're going to be disappointed. There's no *should learn* next method at all. Indeed, you could go straight on to Stedman, Kent or Cambridge if you wanted to, and lots of ringers do.

But if, like me, you enjoy ringing at District meetings and local practices, then a knowledge of any or all of the following methods will definitely come in handy. This chapter is a whistle stop tour of all the Plain Minor methods that are rung and loved in lots of places.

Little Bob

Little Bob has the great advantage that the treble only goes out to fourths place. That makes it good for inexperienced treble ringers and *short*. Indeed, the plain course is so short – 40 changes – that it fits neatly down the side of this page.

Many people learn it as one blue line but many more learn it by *the three rules*.

1. You always dodge 5-6 up and 5-6 down.

2. You always make seconds over the treble if it takes you off.

And,

3. You always dodge 3-4 up and 3-4 down ***unless*** you ring over the treble in fourths place. If you ***do***, you hunt straight through – either up or down – instead.

Getting Little Bob right isn't always easy, and ringers often find themselves dodging 3-4 when they shouldn't and not dodging 3-4 when they should. treble ringers often get out to the back by mistake too.

Curiously, mistakes in Little Bob are often regarded as an entertainment, and many ringers simply love to find the treble in fifths place. "***Get down, treble!***"

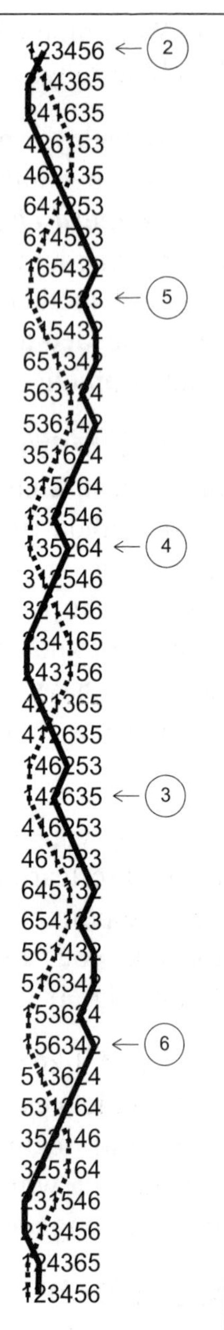

Little Bob

they roar, with huge grins on their faces as though they were playing a game of ***Simon Says.***

Bobs and singles are just like Bob Minor bobs and singles, although it can be difficult to work out where you've got to afterwards. So you either have to learn that by rote, or you have to ring by the three rules. If you do the latter, though, remember that, contrary to the third rule, if you run out at a bob or make reverse thirds at a single, you ***don't*** dodge in 3-4 up afterwards even though you don't meet the treble there.

Little Bob is often spliced with Plain Bob, and there's more about that in Chapter 31.

St Clement's

St Clement's – or to give it its full name, ***St Clement's College Bob*** – is hugely popular and very widely rung. The picture is on the next page, and essentially the method consists of two bells dodging on the front from the time the treble leaves them, to the time it gets back again. The other bells, meanwhile, hunt up and down between thirds and sixths place.

At the lead end, one bell makes seconds and the others dodge – just as they do in Bob Minor – but the order you come to the dodges is the *reverse* of their Bob Minor order.

You ***can*** ring it by a set of rules and watching the treble, but not many people do. Most just learn the blue line. Fortunately, it's one of the few methods that nearly everybody finds easier in the actuality than they do in the theory, and the biggest problems are counting up to three in the dodges and remembering what comes next on the back.

Forgetting to turn round in thirds can also be a trouble,

but, unlike when the treble gets too high in Little Bob, no one finds this the least bit funny. In any case, getting right again afterwards is a nightmare, so it's best to *stay* right.

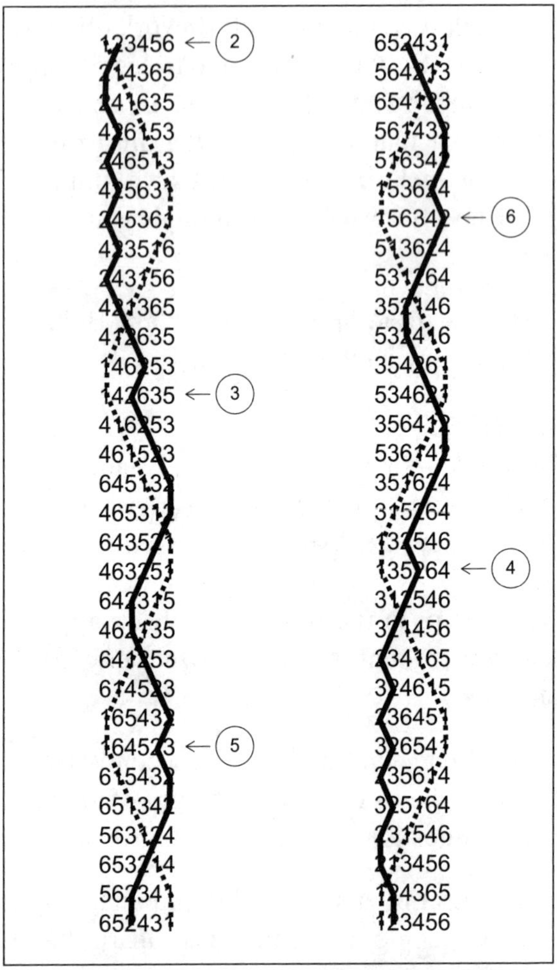

123456 ← (2)	652431
214365	564213
241635	654123
426153	561432
246513	516342
425631	153624
245361	156342 ← (6)
423516	513624
243156	531264
421365	352146
412635	532416
146253	354261
142635 ← (3)	534621
416253	356412
461523	536142
645132	351624
465312	315264
643521	132546
463251	135264 ← (4)
642315	312546
462135	321456
641253	234165
614523	324615
165432	236451
164523 ← (5)	326541
615432	235614
651342	325164
563124	231546
653214	213456
562341	124365
652431	123456

St Clement's Minor

Bobs and singles, once again, are like Bob Minor, but you need to learn the work afterwards very carefully. It's knowing exactly how you join and leave the frontwork that causes the most problems, so I'm putting in a couple of pictures to help. Take careful note that when you run in, you only do the *second* half of the frontwork, but when you make the bob, you do the *whole* of the frontwork over again. If you make thirds at a single, you miss out the frontwork entirely.

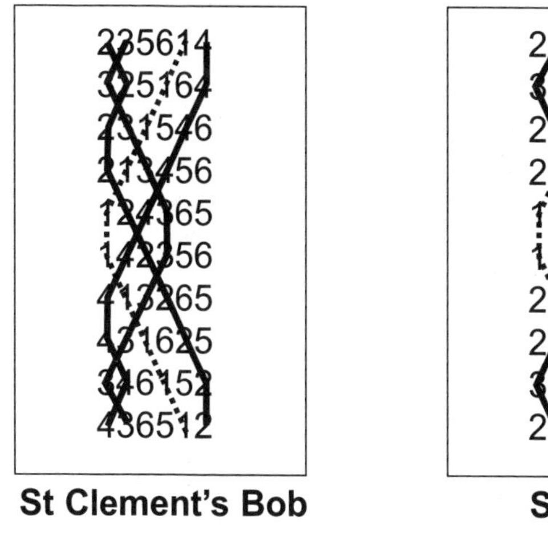

St Clement's Bob

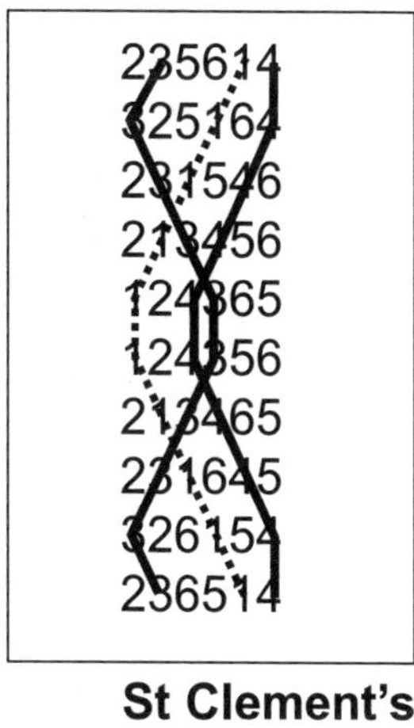

St Clement's Single

The great thing about St Clement's is that it's very musical. Listen to it and enjoy it.

Single Oxford

For most ringers, ***Single Oxford*** is another of those *ring-it-by-the-rules* methods. They think of it as ringing Plain Bob Minimus on the front four unless by the time they get to fourths place, they still haven't passed the treble. If they haven't, they go out to the back and do three dodges with whoever they find there when the treble's gone.

Simple, isn't it?

Well, some people certainly find it so, but others are never really sure whether they've passed the treble or not. If you come into this latter category, learn the blue line instead. You alone will then be in the right place when the treble goes wrong.

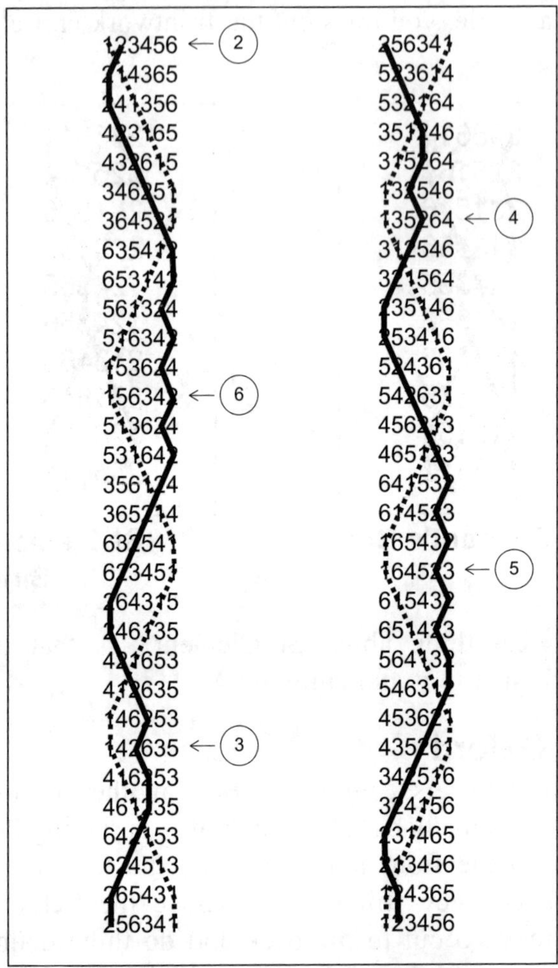

Single Oxford Minor

Single Oxford is another method with Bob Minor bobs and singles. But when you run out or make reverse thirds at a single, don't forget to make fourths at once.

Double Oxford

Double Oxford is a there-and-back method. If you start on the front, you go up to the back, come back down to the front, and that's it. You aren't continually rushing up and down like you are in Plain Bob and most other methods, but the quid pro quo is that you stay everywhere much longer.

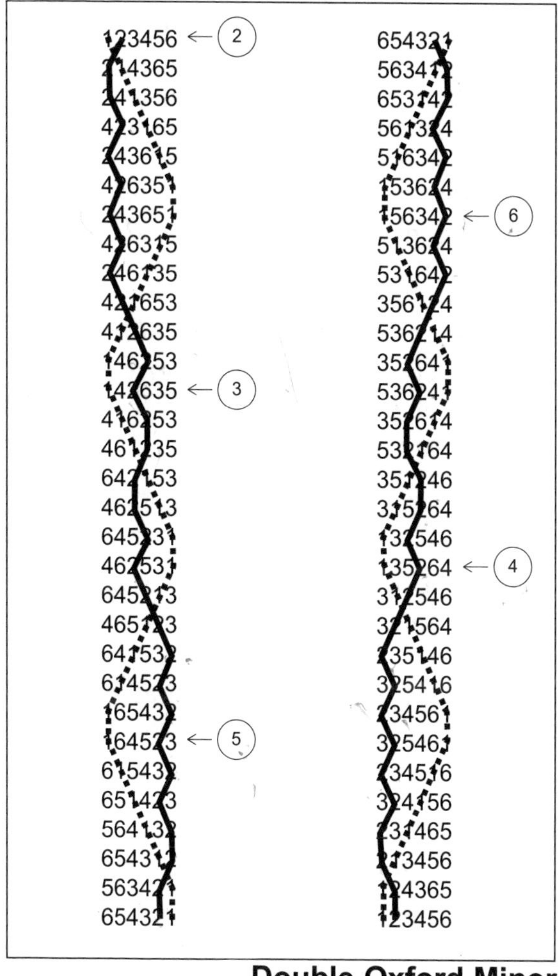

Double Oxford Minor

As well as the blue line, you need to learn the order of the work, which goes

frontwork
places up
backwork
places down

And although that *seems* easy, you must also learn that the ***frontwork*** is three dodges 1-2 down, lead, seconds, lead, three dodges 1-2 up, just like St Clement's; and the ***backwork*** – which is, in fact, the same thing upside down – is three dodges 5-6 up, lie, fifths, lie, three dodges 5-6 down.

Similarly, you must learn that ***places up*** are dodge 3-4 up, fourths, thirds, dodge 3-4 up; and ***places down*** are dodge 3-4 down, thirds, fourths, dodge 3-4 down.

These ***places*** are often called ***Yorkshire places*** because they occur profusely in Yorkshire Surprise Major. The treble always passes through the middle of them in Double Oxford – although it doesn't in Yorkshire.

Interestingly, this is the first ***double*** method we've come across. You can read more about double methods in Chapter 26, but because Double Oxford *is* double, it has several interesting properties. Both upside down and back to front it looks the same, and if you hold this page up to the light and look through at the picture on the previous one, it looks exactly the same as it does from the other side. In addition, because it's double, you could just learn a quarter of the blue line and then ring that quarter four ways:

the right way,
upside down and backwards,
upside down and forwards,
and **the right way up but backwards**.

After which, you'd be back to the beginning again. And although not many people ring Double Oxford this way, they *do* ring two other double methods, ***Double Norwich Major*** and ***Bristol Surprise Major***, that way.

Personally, I enjoy Double Oxford very much. It's oddly satisfying to ring and extremely pleasant to listen to. The biggest problem for most people, is getting the fifths in the middle of the backwork, right.

The bobs and singles are as in Bob Minor, but since not many bands ring them often, they need careful study.

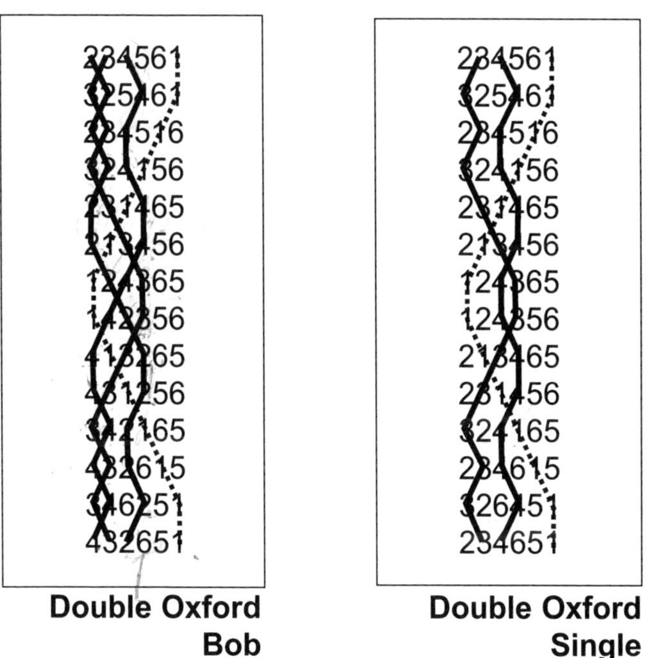

Double Oxford Bob

Double Oxford Single

Remembering to miss off the dodge at the end of the places when running in – or the beginning of the places when running out – is the hard part, but you may also have trouble joining your two sets of places with reverse thirds at a single.

Double Court

And after our *first* double method, here's our second – ***Double Court***. It is a classic method with an elegant structure and a long pedigree, but most people find it so horrendously difficult to keep right in, that it's no longer rung as much as it used to be. Nevertheless, the blue line isn't really too bad.

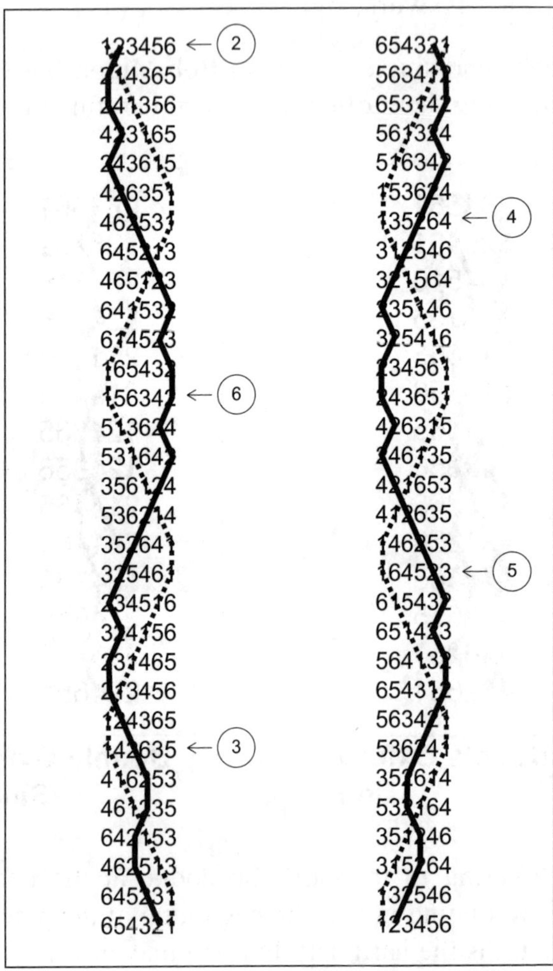

Double Court Minor

Most people, though, don't ring it by the blue line, they ring it by the treble. They remember the rules,

> Always dodge in 1-2 and 5-6 – both up and down – unless the treble stops you.

And,

> If the treble turns you from the front or back, make places. Otherwise, hunt straight through.

Your ***places***, though, are not Yorkshire places but ***court places***. They are simply fourths and thirds if you're going up, or thirds and fourths if you're coming down. Have a look at them in the picture opposite.

Bobs, if anyone has the temerity to call them, are definitely ***not*** Bob Minor bobs. And if you think they look bad, the singles are even worse. It's the bells near the back that are affected, not those going onto or leaving the front.

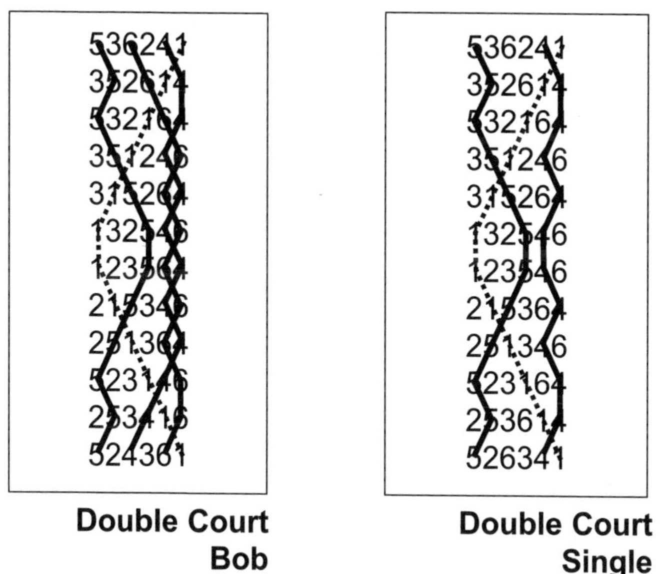

Double Court Bob

Double Court Single

Essentially, the bells in 5-6 do two extra dodges at a bob – making three in all. The bell dodging ***down*** then goes straight down to the front, and the bell dodging ***up***, lies and makes places. The bell that has just done its dodge, lead, dodge on the front, makes fourths, and does it again.

At a single, one bell makes fourths exactly as at a bob, and another makes sixths unaffected. The bell that has just made places up, lies, dodges and makes ***fifths***, and then dodges, lies and makes places down. That's really tricky, so if you're ever likely to ring a single, learn it carefully. But even if you never ring a touch, do have a go at a plain course.

Double Bob

And lastly, ***Double Bob***, a method which District ringing masters sometimes choose as a ***special*** method, normally, I suspect, to catch everybody out. In theory, you ring Bob Minor when you're above the treble, and you ring Bob Minor ***upside down*** – ***Reverse Bob Minor***, as it's called – when you're below the treble. In practice, though, the dodges below the treble are almost everyone's bête noire.

I suppose Double Bob is good training for something, although I'm not exactly sure what. If you really *can* hear when the treble is about to make sixths – and you can dodge underneath it as a result – you undoubtedly have very acute hearing indeed. So acute, that you probably don't need to practise it on Double Bob. And if you *can't*, ringing Double Bob probably won't improve matters. So if you can't, don't worry. Hardly anyone else can either.

Mind you, *your* advantage is that I'm including the blue line on the page opposite for you to study beforehand. Bone up on it but don't tell anyone. Then, the next time your ringing master calls for it, he'll be struck dumb by your listening prowess.

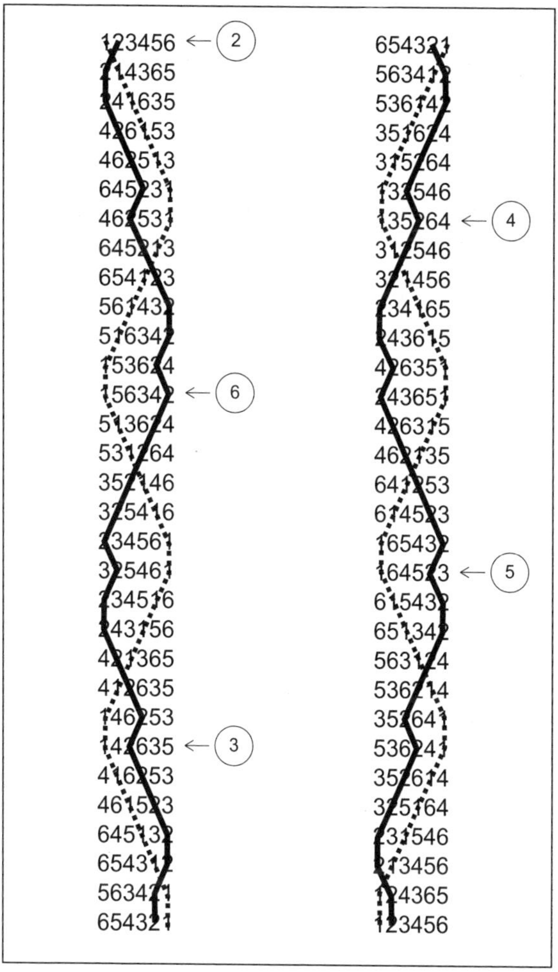

123456 ← (2)	654321
214365	563412
241635	536142
426153	351624
462513	315264
645231	132546
462531	135264 ← (4)
645213	312546
654123	321456
561432	234165
516342	243615
153624	426351
156342 ← (6)	243651
513624	426315
531264	462135
352146	641253
325416	614523
234561	165432
325461	164523 ← (5)
234516	615432
243156	651342
421365	563124
412635	536214
146253	352641
142635 ← (3)	536241
416253	352614
461523	325164
645132	231546
654312	213456
563421	124365
654321	123456

Double Bob Minor

There have been quite a lot of blue lines in this chapter and there will be a good few more in the next, and by the time you've got this far, they're probably becoming second nature to you. But a Mr F. E. Warboys once wrote a most interesting article in The Ringing World *about a rather different system. He uses what he calls* **ideograms**, *which are collections of* *short, horizontal, vertical, and sloping or curved lines, representing hunting, making places and dodging. I couldn't possibly do his article justice in a few words but there must certainly be some ringers who would find his system far easier than blue lines. The trouble is, though, that if they find blue lines difficult, they probably haven't progressed beyond Bob Doubles anyway.*

But if you have trouble with blue lines yourself – or you have a learner in your tower who does – why not experiment with an alternative system yourself. As Mr Warboys said, if nothing else, you'll learn a tremendous amount about the methods you're studying.

11. The Other Doubles

A couple of months ago my friend and I went to a neighbouring tower's practice night. Were we ringers? We were. Did we ring Doubles? We did. Did we ring St Simon's? We didn't – but we'd look it up for next time. Did we ring Reverse Canterbury? We'd look that up too. And we did.

But next time it was, did we ring St Martin's? And then, did we ring St Nicholas? And the time after that it was, did we ring New Bob?

Oh dear, oh dear! Please tell us all the Doubles methods we need to know.

S.T.
Sussex

There are an awful lot of Doubles methods. Not everybody counts them the same way, but the number of plain, symmetrical Doubles methods in the 1980 *Central Council* collection was 183, and my own experience is that at least 60% of them are rung regularly somewhere. That doesn't mean that they're rung in most towers – or even in many towers, but there are certainly a sizeable minority of towers, spread throughout the country, where all sorts of Doubles methods are regularly rung.

We will look at how to stay afloat in the specialist

towers in a moment. But first, let's look at the most common methods. I'm using their most common names too, but you may come across them under other names. This is partly local tradition and partly because in recent times the *Central Council Methods Committee* researched the names by which all methods were first rung to peals. Effectively, this resulted in substantial renaming, so the books and diaries of a few years ago have some different names to the books and diaries of today.

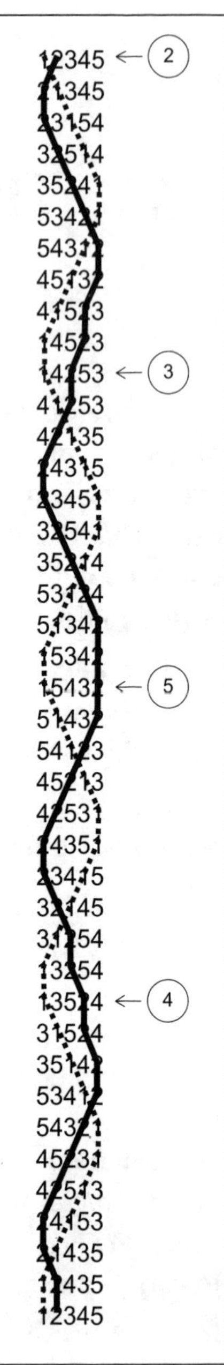

Reverse Canterbury

Reverse Canterbury

Reverse Canterbury – or ***Reverse Canterbury Pleasure Bob Doubles*** to give it its full name – is by far and away the third most commonly rung method. It has a long history of huge popularity among ordinary ringers and huge condescension among posh ones. Indeed, Jasper Snowdon called it ***Plain Bob spoilt***. The plain course is easy because it's exactly the same as Bob Doubles except that you do fourths and thirds – and thirds and fourths – instead of dodging 3-4 down and 3-4 up.

The 3-4 places are known as ***Reverse Canterbury places*** when you ring them in Reverse Canterbury, although they're known as ***Kent places*** when you ring them in ***Kent***. If you've never rung them before, the most difficult bit is getting them at the right stroke. Each place is made backstroke-handstroke rather than handstroke-backstroke.

The ropesight can also be difficult. Take note that the fourths is always over ***the same bell***, whilst the thirds is always over ***different*** bells, one of which is the treble.

And since the method starts in the middle of a set of places, be very careful if you're ringing the Three or Four. The Three starts by making one more blow in thirds and going down – and then does long fifths next time. The Four starts by making one more blow in fourths and going up – and then makes seconds next time.

The bobs – and there aren't normally any singles – add extra interest because they look like this.

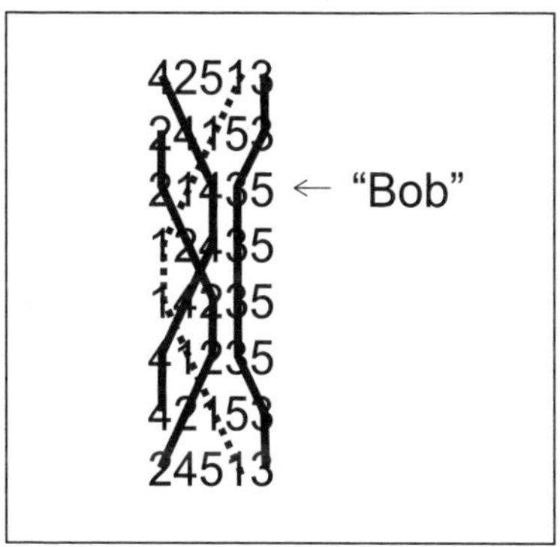

Reverse Canterbury Bob

The bell doing four blows behind is unaffected – just as it is in Bob Doubles – but the bell that would have done its places down does four blows in fourths and lies behind again. It then does seconds next time. The other two bells do thirds and back as in a Grandsire bob. The one that takes the treble off, does places down next time, and the one that doesn't, does long fifths next time.

Not surprisingly the bobs can be a bit of a puzzle and need practice. Even more of a puzzle is that conductors often call the bobs a blow early, probably because the bobs are so Grandsire-like. So be prepared for the unexpected.

St Simon's

And now for something radically different – ***St Simon's***. If you already ring St Clement's Minor, it's easy, but if you don't, it isn't. All the same, it's still hugely popular. Think of it as ***the frontwork*** and ***the backwork***, and learn them separately. Not only will that help you ring it, it will also help you with lots of other methods as well.

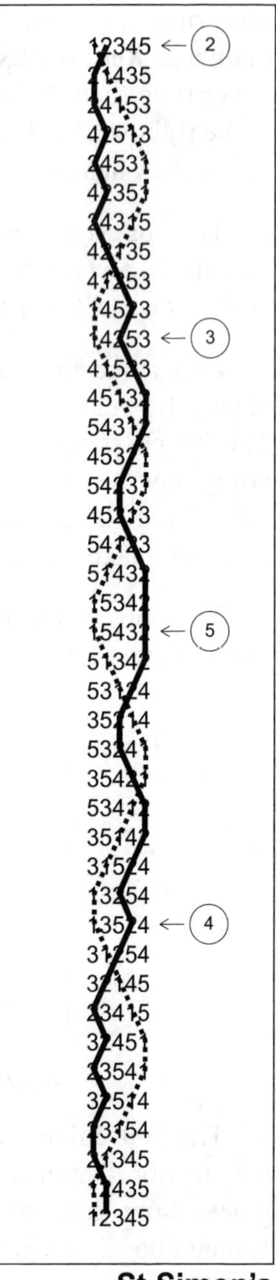

St Simon's

The backwork is

3-4 up
fifths
thirds
long fifths
thirds
fifths
3-4 down

and the hardest part is remembering always to turn round

in thirds. The hardest part of the frontwork, on the other hand, is getting your dodging and leading the right way round. The frontwork is

double dodge 1-2 down
lead, seconds, lead
double dodge 1-2 up

Bobs – and, once again, there are normally no singles – are Bob Doubles bobs, but they send you into unlikely places.

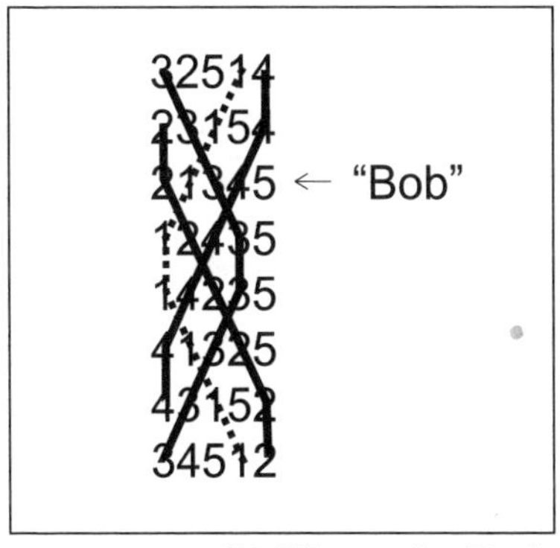

St Simon's Bob

The bell that was going to make seconds, ***runs out*** and does the whole of the backwork ***except for the first dodge***.

The bell that was going to do the backwork, ***makes the bob*** and then does ***the whole of the frontwork again***.

And the bell that was about to dodge 3-4 down at the end of the backwork, misses out the dodge, ***runs in*** and does the ***second half*** of the frontwork.

All that is hard, certainly, but St Simon's is a popular and entertaining method as well as being the gateway to a whole heap of other entertaining methods. It will fully repay you learning it.

St Martin's

St Martin's is the lazy man's St Simon's. The backwork is exactly the same as the St Simon's backwork but the frontwork has you repeatedly leading and making seconds instead of dodging.

The hardest part is keeping track of the number of times you've made seconds. Think of it as one time over someone, one time over the treble, one time over someone else, and that's the end.

Bobs are as in St Simon's, and, once again, there aren't normally any singles.

St Nicholas

St Nicholas is a cross between St Simon's and Reverse Canterbury. What Jasper Snowdon – if the method had been rung then – would have called, ***St Simon's spoilt***.

The plain course – and there is a picture on the page opposite – is exactly like St Simon's but has Reverse Canterbury places instead of 3-4 dodges. The bobs are Reverse Canterbury bobs, and that means that the two bells which have been dodging on the front, both make thirds and dodge together on the front again.

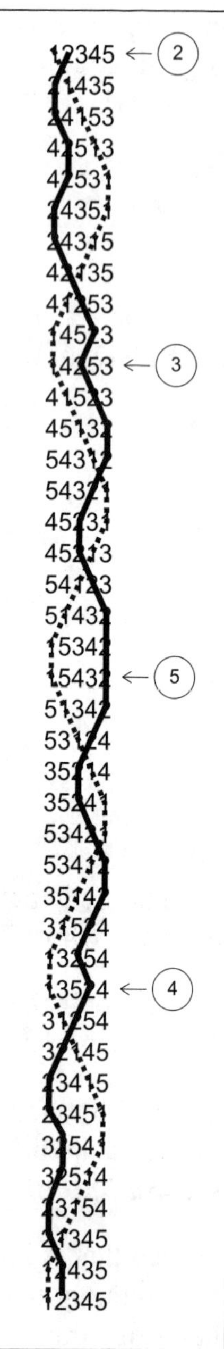

St Martin's

Winchendon Place

Winchendon Place is St Martin's with Reverse Canterbury places just as St Nicholas is St Simon's with Reverse Canterbury places. Bobs, once again, are Reverse Canterbury bobs. What more need I say?

St Osmund & Eynesbury

St Osmund is another St Simon's type method, but it has a different frontwork. The frontwork is

seconds
dodge 1-2 down
three blows lead
seconds over the treble
three blows lead
dodge 1-2 up
seconds

So the frontwork blue line is this

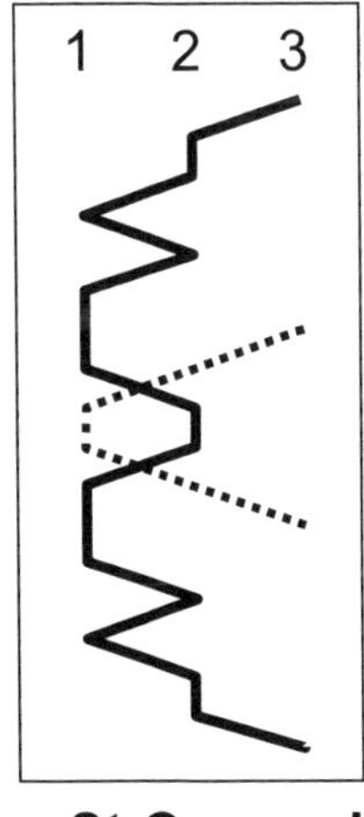

St Osmund

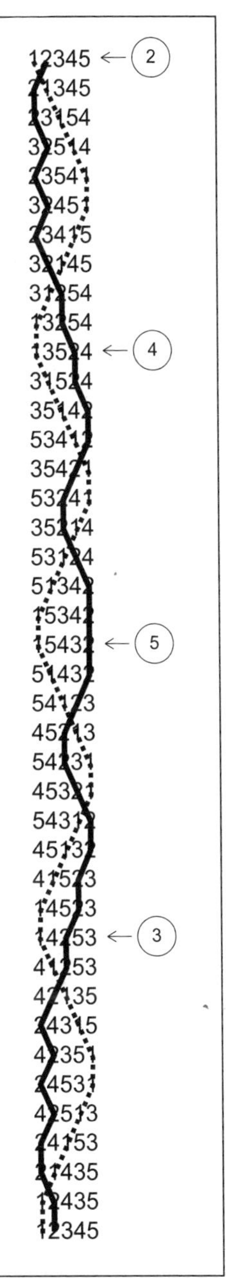

St Nicholas

Watch out that the seconds at the beginning and end are made backstroke-handstroke, and the 1-2 dodges are ***handstroke*** dodges rather than backstroke ones. In addition, after you've made the last lot of seconds, be careful to go up to 3-4 ***without*** leading again.

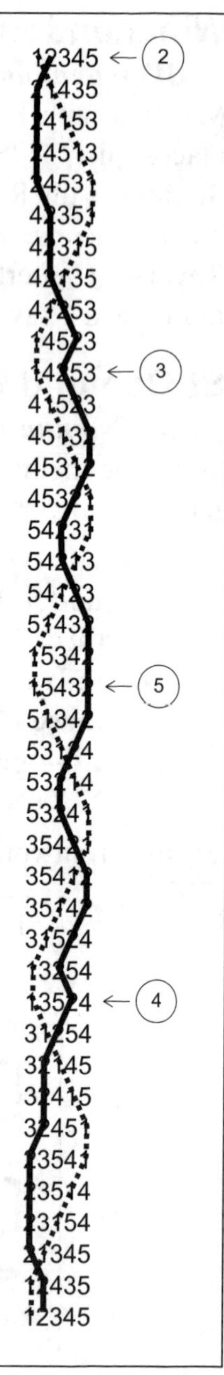

Eynesbury

Eynesbury is a method in which yet another frontwork is coupled with the St Simon's backwork. The frontwork is

three blows in seconds
four blows lead
seconds over the treble
four blows lead
three blows in seconds

and you can see it in the picture. Surprisingly, the hard part is getting yourself to do four blows at lead. Somehow, it feels very unnatural.

The bobs for both St Osmund and Eynesbury are the same as for St Simon's.

And not surprisingly, you can ring St Osmund with Reverse Canterbury places instead of dodging – which is ***St Remigius*** – and Eynesbury with Reverse Canterbury places – which is ***Huntley***.

Union Bob

And now for something very different but still widely rung – ***Union Bob***.

As ever, there's a frontwork and a backwork. The frontwork is plain hunt on three – going up to thirds and back three times – and the backwork – believe it or not – is upside down St Simon's frontwork – although most people think of it as

double dodge 4-5 up
fifths, fourths, fifths
double dodge 4-5 down

Bobs only affect the bells in 4-5, and rather horrendously, they look like this.

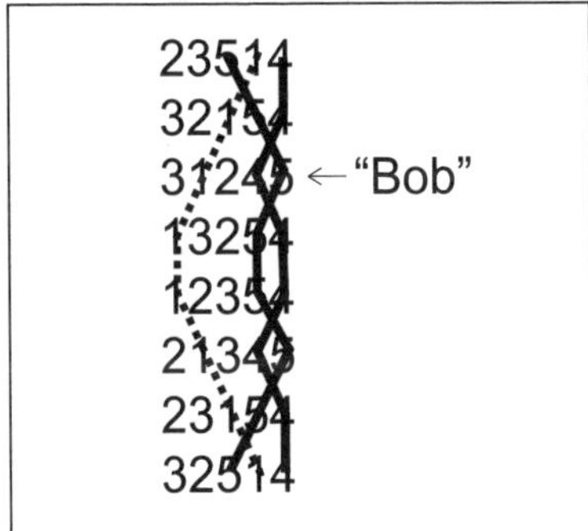

Union Bob Bob

They're rather similar to Stedman Doubles singles – if you've rung those yet – but they take a fair bit of learning. Watch out for the

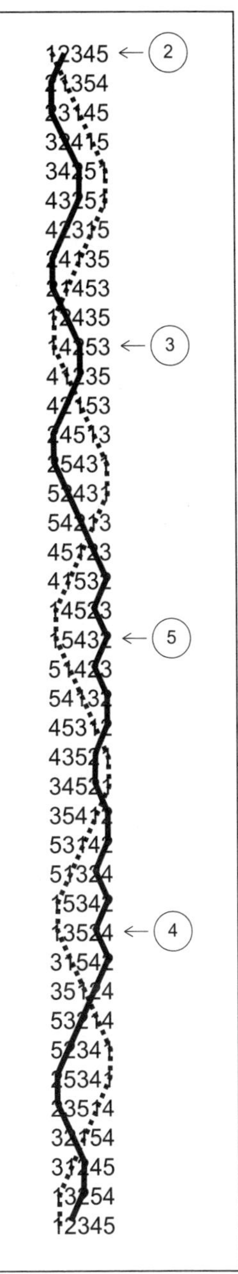

Union Bob

fact that the bell that makes fifths at the bob, stays at the back for another lot of fifths, fourths, fifths.

And if you're going to ring Union with an inexperienced treble ringer, let him know in advance that ***both blows*** in fifths are over ***the same bell***.

Reverse St Bartholomew's

Reverse St Bartholomew's – now officially known as ***St Augustine Bob*** although it's hardly ever called that – is much rung and hugely popular. Since the plain course is exactly like a touch of Grandsire with a single at every lead, it's an easy but splendid step on.

The official bob looks like this.

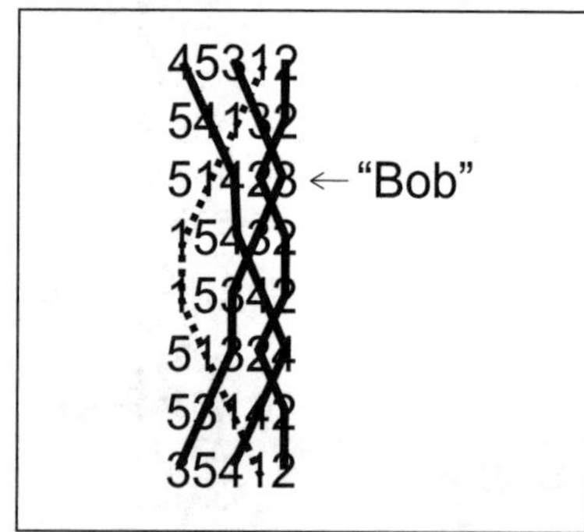

Official St Augustine Bob

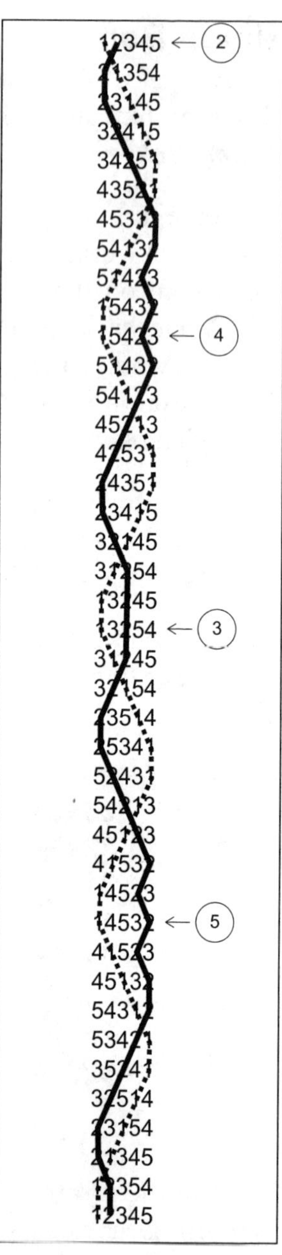

Reverse St Bartholomew's

But although it's very exciting and distinctly complex, very few bands actually ring it. Instead, they ring this, which is a plain lead of Bob Doubles, so the moral is to ask about bobs before you start.

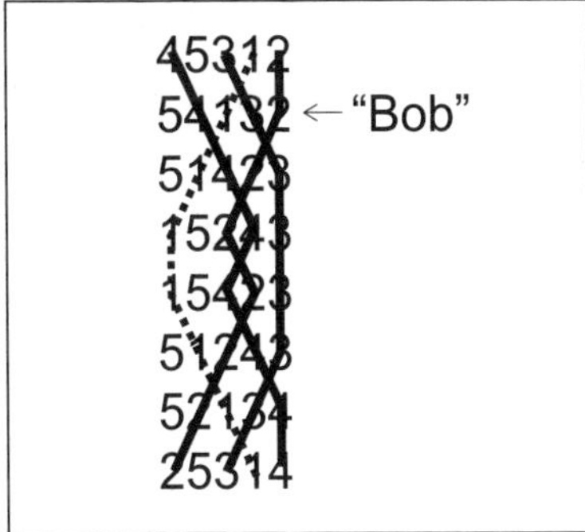

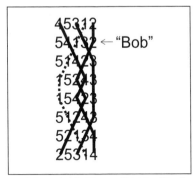

Normal Rev. St B. Bob

But watch out if you're going to ***call*** a 120 using this bob. It affects several changes around the lead end, so your first bob can't be at the end of the plain course.

Shipway's Place

Shipway's Place is nothing like anything we've looked at so far. Once rather more popular than today, there are ***three*** blows in fifths either side of the seconds, and a couple of odd sets of thirds. You also do fourths, fifths, fourths in the middle. The bob is a bit like a Reverse Canterbury bob but needs careful thought in advance. The picture is at the bottom of the next page.

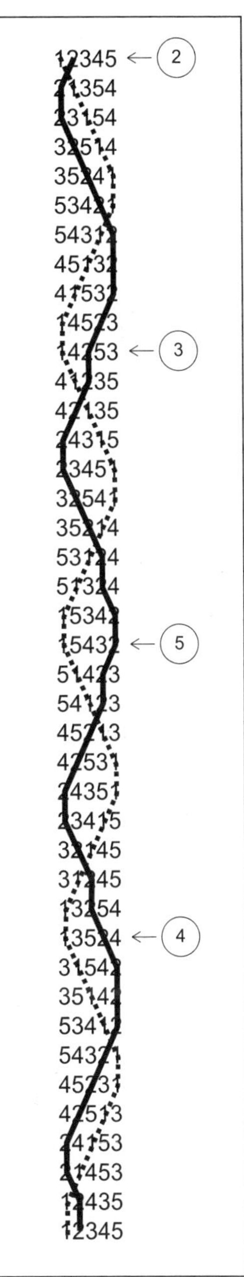

Shipway's Place

The St Hilary Family

That's now twelve methods in ten pages, and yet we've only just started. But by the time you've got this far, you can start putting bits of those twelve together in different ways to get a whole lot more. For example, if you combine St Simon's frontwork with Shipway's Place, you get the method on the right, which is called ***Westminster II Bob***.

If you ring Westminster II Bob with St Martin's frontwork you get ***Blackburn Place***; if you ring it with St Osmund frontwork you get ***St Hilary Bob***; and if you ring it with Eynesbury frontwork you get ***Dragon Place***.

The bob for the St Hilary family is a Shipway's bob, and it looks like this. Doing the fifths, fourths, fifths, is the problem.

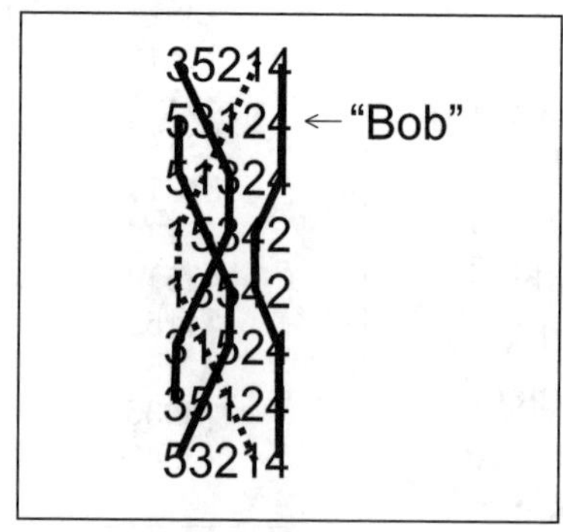

Shipway's Bob

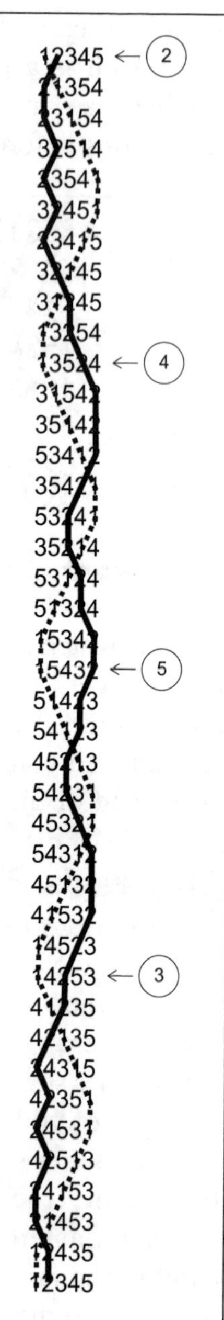

Westminster II

The New Bob Family

And in a similar way we can put St Simon's frontwork with another backwork we haven't seen yet, and get the method on the right called ***New Bob***.

It's not an easy backwork this, but once again, you can substitute St Martin's frontwork, St Osmund frontwork and Eynesbury frontwork to get ***Huntspill, St Vedast*** and ***Blaisdon***. The bob is the same as the Union Bob bob on page 107.

And After

And for the remaining 130 plus methods it's just a question of learning the occasional new backwork or frontwork and then putting them all together in different combinations. I say ***just*** but in reality you'll quickly find your head beginning to spin. With luck, though, sufficient of each will stick, for you to re-learn it fairly quickly in the tower.

One thing's for sure, though. Unless you're a grade one genius you'll never remember all the names.

"***But you rang Thurlby last week!***" someone told me in exasperation recently. "***Did I?***" I said.

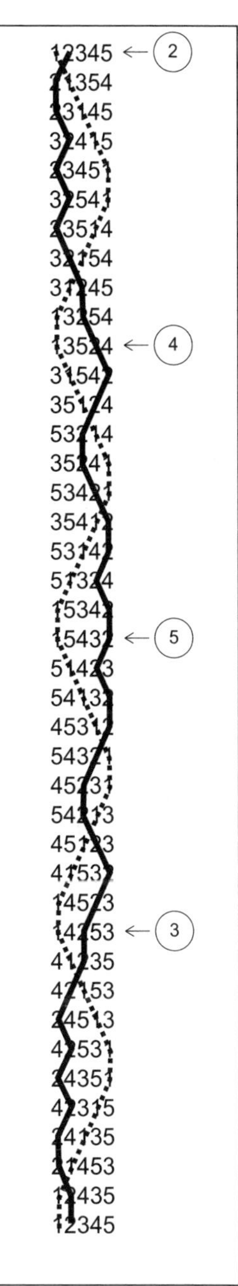

New Bob

I have a warm feeling for Reverse Canterbury. In 1985 the ***Central Council Methods Committee*** *found through meticulous research that when first rung to a peal, it had in fact been called* ***Canterbury****, so they declared that in future Reverse Canterbury would be called Canterbury – and Canterbury would be called Reverse Canterbury.*

To be fair to them, this was entirely in accordance with the Council's decisions on method names, but to me it seemed totally bizarre. I imagined dozens of confusing conversations.

"Do you ***mean*** *Reverse Canterbury or do you* ***really*** *mean Canterbury?" and, "Is that* ***old*** *Canterbury or* ***new*** *Canterbury?" or, "Is it* ***Canterbury*** *Canterbury we're ringing or* ***Reverse Canterbury*** *Canterbury?"*

So at the Central Council annual meeting in what people were kind enough to say was a witty and entertaining speech, I proposed that, "Plain Bob Doubles with imperial places at the lead end, retain its name of Reverse Canterbury."

A heated debate followed. ***The College Youths*** *spoke up strongly for the traditional name – showing what grand chaps they really are – and the* ***Bath and Wells*** *said they'd been mandated by their AGM to propose the same motion. Eventually, the voting was about 200 for and five against –* "Enough to make up a band to ring it under the wrong name," *said the College Youth sitting behind me – although the official minutes recorded only four against.*

At the time, I was pleased to have done my bit in support of common sense and tradition. But on reflection, I doubt that common sense and tradition really needed my support. No doubt everyone would have carried on calling it Reverse Canterbury anyway because ringing vernacular and customs are extremely robust. In the long term the Central Council has little option but to go along with them, as they did with our next topic – **This Variations Business**.

12. This Variations Business

Please explain to me what a Doubles *variation* is. Please also explain what *m/v* means in the quarter peal columns, and why there's been so much fuss about it all in recent years.

R.C.B.
East Anglia

Only in Doubles do people ring variations. They *could* ring them on any number of bells, but no one does except on five. To the purists they've caused irritation, frustration, and even anger, but to the ordinary Doubles ringer they're simply a pleasant and musical way of producing some ... well ... *variations* in their day to day ringing.

What is a Variation

We'll start with a definition. Quite simply, a ***variation*** is a method rung with the bob – and/or single – of another method instead of the normal one. So the popular variation ***Kennington*** is Bob Doubles rung with a Reverse Canterbury bob instead of a Bob Doubles one. And that means that when a bob is called, you do the whole of the work of a Reverse Canterbury bob. That's thirds and back if you're near the front, four blows in fourths if you were going to dodge 3-4 down, and four blows in fifths unaffected. But if no bob is called, you just ring Bob Doubles entirely as normal.

Equally, ***Southrepps*** is Reverse Canterbury with a Bob Doubles bob. So you ring Reverse Canterbury at all times except when a bob was called. Then, you ring the whole of a normal Bob Doubles bob.

Simple isn't it?

Ringing Them

Well, it's simple enough in theory, but it's far more difficult in practice, and that, of course, is why Doubles bands ring them. If you never rang anything but Bob Doubles, Reverse Canterbury, Kennington and Southrepps, you could learn all the possible ways of being affected *and* what your next work would be – just as you did for Bob Doubles. But by the time you're ringing more than half a dozen variations, that becomes too much to cope with, and you have to work out what to do as you go along.

So how do you do that?

Well there are various ways, but most people do it by noticing where they pass the treble. They ***ring by the treble*** as it's known, and for every call and every type of plain lead, they learn what they should do after each passing position. So for a ***Reverse Canterbury bob*** they learn,

Pass treble	Work
1-2	Thirds and back
2-3	Thirds and back
3-4	Four blows behind
4-5	Four blows in fourths.

And for a Grandsire single they learn,

Pass treble	Work
1-2	Seconds
2-3	Long thirds
3-4	Double dodge 4-5 up
4-5	Double dodge 4-5 down.

Of course, they also have to remember which variation is which, and there's quite an entertainment in that as well. When someone calls for ***Stoke Rochford*** you need to be able to bring instantly to mind that it's St Hilary with a Shipway's bob and a Grandsire single.

What's more, the bobs and singles are often called rather earlier than normal. That's because some of the affected bells start their work well before the treble leads. In Kennington, for example, the bob must be called when the treble's in thirds place because otherwise there isn't sufficient warning for the bells in the middle to make thirds and fourths. Similarly, with a ***Pinks*** single – named after the flower, not the colour – which normally has to be called when the treble's in fourths place if the back bells are to have enough warning.

The Various Calls

And while we're on the subject of a Pinks single, you'd best know that there are a vast number of possible bobs and singles, many of which are not even symmetrical. On the next two pages are pictures of twelve of the most popular. You certainly don't need to learn them all, but you can use them to ring the variations listed on the page after.

Some Variations

And it's *those* variations that you might like to try. Five of them, ***April Day, May Day, Kennington, Southrepps*** and ***Old Bob*** are rung very widely indeed, and many of the others are fairly popular too. But they're only a handful of the really huge number of possibilities.

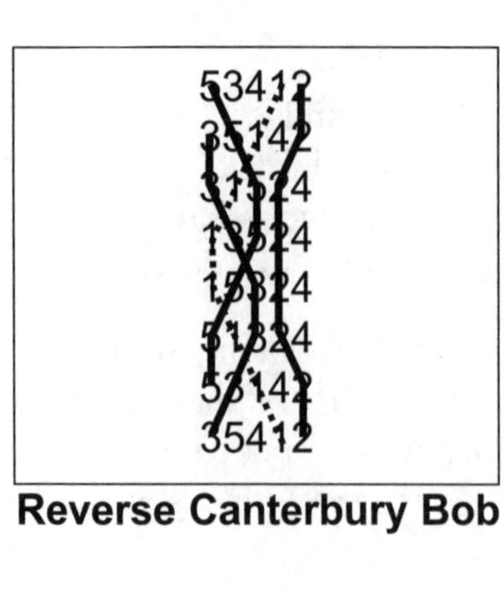

Reverse Canterbury Bob

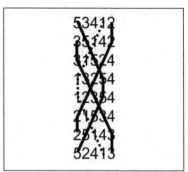

53412
35142
31524
13254
12354
21534
25143
52413

Plain Bob Bob

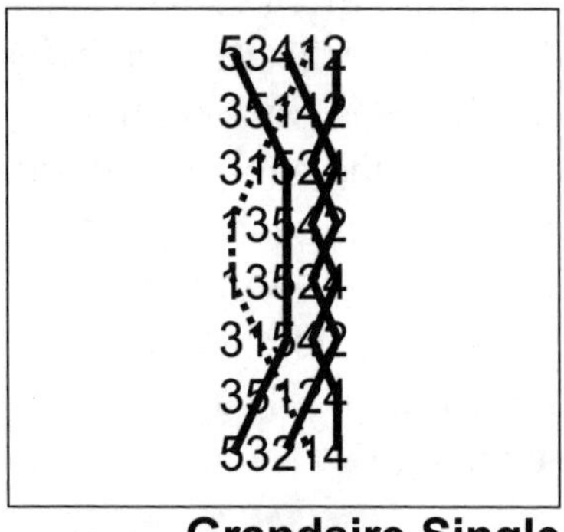

Grandsire Single

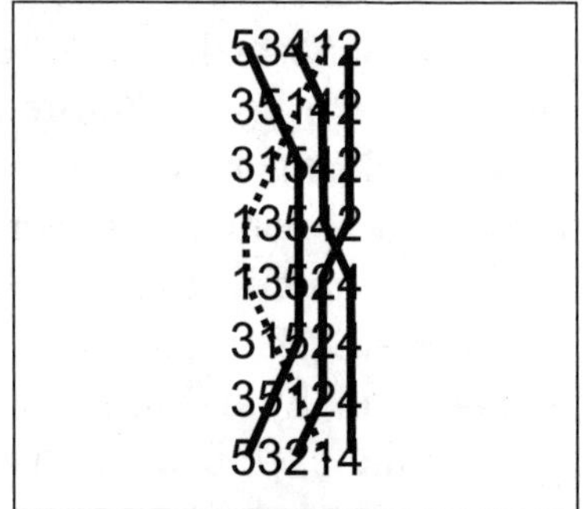

Pinks Single

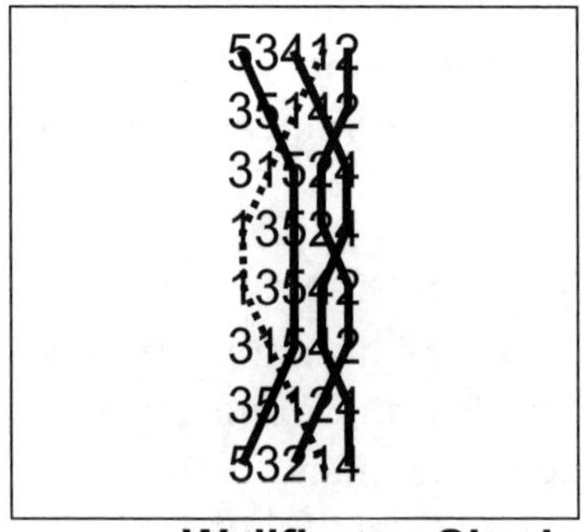

Wallflower Single

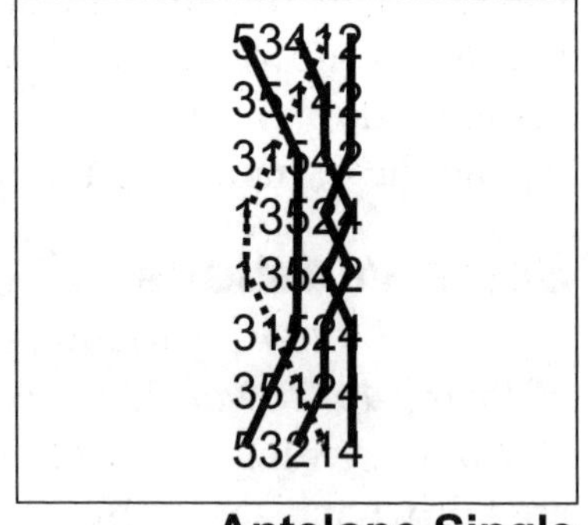

Antelope Single

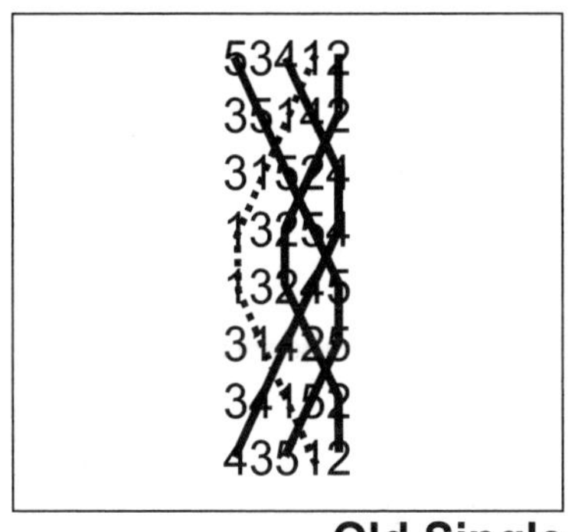

Old Single

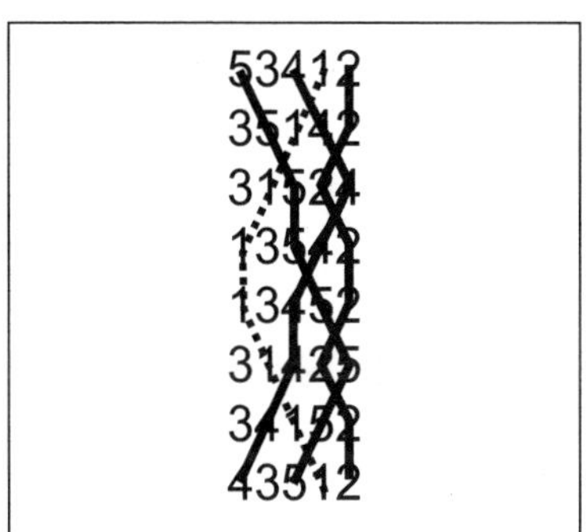

Grandsire Extreme

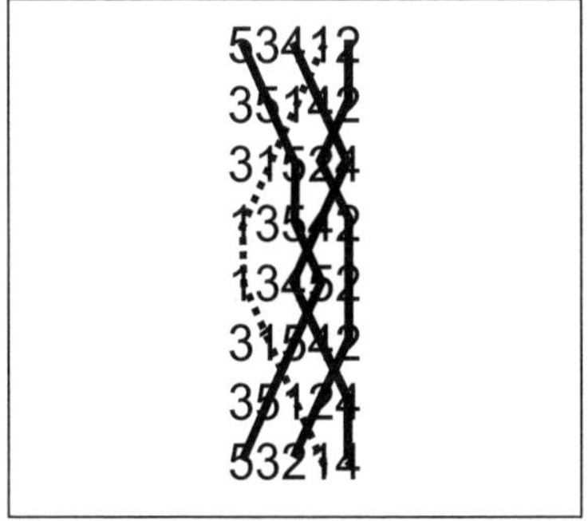

Ready Money Single

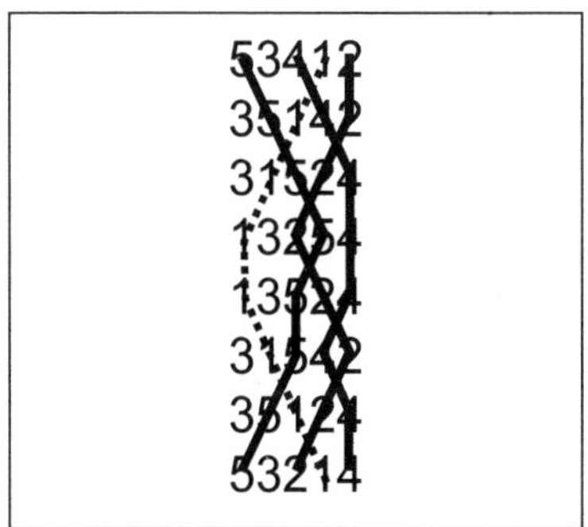

Old Hudibras Single

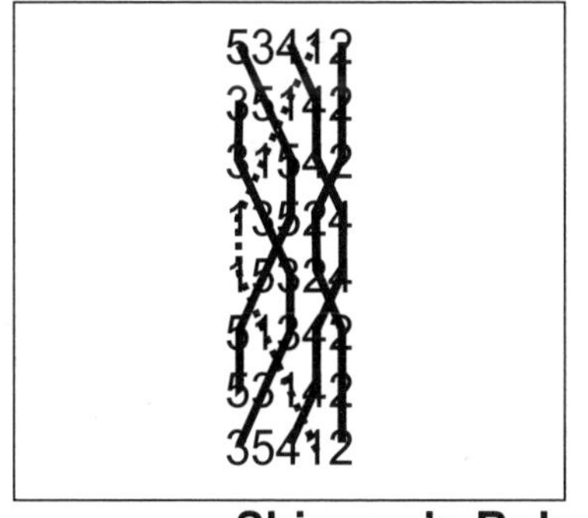

Shipway's Bob

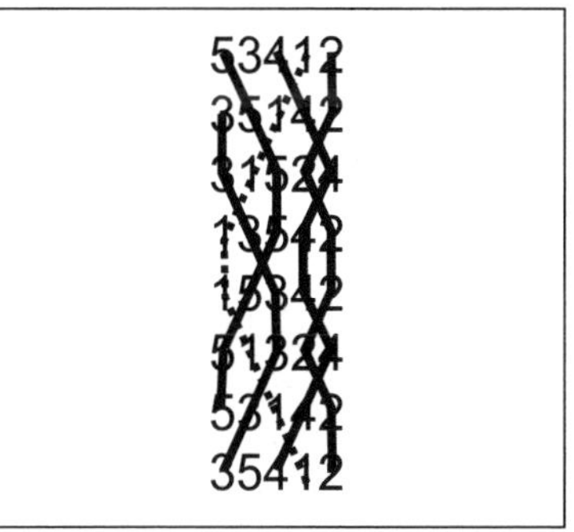

New Bob Bob

Name	Plain Course	Bob	Single
April Day	Plain Bob	-	Grandsire
May Day	Plain Bob	-	Pinks
Kennington	Plain Bob	Rev. Cant.	-
Old Bob	Plain Bob	-	Old
Ready Money	Plain Bob	-	Ready Money
Old Hudibras	Plain Bob	-	Old Hudibras
Wollaston	Plain Bob	Rev. Cant.	Wallflower
Southrepps	Rev. Cant.	Plain Bob	-
Campion	Rev. Cant.	-	Gr. Extreme
St David	Rev. Cant.	-	Antelope
Inkpen	Rev. Cant.	Plain Bob	Gr. Extreme
St Ignatius	St Simon's	-	Pinks
St Alban	St Simon's	Rev. Cant.	-
Austrey	St Martin's	-	Wallflower
St Laurence	St Martin's	-	Antelope
St Peter	St Martin's	-	Old
Stoke Rochford	St Hilary	Shipway's	Grandsire
Alvaston	New	New	Pinks

The Problem

But the fact that so many changes are affected by a bob or single, leads us to a technical problem. I said in Chapter 5 that a bob is no more than then the smallest possible hiccup in the plain course, but a Pinks single, for example, isn't a small hiccup, it's a major eruption. For about eight or ten changes, you're really ringing an entirely different method.

Of course, that doesn't bother you and me, but it *does* bother ringing technicians who find it extremely unsatisfying. "How do you know," they ask, "whether you're ringing Kennington or whether you're ringing Bob Doubles spliced at the half-lead with Reverse Canterbury?"

Certainly, that's a deep philosophical question, and

whether you can be bothered to answer it or not depends on your personality. Most people reply, "If we *say* we're ringing Kennington then we *are* ringing Kennington," and indeed, that's probably right. After all, when you're ringing a plain course of Grandsire, you're ringing a plain course of Grandsire. No one would suggest that you were ringing a silent and unconducted touch of Original – see page 395 – with a bob every ten changes.

And Then

But the problem got particularly tricky when people started ringing a number of variations in the same 120. If you ring several different methods with several different bobs, which goes with which? Could you, perhaps, ring six leads of different methods, and six leads of different bobs, and say that you were ringing 6 x 6 = 36 different variations? That could be 1,512 variations to a peal.

Well, most people think that's plainly ridiculous and a line should be drawn somewhere. So the *Central Council* drew up some rules for peals. As with all rules, they don't please everybody, and they certainly aren't perfect, but they're a pretty good attempt, and most Doubles ringers are fairly happy with them. You can obtain a copy of the rules by buying a copy of ***Central Council Decisions*** from *Central Council Publications* or by looking them up on the Central Council website. Essentially, they say that,

> ***Either*** all the variations in an extent must have the same call or calls and there is at least one plain lead of each. ***Or*** all the variations and methods in an extent must have the same plain course and no call or calls are the same for any two of them.

But as with the all newish legislation, you can find

yourself inadvertently transgressing whilst doing something which at one time was perfectly legal, and peal bands sometimes do. Normally, it doesn't alter the fact that they've rung a peal, it just means that they've rung fewer variations than they thought.

Naturally, no one likes being caught out in that kind of mistake, and some conductors have complained vigorously, both about the rules and about being checked up on.

The Background

Interestingly, though, much of the controversy about variations arose through a few high-brow ringers getting out of touch with grass roots ringing. They apparently believed that variations were a new and unwelcome innovation after the Second World War, whereas in fact, they date back to the dawn of method ringing.

Certainly, ***St Dunstan's*** – Grandsire with a Grandsire bob, Grandsire single and Grandsire extreme – was rung in the 1600s. Indeed, it was possibly named by Fabian Stedman himself, since the first ever ringing book, ***Tintinnalogia***, was published – although not written – by him, and printed in premises in St Dunstan's churchyard, Fleet Street.

Similarly, ***Old Hudibras*** was rung in the seventeenth century, although then it was just called ***Hudibras***.

Even more interesting is the way these variations survived. St Dunstan's has unquestionably been rung regularly in my own area for at least the past century, apparently without anyone having access to any written material on it at all. It's rather like the way one of the earliest call change sequences, the ***Twenty All Over***, has survived for 400 years almost entirely by oral tradition.

M's and V's

And as for what **m/v** means, **m** means method, and **v** means variation. So if someone says they rang a quarter peal of 11 m/v, they mean that they rang 11 methods and/or variations. It could have been 1 method and 10 variations, or 6 methods and 5 variations, but altogether it was 11.

And when you come to think of it, that's very handy. Because by the time you get past a couple of dozen m/v, it's jolly hard to remember quite *what* you've rung.

Of course, this isn't really a conducting book, but it would be no good me telling you about these variations if I didn't also tell you how to call them. Essentially, it's fairly simple. For all the variations I've listed with ***one*** *call – be it a bob or single – you can call a 120 by calling a call every fourth lead. That's exactly as you would call Bob Doubles. So you can call,* ***(Plain, Plain, Single, Plain)*** x ***3****, for example. For variations with two calls, you can call* ***(Single, Plain, Bob, Plain)*** x ***3****, etc.*

But watch out for a major elephant pit. You cannot normally call your last call at the end of the 120. That's because the call affects changes after the lead end as well as before, and your touch will either come round at handstroke or not at all. So in general, ***don't*** *call Plain, Plain, Plain, Bob or Plain, Single, Plain, Bob, tempting though it is.*

And if you go on to call some of the thousands of variations ***not*** *in this book, there are a few simple calling rules for all of them in* ***The Bob Caller's Companion****.*

And if all this m/v stuff is rather a worry, you can see why so many ringers go straight from Bob Minor to something often rung with no calls at all – **Kent**.

Treble Bob

13. Kent Minor

About six weeks after I took up ringing, someone bought me a copy of *The Nine Tailors* as a present. I didn't understand the ringing parts at all, but I was fascinated by the atmosphere of the peal. Mastering Kent immediately became my goal, and now that I can ring Bob Minor, I feel I'm ready to start on it. Please guide me.

Phillip R.

In the village of Leeds in Kent in the middle of the eighteenth century, there was a first class method ringing band. They rang lots of peals – or, at least, what in those days was lots of peals – and they had a particular taste for very long ones. Their tower captain was a truly remarkable man named James Barham, and under his leadership they actually succeeded in ringing the entire extent of Plain Bob Major – all 40,320 different changes – in 27 hours.

They did it on the 7th and 8th of April 1761, but needless to say, they didn't do it with just eight ringers. They did do it, though, with just 13 ringers who rang in shifts, each of them ringing for many hours at a time. And the conductor was James Barham, who had previously rung for nearly 15 hours continuously in a failed attempt six years earlier.

In the last 50 years many exceptional long lengths have been rung – including the extent of major by only eight ringers at Loughborough Bell Foundry in 1963 – and the skill and endurance of those involved leaves me dumb with admiration. But for me, James Barham's achievement in 1761 stands head and shoulders as the greatest ringing feat of all time. Not only must his strength and staying power have been extraordinary, but his conducting ability must have been way ahead of his time. Most remarkable of all was his determination and vision.

Yet, impressive as James Barham's ringing achievements were, they are virtually unknown to the great majority of ringers today. He came onto the scene, he rang for a great many years, and he made his mark. But he departed leaving us almost nothing.

Almost nothing, that is, except for his great and largely unattributed legacy. He and his band invented ***Kent***.

Treble Bob

Exactly how and why James Barham and his band invented Kent, we'll come to in a moment. But first let's look at ***treble bob*** – which they *didn't* invent – and what *that's* all about.

All the methods we've looked at so far, have the treble plain hunting. In the doubles methods it hunts out to fifths place, and in the minor methods it hunts out to sixths place, but it does nothing more than ***plain*** hunt. In Kent, though – and in other treble bob and Surprise methods – the treble does a ***treble bob hunt***, or as we normally say, it ***treble bobs***.

And in case you've never seen it before, on the next page you can see what the treble's path looks like.

When you first see it, it looks a bit daunting. But if you can manage Plain Bob Minor, it won't take you long to get

Treble Bob

the hang of treble bob. You simply

dodge 1-2 up
dodge 3-4 up
dodge 5-6 up
lie behind
dodge 5-6 down
dodge 3-4 down
dodge 1-2 down
lead

And then you do it all over again and again until someone says, ***that's all***.

I say, ***simply***, but you'll find that dodging in one place so soon after dodging in another, is decidedly breath-taking to begin with. And in addition, dodging in 1-2, as well as being very difficult to get used to, is extremely easy to forget, particularly when you're dodging down.

Some people think of treble bob as taking three steps forward and one back – like life – but most ringers find it easier to remember the dodging positions.

Treble Bob Practice

And since it's so difficult to begin with, you and your band may well want some treble bob practice before launching into Kent proper. And to get that practice, a course of ***pure treble bob*** will do very well. Here's a picture.

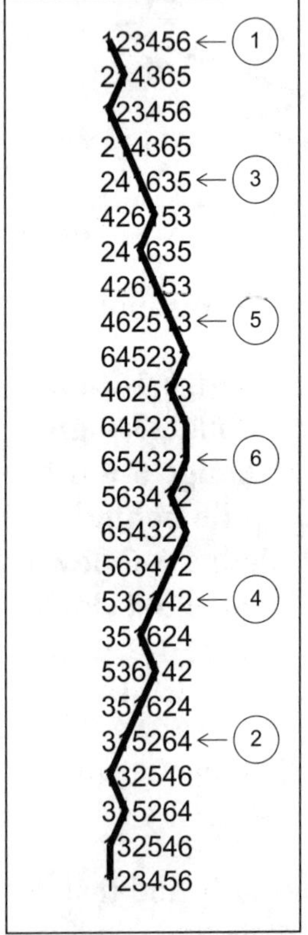

Pure Treble Bob

A moment's study will show you three things. It's short,

so there's no need to concentrate too long; everyone does the same thing, so you all practise what the treble does in Kent; and it's ***false***, so every change gets rung twice. For that reason some people get a bit snooty about ringing it other than for practice, but as a practice method it serves very well.

It is, though, pleasantly musical. And if your band want to ring it over and over again on a Sunday morning, go ahead.

The Method Itself

And now for Kent itself. There's a whole blue line on the next page, and when you've got to the end of this paragraph you can turn over and have a look at it. But don't start learning it yet, as I'm going to talk you through it.

You can see that there's a lot of treble bobbing but there's also some other stuff that doesn't look much like treble bobbing at all. Nevertheless, it really isn't anywhere near as difficult as it looks at first glance, and to make it even easier, we're going to divide it up.

The Slow

First, ***the slow***. This ***slow*** is nothing whatever like ***the slow*** in Stedman, but it's called ***the slow*** nonetheless. At one time it used to be called ***the slow hunt bell***, but although you may find the term in older books, almost no one calls it that nowadays. When you're in the slow, you're said to be the ***slow bell***, and if you don't ring it when you ought to, people will shout, ***"Slow bell,"*** at you. This won't be a comment on your striking but a statement of where you should be.

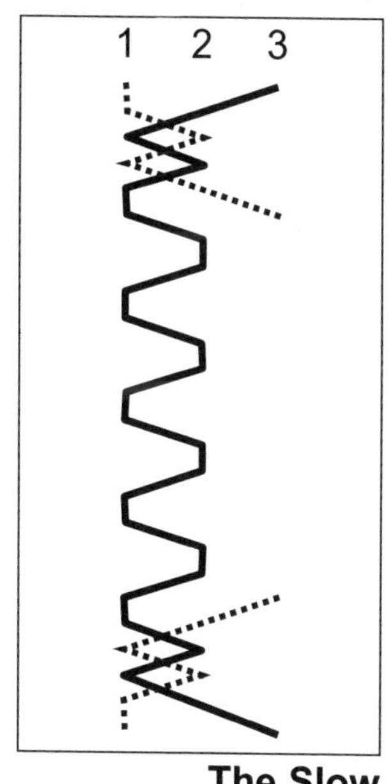

The Slow

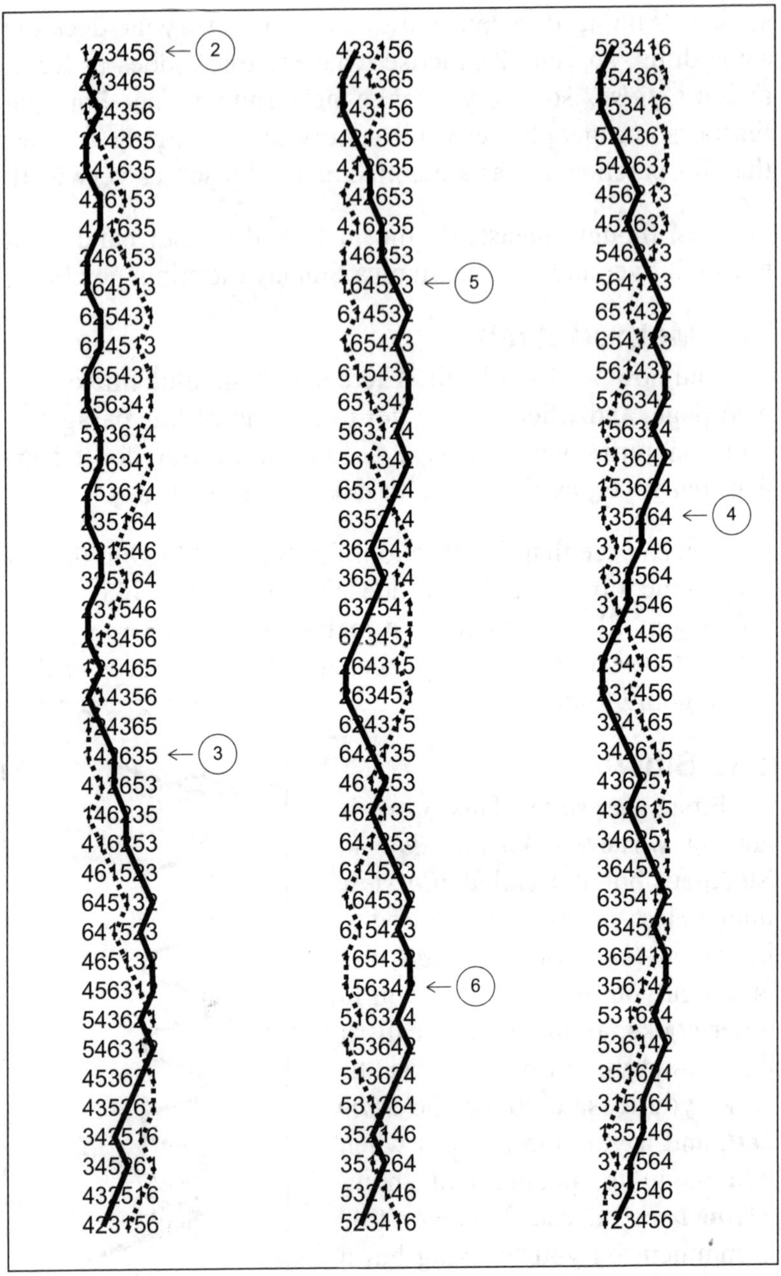

123456 ← (2)	423156	523416
213465	241365	254361
124356	243156	253416
214365	421365	524361
241635	412635	542631
426153	142653	456213
421635	416235	452631
246153	146253	546213
264513	164523 ← (5)	564123
625431	614532	651432
624513	165423	654123
265431	615432	561432
256341	651342	516342
523614	563124	156324
526341	561342	513642
253614	653124	153624
235164	635214	135264 ← (4)
321546	362541	315246
325164	365214	132564
231546	632541	312546
213456	623451	321456
123465	264315	234165
214356	263451	231456
124365	624315	324165
142635 ← (3)	642135	342615
412653	461253	436251
146235	462135	432615
416253	641253	346251
461523	614523	364521
645132	164532	635412
641523	615423	634521
465132	165432	365412
456312	156342 ← (6)	356142
543621	516324	531624
546312	153642	536142
453621	513624	351624
435261	531264	315264
342516	352146	135246
345261	351264	312564
432516	532146	132546
423156	523416	123456

Kent Treble Bob Minor

Learn it as a piece of work all by itself. It starts when you get down to the front and find the treble there waiting for you. You then

> **dodge with the treble,**
>
> **lead and make seconds repeatedly until the treble comes back down to join you again,**

and,

> **dodge with the treble once more, before going back up to 3-4.**

All that shouldn't be too hard, and in fact it isn't. As long as you know when to start it and when to finish it, the rest comes easily enough. Some people remember where the slow comes in the rest of the blue line, but whether you do that or not, make a special effort to cement in your mind which bell is the treble. Every time you get to lead, ask yourself, "Am I taking the treble off?" If you are, dodge with it and carry on with the slow.

Of course, you have to finish the slow as well as start it, and you may find it all too easy to keep on doing lead, seconds, lead, seconds, ad infinitum. So to avoid this, remember that the end makes itself known by two signals:

> ***the treble takes you off,***

and,

> ***you've made seconds over all the other working bells in turn.***

Most Kent ringers look for both signals. They look to make seconds over everyone, and then they see the treble joining them on the front.

Interestingly, very few Kent ringers actually count the number of their sets of seconds. If you want to know, in Minor there are four, but you'll find it astonishingly difficult to keep count of them.

The Rest of It

And except when it isn't, the *rest* of Kent is treble bob ***without any dodges in 1-2***. You dodge in 3-4 up, 5-6 up, 5-6 down and 3-4 down, but you do a normal whole pull lead on the front without any 1-2 dodging at all.

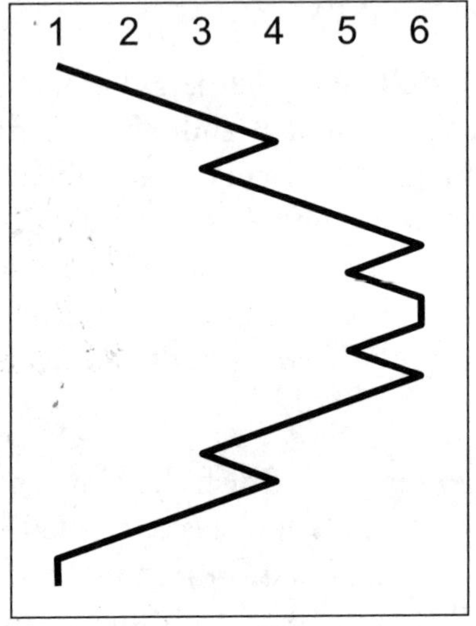

General Kent Work

That's so straightforward after your treble bob practice that I shall say nothing more about it.

The Places

And that leaves us with the bits where you aren't treble bobbing – ***the places***. These all occur in 3-4. ***Places down*** are in the picture at the top left opposite, and ***places up*** are at the top right.

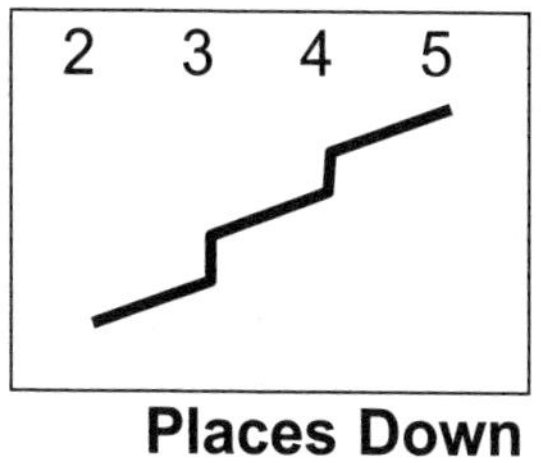

Places Down

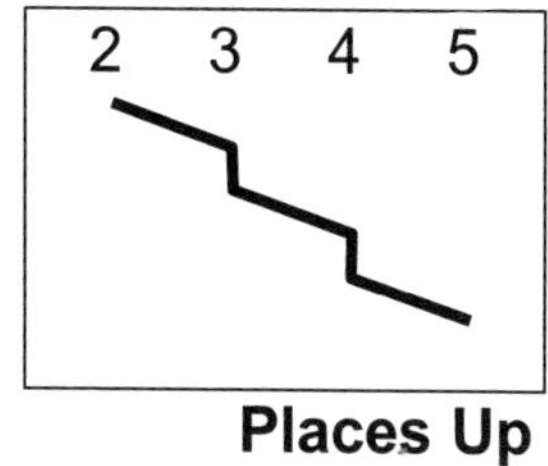

Places Up

They are absolutely identical to the places you ring in Reverse Canterbury Doubles and they're quite easy to remember. The difficulties are putting them in at the right time and ringing them correctly.

When to Ring Them

Let's look at the first problem first. The essential point is that a set of Kent places takes exactly the same number of changes to complete as a dodge, and they put the bells into exactly the same position afterwards that a dodge would. The two pictures below show that's true.

But the places are needed because they prevent the repetition of changes that would occur during a dodge. In the second picture rounds occurs twice – as does 214365 – but in the first it doesn't.

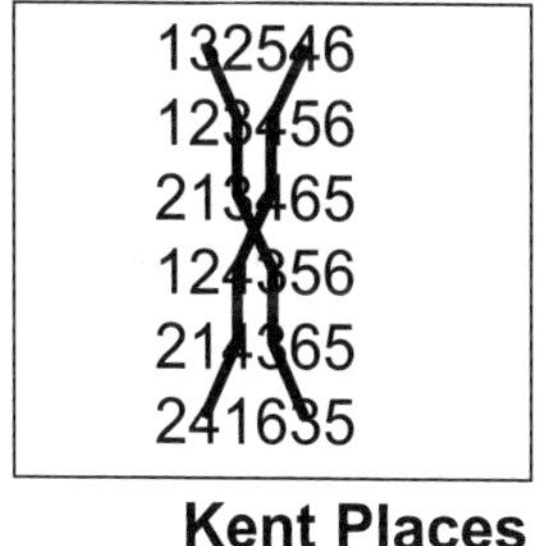

Kent Places

132546
123456
214365
123456
214365
241635

A Dodge

So the essence of Kent is that some 3-4 dodges are replaced by places, and that is James Barham's great legacy. He invented a method in which instead of doing your places, you can dodge by mistake, and apart from a crunch at the time, it will make absolutely no difference a moment later.

Interestingly, by the time he invented Kent in the early 1770s, ***Oxford Treble Bob*** – then often known as ***Union Treble Bob*** – had been around for many years. But the places in Oxford have to be got right or the bells immediately get into a real pickle, whereas Kent places can be got wrong with impunity. In effect, James Barham invented ***the fudger's charter***, and there will be times when you are as grateful to him as all other Kent ringers have been.

Avoiding the Crunches

But even though you *can* crunch with impunity, you would obviously far rather not. So how do you remember which 3-4 dodges should be replaced by places and which shouldn't? There are three systems.

The first and most widely used, is to notice whether the treble is ***below you*** when you are in 3-4. And by ***below you*** I mean whether it's in 1-2. If it is, you make places. If it isn't, you dodge. And a look at the picture on page 130 will confirm that.

But this begs the question, how do you *know* whether the treble is below you? And the answer is that, on your way ***up*** from the front, you check to see whether you have rung over the treble by the time you get to thirds place. If you have, it's below you. If you haven't, it isn't.

Similarly, on your way ***down***, you check to see whether you've rung over the treble by the time you get to fourths. If you have, the treble is above you. If you haven't, it's below you.

If you actually ring over the treble ***in*** fourths, ***don't*** make places. Dodge with the treble instead. It may be below you when you are in fourths but it will not be below you when you are in thirds. Besides, you know that it must dodge with you because it never makes places, so *you* must dodge with *it*.

The Second Method

The second method is nothing to do with the treble. You remember that after ringing the slow, your next two times in 3-4 up will be places. Check this with the picture. Your 3-4 up after that, is a dodge, and so is the following 3-4 down. But the subsequent two 3-4 downs after *that* are places. The slow then comes immediately after the last places down.

This method isn't easy, and it takes a lot of concentration, but some people like it.

The Third Method

And the third method is the same as the second method except that you don't try to remember when the places down begin. Instead, you just look out for when you dodge 3-4 down with the treble. The next two 3-4 downs are then places.

This last method, like the first, works just as well for Kent Major, Royal and Maximus as it does for Minor. Many ringers use it.

Making the Places

But even when you ring the places at the right times, you can still find the ropesight extremely tricky. So if you have this problem yourself, these rules should help.

> The two blows in fourths are always over ***the same bell.***

> The two blows in thirds are always over ***different*** bells, one of which is the treble.

And,

> You take the treble at your ***second*** blow in thirds in your ***first*** places down and ***first*** places up, and at your ***first*** blow in thirds in your ***second*** places down and ***second*** places up.

Of course, if you don't have ropesight problems, you won't need to bother with this, but if you do, Kent places can be a nightmare.

The Bobs

And that brings us to the bobs – and, fortunately, there are no singles. The great majority of Kent Minor is rung in plain courses, so if you take a while before learning the bobs, no one will mind very much. But when you eventually do get round to them, you'll find them very different from Bob Minor bobs.

Here is the picture, but in case you think it looks too awful to learn anything from, the rules are these.

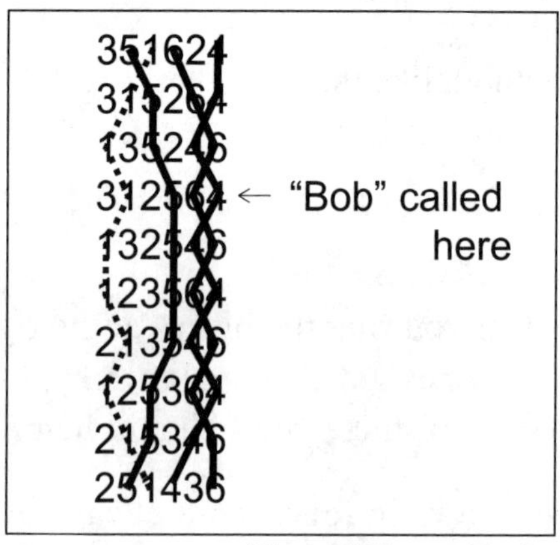

Kent Minor Bob

1. The bell leaving the slow is unaffected.
2. The bell going into the slow is unaffected.
3. The bell doing its ***second*** lot of places up, immediately adds on its ***first*** lot of places down, and so does,

   two blows in thirds,
   four blows in fourths,
   two blows in thirds,

   and then goes back down to lead again. This is rather like ringing a stepladder and it's definitely fun when you've cracked it.
4. The bell dodging 5-6 up when the bob's called, does ***two more*** dodges in 5-6 up, making three dodges in all.
5. And, the bell dodging 5-6 down when the bob's called, does ***two more*** dodges in 5-6 down, making three dodges in all.

Not surprisingly, these last two ways of being affected are the most difficult. To begin with, most ringers find it very hard indeed to count three dodges, and they often end up ringing two or four instead. Even when they get it right, they find it a real puzzle to work out when their next lot of places are due.

Indeed, it is *so* difficult, that I really do recommend you trying to come to terms with the first or third methods on pages 134 and 135. If you can't, though, you'll need to remember that each bob delays the onset of your places down by exactly ***one*** 3-4 down occasion.

Giving it a Go

And if you've got all the way to this paragraph, you're probably very serious about giving Kent a go – and a jolly good thing too. It's a step forward, it's a challenge and it's a real pleasure as well. Think of those eighteenth century men of Kent delighting in the novelty they'd just created, and wondering if anyone would still be ringing it in 250 years time. With a bit of practice ***you*** will be.

A couple of years ago a lady wrote me a letter headed ***A Kent Lament****.*

> "I love Kent," *she said,* "but I dread the slow. In no method do I lead well, but at least I don't have to do it often. In the slow in Kent I have to do it over and over again, and I can sense everybody willing it to end. When the treble takes me off, it's a real relief."

If that's **your** *problem, worrying about it will only make it worse. The Striking chapters later on may help, but in any event, leading for five whole pulls in quick succession might actually help you* **improve** *your leading, especially if you approach it in a positive spirit. I certainly hope so, because there's Kent slow work in our next method too –* **Oxford**.

14. Oxford Minor

Now and again I say to our District ringing master, "What about a course of Oxford Treble Bob?"

"Oh dear no!" he replies, "We haven't got enough," or "We couldn't manage it," or "It would take too long for people to look it up," and we ring Kent instead. Some day he may say, "Yes," and when he does, I must be ready.

F.B.P.
Surrey

For various reasons, there are *lots* of methods called Oxford – Single Oxford, Double Oxford, Old Oxford Delight, Oxford Bob Triples, Oxford Imperial Bob, etc. But when people just say, ***Oxford***, they mean Oxford Treble Bob.

Oxford was traditionally regarded as the next step on from Kent. But as I pointed out in the last chapter, Oxford was in fact invented *before* Kent. ***The Union Scholars***, a group of London ringers, invented it in the early eighteenth century and called it ***Union Treble Bob***.

But somewhere along the way, it got to be called Oxford Treble Bob instead, and it also became substantially eclipsed by Kent because Kent was so much easier. Nevertheless, it's a pleasant and challenging method, and if you want to be a well rounded method ringer, you'll definitely want it in your repertoire.

The Method

And if you're still catching your breath after that long Kent chapter, you'll be pleased to know that this is going to be a very short one. You know how to treble bob and you know how to ring the slow, and that means that 95% of the necessary learning is already done. But all the same, Oxford has something entirely new.

Take a look at the picture opposite. The slow is there plainly enough, and so too is the treble bobbing. But the treble bobbing is interfered with by fourths and back and thirds and back, apparently stuck in at random.

So what are these thirds and fourths all about?

Well, to understand this, let's look at the six changes of Kent around the start of the method and compare them with the equivalent six changes of Oxford.

Kent Places	Oxford Places
132546	132546
123456	123456
213465	214365
124356	124356
214365	213465
241635	231645

You can see that both sets have a lot of similarities. Indeed, the work of the treble, Two, Five and Six is exactly the same in each of them. But the Three and Four not only do different work, they also end up going in different directions.

Both these pieces of work are called ***places***. The first, where the three and four do Reverse Canterbury type work and carry on in the same direction, are known as ***Kent***

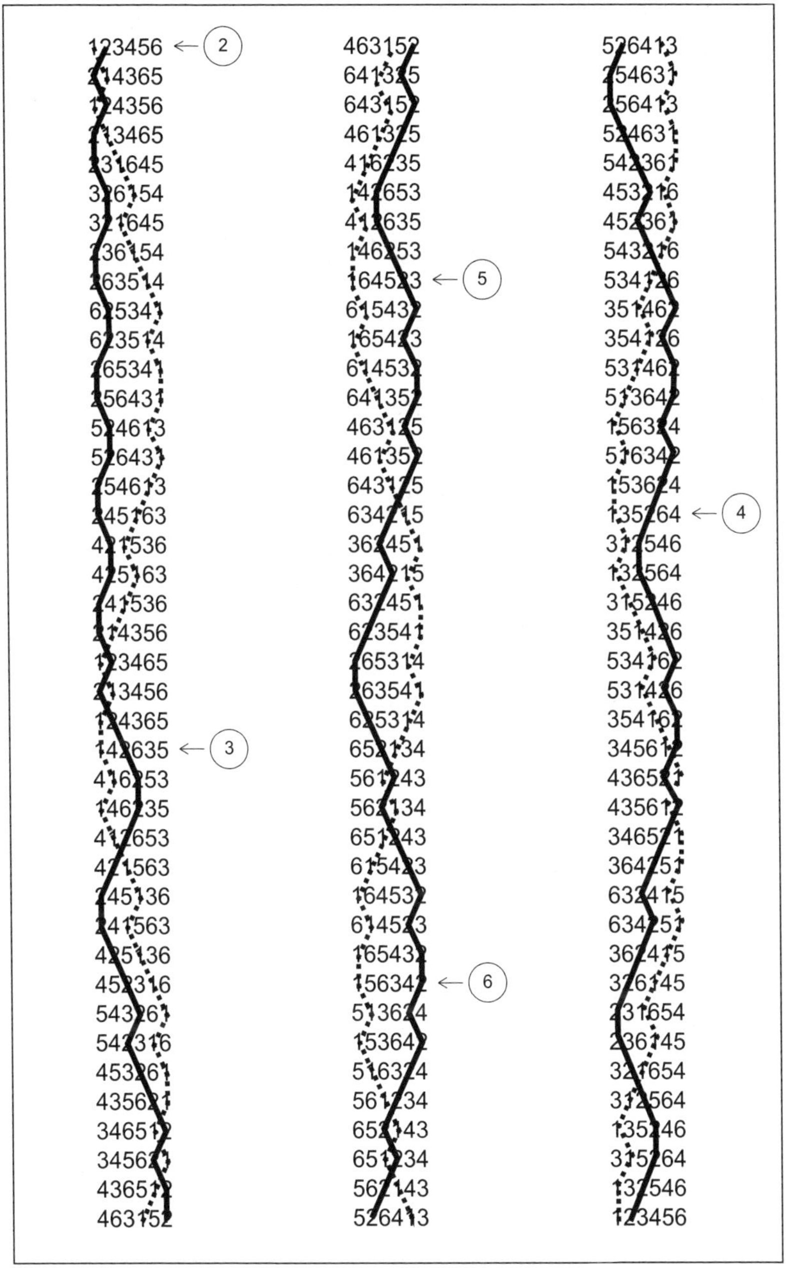

123456 ← (2)
214365
124356
213465
231645
326154
321645
236154
263514
625341
623514
265341
256431
524613
526431
254613
245163
421536
425163
241536
214356
123465
213456
124365
142635 ← (3)
416253
146235
412653
421563
245136
241563
425136
452316
543261
542316
453261
435621
346512
345621
436512
463152

463152
641325
643152
461325
416235
142653
412635
146253
164523 ← (5)
615432
165423
614532
641352
463125
461352
643125
634215
362451
364215
632451
623541
265314
263541
625314
652134
561243
562134
651243
615423
164532
614523
165432
156342 ← (6)
513624
153642
516324
561234
652143
651234
562143
526413

526413
254631
256413
524631
542361
453216
452361
543216
534126
351462
354126
531462
513642
156324
516342
153624
135264 ← (4)
312546
132564
315246
351426
534162
531426
354162
345612
436521
435612
346521
364251
632415
634251
362415
326145
231654
236145
321654
312564
135246
315264
132546
123456

Oxford Treble Bob Minor

places. And the second, where one bell does fourths and back and the other bell does thirds and back, are known as ***Oxford places***.

Structurally the two methods are **exactly** the same except that Kent has Kent places either side of the lead end, and Oxford has Oxford places there. It's only in those brief moments when the treble is dodging 1-2 up and 1-2 down that the methods differ, but even so, coping with Oxford can be a real problem.

The Order of the Work

You can, if you like, remember Oxford by learning the order of the work. You can learn

slow work
fourths and back
treble bob up to the back and down to thirds
reverse thirds
treble bob up and down 2½ times
reverse thirds
treble bob up and down
fourths and back

or something like that.

At first sight that seems like the safest system because you need rely on no one but yourself. But somehow, it's terribly hard trying to remember how many times you've treble bobbed up and down in the middle.

The Second System

So because the order of the work is so hard, many ringers use a different system. They ring Oxford entirely by the treble. They use the first Kent system on page 134 and simply treble bob until they find themselves in 3-4 with the treble below them. Then, if they're on their way down, they make thirds and go back up again, and if they're on their way up, they make fourths and go back down again.

Think of it as making a handbrake turn in 3-4 whenever the treble is below you, and you can't go wrong.

The Third System

And the third system is to remember the fourths and thirds ***after*** the slow, and then to treble bob until you find yourself dodging 3-4 down with the treble. Your ***next*** time down from the back has the reverse thirds, and the fourths and the slow follow soon after.

Bobs

And now for the bobs – and, fortunately, once again, there are no singles. Even more so than with Kent, touches of Oxford are far rarer than plain courses, but when you come to them, the bobs are very similar to Kent bobs.

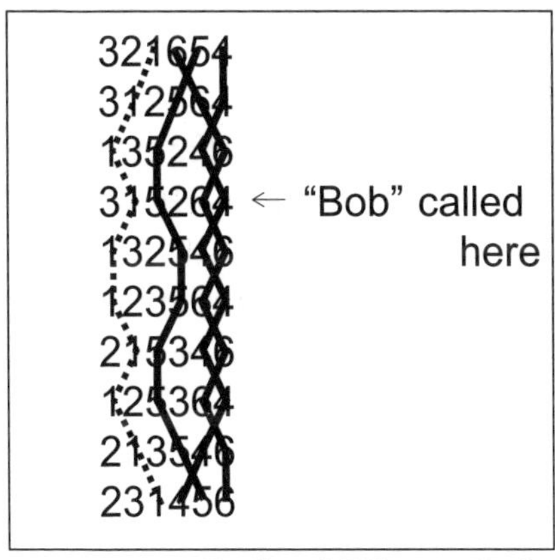

Oxford Minor Bob

You can see that, as in Kent, the bells going in and out of the slow are unaffected. Similarly, the bell in 5-6 up does two more dodges, making three in all, and the bell in 5-6 down does the same. But the bell that makes the bob, does this.

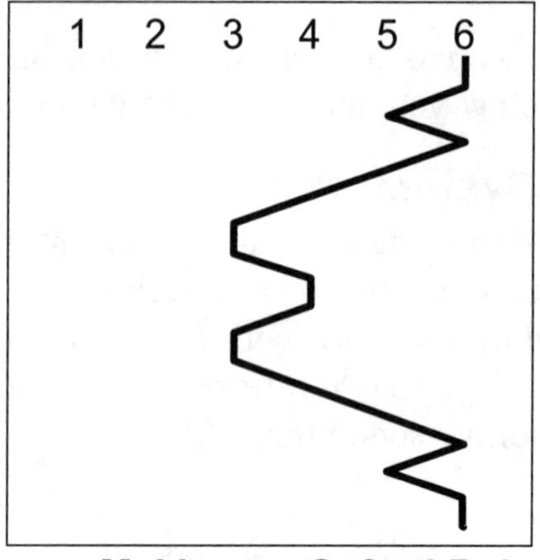

Making an Oxford Bob

It comes down from the back, makes thirds, fourths, thirds – a ***crankshaft***, as some ringers call it – and goes back up to the back again without getting down to lead at all. This is a tricky little manoeuvre which it's best to be prepared for.

Giving Oxford a Go

And that is all there is to it. Quite straightforward, you might think, and definitely not worth all the fear and doubt that traditionally comes with it. Just recap on the basic rules, and then turn the clock back with an error-free course. This time it will be the *Union Scholars* smiling down at you.

"It's all very well you recommending people to ring Oxford," a conductor told me after I had written the last reply, "but I can't put anyone right in it. It would be easier for me if they rang Kent and Oxford spliced instead." Well ...

15. Kent and Oxford

Kent and Oxford – like Cheese and Tomato, and Roast Lamb and Mint Sauce – is one of life's ***classic*** combinations. If you can ring Kent, you can probably ring Oxford, and if you can ring Kent ***and*** Oxford, you can almost certainly splice them together. Don't worry if you and your band have never rung any spliced before. Kent and Oxford is very much the shallow end of multi-method ringing.

How to Ring Kent

There's a picture of Kent Minor on page 130 surrounded by a whole chapter of hints and tips. Just to recap, most ringers learn the blue line like any other method but nonetheless experience the age old 3-4 difficulty. That's when the *passing the treble* rules come in handy. If you can ring Kent but don't use these rules, now's the time to learn them. You'll find them on pages 134 and 135.

How to Ring Oxford

And having learnt Kent by the *passing the treble* rules, learning Oxford the same way is only a little extra. There's a blue line on page 141 and the rules are on pages 142 and 143. As explained there, Oxford places are rather like a Bob Minor single. If you're on the way up, you make two blows in fourths and go back down. If you're on the way down, you make two blows in thirds and go back up.

Ringing them Together

And once you can ring both Oxford *and* Kent by the treble-passing rules, ringing the two methods together is easy. Importantly, *you don't need to know where you entered the method*; you just follow the rules of the method that was last called. So essentially you,

> Always ring Kent unless you are in 3-4 and the treble is below you.
>
> Then, if you *are* in 3-4 and the treble is below you, ***and the conductor last called, "Kent,"*** you do 3-4 Kent places.

But,

> If you're in 3-4 and the treble is below you, ***and the conductor last called, "Oxford,"*** you either do fourths and back or thirds and back depending on which way you're going.

And that's all there is to it. What's more, the rules apply as much to Major, Royal, and Maximus as they do to Minor. Remember, though, that if you dodge 3-4 by mistake for your Kent places, not much harm will be done, but if you miss your Oxford places, chaos will inevitably follow.

A Few Technicalities

But even though you need learn nothing more, you probably want to know *why* you need learn nothing more. After all, people generally make out that spliced ringing is pretty fancy stuff.

Well, there are other chapters about spliced ringing in this book, and the normal way of splicing is for the method to be changed when the treble leads. The new method then begins as the treble goes back up to seconds place after leading full.

But when Kent and Oxford are spliced, the new method is called ***when the treble is dodging 3-4 down***, and the change occurs at once.

That is a particularly good place to change because both methods are exactly the same then and the tricky bits are just about to happen. If they were spliced at the lead end, you would sometimes need to do Oxford and Kent places in quick succession and the whole business would be very much more difficult.

All touches of Kent and Oxford are rung this way, and as a result, sticklers for accuracy used to like to say that the methods were ***combined*** rather than ***spliced***. This always was a bit pedantic, and nowadays most people call them spliced. But if someone in your tower wants to call them ***combined***, there's no point in falling out over it. After all, it's ringing it that's fun.

The Variety

And on another technical point, touches of Kent and Oxford can be rung in many different ways and with enormous variety. You can have touches – indeed whole 720s or quarter peals – with only changes of method and no bobs at all. Equally, you can have touches with bobs only in the Kent or only in the Oxford, or in both.

Because treble bob was the zenith of general ringing for a very long time, much effort went into composing Kent and Oxford touches. The result was a lot of compositions in a format that many conductors – quite rightly – find extremely difficult to understand. So if you see compositions of Kent and Oxford Major with headings such as ***Ilkeston***, ***Killamarsh*** and ***Worcester***, don't be confused into thinking that they're really compositions of something else. Killamarsh compositions are particularly difficult to follow.

The Elephant Pit

And lastly, an elephant pit. A deep and terrible trap that lies in wait for all Kent and Oxford ringers.

When a change of method is called, you'll often be a long way away from being affected – dodging 5-6 up for example. So you say to yourself, "That doesn't matter much to me," and carry on. Several minutes later you arrive in 3-4 with the treble below you, and you can't for the life of you remember what method's being rung at that moment.

If that happens to you, ring Kent. By and large, Kent is rung in longer blocks than Oxford, and it's also rung in greater quantity. Alternatively, ask quietly but clearly, "What method are we in?" Best of all, though, pay close attention to the conductor at all times.

And if you really *can't* rely on your memory, have a go at the tried and trusted ***feet*** method. Put your right foot forward when the conductor calls ***Kent***, and your left foot forward when he calls ***Oxford***. Then, when the places come, a glance at your feet immediately tells you what to do. Indeed, it will be your feet that stop you falling into the elephant pit. And what could be more satisfying than *that*?

A few years ago I wrote a ringing article for The Field *– the well-known, country sports magazine. It was about ringing generally, but it also contained hints aimed at encouraging well-heeled* Field *readers to dig deep into their pockets for belfry restoration.* The Field *took some first class photographs to accompany the article, and overall, I was well pleased.*

Assuming that other ringers would be equally pleased, I sent a paragraph about it to The Ringing World*, suggesting* *that if anyone couldn't afford to buy the magazine – excellent value though it was – they could look out for it in their dentist's waiting room in two years' time.*

One ringer, though, was not at all pleased, and he wrote indignantly to the Editor saying so. He railed at me strongly for promoting sales of a country sports magazine, and although I have never taken part in a country sport myself, it brought home to me how easy it is to upset and offend people on matters about which they feel deeply.

So with there being so many vegetarian ringers nowadays, I was a bit worried about admitting in the last chapter that I enjoyed eating roast lamb and mint sauce. No one complained at the time, though, and I hope you don't mind now. But if you do, I can only apologise. Fortunately, we're now moving on to safer subjects. There's nothing at all about either meat eating ***or*** *fox hunting in* **Ringing Stedman**.

Ringing Stedman

16. Ringing Stedman

The First Steps

I am not an expert ringer. I took a long, long time to learn and I shall never ring Cambridge or anything like that. Grandsire and call changes are my staple fare with the occasional course of Bob Doubles thrown in, but I would *so* like to be able to ring Stedman. If I could manage just a plain course now and again – or maybe even a short touch – I would never want for more. Looking it up is getting me nowhere. Can you help?

E.L.T.
Northamptonshire

There is no doubt that Stedman is ***special***. It is enjoyable, musical and sociable, and for several centuries it was the zenith of ringing achievement everywhere. Indeed, in many areas it still is. When you can turn up at a District practice and effortlessly manage a course of Stedman, you can sit down again afterwards with that comfortable, self-satisfied feeling of having ***arrived***.

But, of course, Stedman isn't easy. If it were, it wouldn't be such an achievement. There are a mass of quirks and pitfalls lurking within it to trap the unwary. But once you've been shown the way through those quirks and pitfalls, it isn't really too difficult either, and hopefully, these chapters will show you the way.

The Method

If you've read any of the other books and articles on Stedman, you'll have noticed that Stedman authors experience an overwhelming urge to explain how the method is constructed. I was a little tempted that way myself, but I

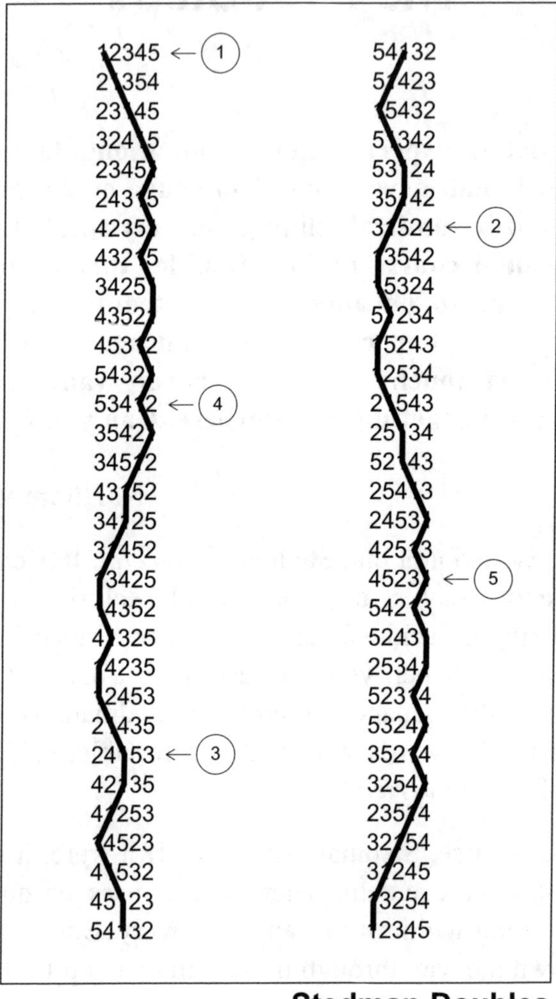

Stedman Doubles

resisted because I didn't think that giving in would help you very much. Instead, I'm defying convention by starting with a picture of the blue line – and there it is on the left.

Dividing it up

If you've seen it before, familiarity may have deadened the shock. But if you've only ever rung Bob Doubles or Grandsire it will look pretty horrific. So horrific, indeed, that you may not want to think any more about it.

And if you don't, I fully understand. But bear with me a moment and I'll show you how you can learn – and, indeed, practise – the different parts of it separately. You can then put those parts together and ring the whole thing with relatively little difficulty.

So we'll begin by dividing it up into four pieces, and we'll learn the names of those pieces as we go along.

The Dodging

First, ***the dodging*** – the work that occurs in 4-5. You've already dodged a fair bit in Plain Bob or Grandsire so you know how to do it. Persuade your tower captain to let you ring the treble to the method on the next page.

It's known as ***Cloister*** or ***St Helen's***, and you can see that it doesn't last very long but it gives you the opportunity to practise exactly the same dodging you do in 4-5 in Stedman. You simply

hunt up to 4-5
do two dodges in 4-5 up
lie behind
do two dodges in 4-5 down
and hunt back down to lead again.

I say ***simply*** but to begin with you may not find it quite *that* simple. Don't be afraid to keep on practising it over and over again until you've got it absolutely right. In particular, take note that the dodges are ***handstroke*** dodges, as in Grandsire, and not ***backstroke*** dodges as in Plain Bob. And to help, I've put little "H"s and "B"s next to the diagram to show which blows are at hand and which are at back. If you have trouble getting it right, check that you're dodging the right way round.

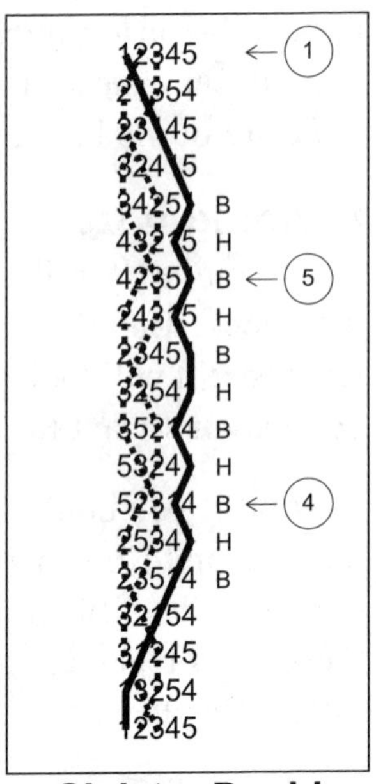

Cloister Doubles

The time you spend practising the dodging will bc time well spent, because although many people think it's the work on the front that makes Stedman difficult, in reality that's rarely the *real* trouble. The frontwork is difficult, certainly, but it's trying to get it right after making a pig's ear of the dodging that's the real scupperer. If you can do the dodging perfectly, you're in with a real chance of getting the frontwork right as well.

The Quick Work

And then it's time for the next bit, and one of the delights of Stedman is coming into contact with some distinctly odd, but pleasantly quirky, terminology. ***The quick work*** or ***the quick*** is an example of this. It sounds rather complicated but in reality it's

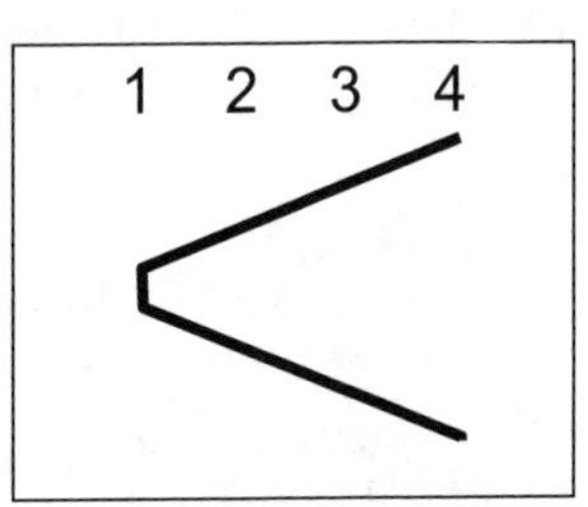

The Quick Work

nothing more nor less than a piece of plain hunting. But even though it really *is* only a piece of plain hunting, you must never call it that because no one ever does. When you're hunting down you're said to be ***going in quick***, and when you're hunting up you're said to be ***going out quick***. Whilst you're doing your quick work you're said to be ***quick bell***, and if all that seems rather odd, you can at least console yourself that *quick* it certainly is. Blink, and you'll miss it.

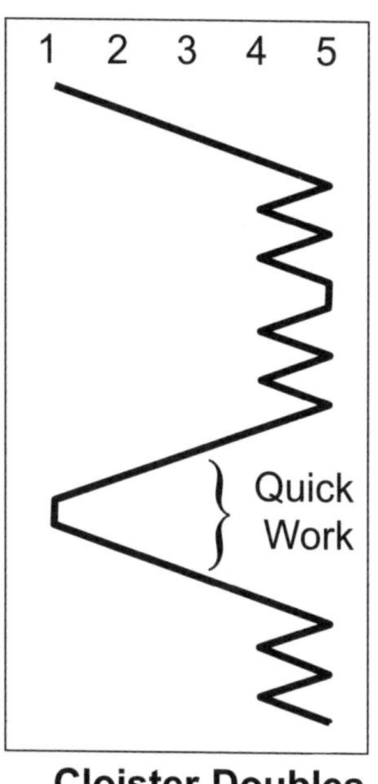

Cloister Doubles

But once you've got over the the terminology, the quick work itself isn't difficult, especially if you get the dodging right before and after. What's more, ringing Cloister will give you lots of practice at it as well as at the dodging because you'll be ringing it over and over again in between.

Over and over again, that is, as long as you keep going at the end of each course as shown on the right.

Next Time

And that's the end of the first chapter. I'm stopping here so that you can get in a good bit of practice at Cloister before you even start *thinking* about the last chunk. That is known as ***the slow work*** and it certainly is the most difficult bit. But by the time you're happy with the dodging and the quick you'll be more than ready to give it a good run for its money next time.

Not long after this chapter appeared in The Ringing World, *I received a most interesting letter from Herbert Taylor, the tower captain of Darley Dale in Derbyshire. He explained that he had discovered Cloister for himself in the late 1940s when looking for a method for his learners, and as the dedication of Darley Dale is St Helen,* **St Helen's** *was what he called it.*

It seems probable that the method spread to a number of areas as a result of visiting bands seeing it on the Darley Dale ringing chamber wall, and Herbert also sent it to The Ringing World *in the 1960s. But where the name* **Cloister** *comes from is by no means clear. It seems to have been around a long time, and it certainly has a seventeenth century feel to it.*

But whatever you call it, Cloister is fun and musical, and we talk about it in more detail in Chapter 46. Certainly, Herbert did us all a good turn by inventing – or re-inventing – it. How curious, though, that his name – like almost all other method composers' names – will only ever be known to a few, yet Stedman's name has struck delight and fear in almost everyone for over three centuries. And that's particularly so when talk comes round to **The Tricky Bits**.

17. Ringing Stedman

The Tricky Bits

If you have the extreme good fortune to be a general, all-round brain-box, you probably learnt Stedman Doubles in 15 minutes and aren't reading this chapter now. But if you're just average like the rest of us, you will need to learn it gently.

Last time, we looked at the first steps in progressing from Plain Bob and Grandsire to Stedman, and we learnt ***the dodging*** and ***the quick work***. In passing, we also learnt ***Cloister***. But the tricky bits we left till this time, and *those* are what we're going to look at now.

The Slow Work

We'll start with the section we haven't yet been introduced to – ***the slow work*** or ***the slow***. Not only is it tricky in itself, but it's made trickier – though more entertaining – by the peculiar terminology that goes with it. Indeed, the term ***slow work*** is itself rather odd. But before we get on to the terminology, take a deep breath and have a quick look at the picture on the next page.

Rather daunting, isn't it? But before you start learning anything, let me guide you a moment.

The whole of the slow work takes place between first place and thirds place. The essence of it is that you repeatedly do thirds, then something on the front, then thirds again, then something else on the front, then thirds again, and so on. It's a bit like plain hunting on three except that you never just do a normal lead. You always do something funny instead.

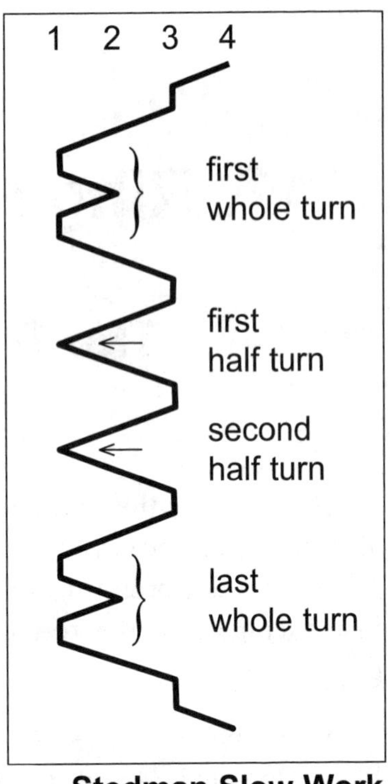

Stedman Slow Work

The Names

These funny sort-of-leads have their own names, and I've written them on the picture. The bits where you do two blows lead, one blow in seconds and two blows lead, are known as ***whole turns***. The first one is called the ***first whole turn*** and the second one is called the ***last whole turn***. I haven't the slightest idea where the name ***whole turn*** comes from, but it's universally used by all Stedman ringers, so you'd do best to use it yourself.

The other times that you get to the front, you do *one blow only* at lead and then go back up to thirds again. Common sense would suggest that you would call these single blows, *point leads* or *one blow leads*, or something like that, but tradition dictates otherwise. In Stedman they are invariably known as ***half turns*** and never as anything else. The first one is known as the ***first half turn*** and the second one is known as the ***second half turn***.

From time to time you may wonder why you should have a ***last*** whole turn but a ***second*** half turn. Certainly *I* do. But it's just one of ringing's great unsolved mysteries and simply the way things are. If you can think of a good reason, please let me know.

Reciting the Slow

And when you recite the slow work to yourself, you do it like this.

Thirds
first whole turn
thirds
first half turn
thirds
second half turn
thirds
last whole turn
thirds
and out to 4-5.

Learn it parrot fashion. Keep on reciting it to yourself and your friends until you – and they – are heartily fed up with it. Recite it on practice night, recite it in the bath, recite it whilst drinking a cup of tea, and recite it anywhere else you can think of. You'll then be in with a real chance of making a fair stab at ringing it when the time comes.

Ringing the Slow

But although learning the order of the slow work is essential, no matter how well you can recite it, you'll probably still have trouble ringing it. And for most people, the main reason is that they get confused about what stroke they should be leading at.

The point is that in Bob Doubles you always lead one

blow at handstroke followed by another blow at backstroke. The same is true in Grandsire Doubles, Bob Minor and many other methods. We call this type of leading, ***leading right***. But in Stedman you must sometimes lead one blow at backstroke followed by one blow at handstroke, and we call this type of leading, ***leading wrong***.

Leading wrong is itself very difficult when you've only ever led right, but in the slow work you have the extra problem that sometimes you must lead right and sometimes you must lead wrong, and *that* is where the trouble lies.

Take another look at the first whole turn and the last whole turn. They both *look* the same. They both *look* like a pair of short trousers turned on their side. But in reality they *aren't* the same because the first whole turn is

lead wrong,
point seconds at backstroke,
lead right,

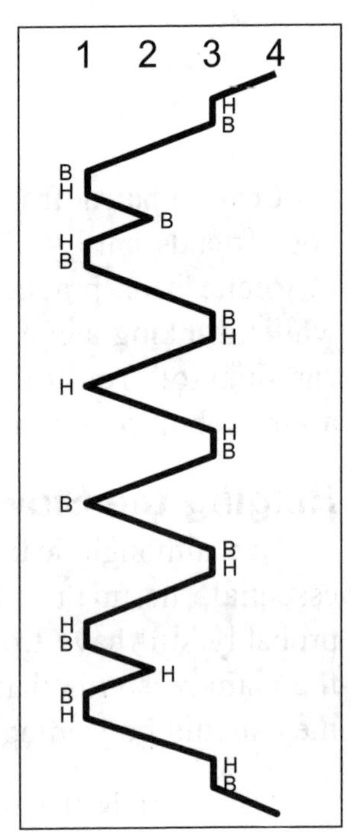

whilst the last whole turn is

lead right,
point seconds at handstroke,
lead wrong.

So the great majority of ringers find that the two whole turns *feel* very different. Similarly, the first half turn is a point lead at ***handstroke*** whilst the second half turn is a point lead at ***backstroke***.

So, just as in the first chapter, I'm including a diagram with little "H"s and "B"s next to it to show which stroke you ring each blow at. There's no need to learn this before you attempt your first plain course, but you'll find it very useful to refer to once you've gone wrong.

Indeed, even if you find you can manage fairly well without it, you'll still find it very useful knowledge for later on. Certainly, you'll never be a *reliable* Stedman ringer without it. Staying right in Stedman is one of life's great difficulties. And that, amongst other things, is what we shall be looking at next time.

Over the ten weeks that this series appeared in The Ringing World, *I received a number of letters from people explaining how* ***they*** *thought of Stedman. I was very grateful for these, and most of the ways were entirely sensible even if a little different from my own. Interestingly, though, there were one or two which were so astoundingly complex that – to me – they bordered on the bizarre. One was particularly remarkable for coming on a sheet of paper several feet long and sellotaped to itself in several places* "... in order to make the system completely clear."

The moral seems to be that there are many ways of thinking about Stedman, and whenever you're ringing it, the other ringers may all be thinking about it completely differently. And that is all the more reason to put every effort into **Staying Right**.

18. Ringing Stedman

Staying Right

Time has passed, and we have arrived at Chapter 18. With luck you've now had the time to study the method and the opportunity to practise it. You may be finding it difficult, but the more you practise, the better you'll get.

The trouble is, though, that practice alone isn't sufficient. No matter how many years you spend ringing Stedman, there will always be occasions when you completely lose track of what you're doing. Time and wisdom will not cure it. Age and experience just cannot seem to wither the boundless propensity we all have for going wrong.

What's more, in Stedman Doubles the problem is particularly acute. One moment a touch is being rung perfectly, the next it evaporates as though hit by a gas explosion. Quite often, everyone goes wrong simultaneously, each person blasting themselves into an orbit light years from everyone else.

The extreme rarity of Stedman Doubles quarter peals demonstrates how severe the problem is. Indeed, it's so severe that it can never be completely overcome. But even if you can't overcome it, you can at least reduce it. And that is what this chapter is about.

The Problem

Way back in Chapter 16, I resisted the temptation to go into the technical details of how Stedman is constructed, and I'm going to continue resisting now. Suffice it to say, though, that when Fabian Stedman invented the method, he wasn't setting out to produce an entertaining blue line. He wasn't even trying to invent something which would provide enjoyment and interest for four hundred years to come. Indeed, he wasn't even *thinking* of the blue line because blue lines were still two centuries in the future. Instead, he was simply trying to devise a system which would produce all the 120 different changes on five bells.

In doing this he might have arranged for one bell to plain hunt all the time as the treble does in Grandsire and Plain Bob. But he didn't. Instead, he took the front three bells and permuted them all of the six different ways round whilst at the same time making the other two bells dodge. He then swapped one bell from the front with one from the back, and did it all over again. And again. And so on.

As it happens, there are several different ways of doing this, and he may well have invented Cloister Doubles – which we looked at in Chapter 16 – and Erin Doubles – which is the Doubles form of Erin *Triples* included in Chapter 30 – on the way. If so, he probably dismissed them as being incapable of producing all the 120 different changes. Eventually, though, he invented Stedman, and so assured himself of the most famous niche in the whole of ringing history.

But the trouble is that, clever as he was, Fabian Stedman invented a method ***in which the treble doesn't plain hunt***. ***All*** the bells ring ***all*** of the method ***all*** of the time. There is no underlying structure to hang on to, no treble to guide you, and nothing to help you decide what to do next. When you ring Stedman, you're on your own without a safety net, and that is where the problem lies.

Methods and Principles

But although that's the problem, we'll pause a moment before looking at solutions. First, I'll belabour you with one last piece of terminology. In strictness, Stedman is not a ***method***, it's a ***principle***.

And in case you want to know the difference, a method is a ***method*** if one bell plain hunts – or does other regular work – throughout, but a method is a ***principle*** if everyone – including the treble – all have their go.

Nowadays it's rather pedantic to make the distinction in normal speech, and most people call Stedman a ***method***. But at some time or other you're bound to come across a stickler for accuracy who pulls you up on it. So you might as well know what he's talking about.

The Commonest Mistake

And now for some assistance. Let's start with Stedman's commonest mistake – the last whole turn. As we discussed before, it consists of a whole pull ***right***, a point blow in seconds place at handstroke, and a whole pull ***wrong***.

By far and away the commonest mistake in Stedman is to lead right and then go straight out to 4-5 without leading wrong – or, indeed, making thirds – at all. The lead right overcomes you, and you lapse into your Bob Doubles autopilot and go ***out quick***.

Indeed, this is such a common mistake that I always advise novice Stedman conductors to shout, "Finish your whole turn," whenever there's a hiatus on the front. Nine times out of ten the ringing then comes right again as if by magic.

As regards keeping yourself right, there's no easy solution. The best you can do is simply apply greater concentration to your last whole turn than any other part of the method. Every time you approach it, you must say to yourself,

> "My word! This is that dreadful last whole turn approaching and I must jolly well get it right."

Shallow advice, I know. But applying it will do more to keep you right in Stedman than anything else.

Other Slow Mistakes

The last whole turn, though, is not the only piece of the slow work you can get wrong. *Any* of the turns can be converted into mistakes.

For example, you might do your second half turn and then go straight out to 4-5; or you might do a last whole turn when you should be doing a first half turn; or you might do three half turns instead of two; or you might even get your last whole turn confused with your first whole turn and do the slow work all over again.

Some people are more prone to this kind of mistake than others, and extra concentration helps. But over and above that, the greatest assistance you can give yourself, is to know, for each blow of your slow work, whether it's at handstroke or backstroke.

Knowing the Strokes

We looked at this last time, and I included an annotated picture to help. You can find it on page 162. There are three ways that knowledge of the strokes can assist you. First, it can give you an added dimension to your slow work litany. Simply by saying,

"... first half turn at ***handstroke***,
seconds,
thirds at ***hand and back***,
seconds,
second half turn at ***backstroke*** ..." etc,

you'll be cementing it more securely into place.

Second, it will enable you to differentiate more clearly between the different parts. If you start to lead at handstroke and ***you've already done a half turn***, you must be doing your last whole turn. You don't need to know you've already done two half turns because, *by the stroke alone*, a handstroke lead cannot be your ***second*** half turn.

Similarly, you cannot do two consecutive lots of slow work because the last whole turn is so different from the first whole turn.

And the third advantage is that, when all else fails, you have fewer alternatives to choose from. For example, if you come down to lead at handstroke and your mind is a total blank, you can only do either the first half turn or the last whole turn ***and nothing else***. You therefore have a one in two chance of being right, and that's heaps better than a one in four chance.

Small comfort perhaps. But anything that increases your chances in Stedman must be good.

Frontwork Ropesight

Yet even when you're absolutely rock-sure of what you're doing, you can still get things wrong. And the more Bob Doubles and Grandsire you've rung, the more likely that is because, quite simply, you look the wrong way.

In Plain Bob and Grandsire, the bell that takes you from

lead is almost invariably different from the bell which you took from lead. You may know this consciously or you may not, but in either event you will ***automatically*** expect it to be so.

In Stedman, though, it is *not* always so, because when you do a half turn, the bell which you took off, takes you off. And there are also other ropesight oddities which can repeatedly catch you unawares.

So be prepared for Stedman ropesight to be different, and be prepared to go back to the picture and look at the numbers in the bits that you keep getting wrong. You can then see if your problem is that you always look the wrong way.

And over and above that, remember the two golden rules of the slow work ropesight.

> When you go up to thirds and back down to lead, you always ring over exactly ***two*** other bells ***and no more.***

And,

> One of those bells is one of the two bells of your previous trip to thirds, and one is different.

The Dodging

And the last thing we'll look at is the dodging. It is essential to remember that there are ***two*** dodges – not three – and that you have to step back twice at ***handstroke***.

The best method is to count the dodges at handstroke, saying something like, "back once, back twice," as you do them. This will not only help you get the dodges right, it will also enable you to correct yourself if you miss the thirds as you come out of the slow.

That is another common mistake, and when you make it you will automatically start to do ***backstroke*** dodges instead of handstroke ones. But if you know that your dodges must be at ***handstroke***, you'll be able to put yourself right again without too much trouble.

Next Time

And there, for the moment, we'll pause. We've covered most of the possible mistakes and you'll have plenty to work on during the next couple of weeks. But there's one great difficulty that we haven't yet talked about. Perhaps you already know what it is and perhaps you don't. But either way, I'll let you go away and do some deep breathing so you'll be fresh and ready for **Stedman's Greatest Problem** next time.

Speak it only in a whisper, but Fabian Stedman seems to have been a bit of a snob. In his book, ***Campanalogia****, published in 1677, he tells us that he was able to follow all the bells through all the methods by ear alone, and that this was how he worked out what to do next. He also suggests that all other good ringers of the time were doing the same – although elsewhere he implies that most of the ringers* ***he*** *knew, didn't.*

Some people have suggested that this shows how musical the ringers of the seventeenth century were, but my own view is that it simply shows what a yarn spinner Stedman was. The book was addressed to a group of wealthy and influential young gentlemen, and the early part has a deal of flattery of one kind and another. His suggestion that they all possessed listening excellence was probably just another example of it.

Of course, at that time, the blue line was still 200 years in the future, and it may well be that the ringers then relied a lot more on listening to the hunt bell than they do today. But it also seems clear from other things he had to say, that ropesight of a kind **was** *used, even if not by him. Other writers of the time appear to confirm this.*

But whatever the truth, he definitely didn't think of his great invention in anything like the way we think of it today. If he could come back now and read the discussion in the next chapter, it would leave him totally bemused. Whereas for us, it often seems that nothing could be more important ...

19. Ringing Stedman

Stedman's Greatest Problem

There is a great and fundamental problem that has been troubling Stedman ringers for generations. Throughout the centuries they have discussed it, pondered it, and analysed it more than anything else in ringing. "How do you know," they have all asked each other, "whether to go in Quick or whether to go in Slow?"

And indeed, how *do* you know? The greatest of minds have been plumbed for an answer and found wanting. Yet over the years a multitude of patent tips and systems have grown up, so that now there is one to suit every taste. And it is those tips that we are looking at this time.

The Standard Rule

Primarily, of course, there is ***The Standard Rule***.

> If you ***came out quick last time*** – and you are not affected by a call – you must ***go in slow next time***.

And,

> If you ***came out slow last time*** – and you are not affected by a call – you must ***go in quick next time***.

You probably realised that about two chapters ago, but the trouble is that practice isn't nearly as simple as theory. Even in a plain course it's very easy to forget which way you last came out, and in touches, the bobs and singles – which we'll be looking at later on – muck it around no end. So if you're among the 99% of Stedman ringers who find *the standard rule* isn't enough, one of the following tips might help.

Using your Feet

A lot of Stedman ringers shuffle. Sometimes this is because they're nervous, but more often it's because they're using their feet to tell them what to do next.

When they go ***out quick*** they put their ***right foot forward***, and when they go ***out slow*** they put their ***left foot forward***. If they are affected by a call, they move one foot forward and the other back. When they get to the end of 4-5 down, they look at their feet. If the right one is forward they go in slow, and if the left one is forward they go in quick. And that is that.

Simple, isn't it?

Well, some people certainly find it so. Others get confused about which foot is which, or they move the same foot twice or not at all. Other ringers can never remember to move one foot back and so they gradually shuffle into the middle of the ringing chamber. And yet others get so worried about their feet they can't ring the method at all.

Certainly the system is well worth trying. But if you're going to rely on it, make sure that you always move your feet ***at exactly the same point*** every time you ring the method.

Incidentally, if you were to use the system while ringing peals, it could be said that you were using a ***physical aid to***

memory and so the peal should be disallowed. Mind you, I suspect that only a few purists would go that far, but you might do best to keep it to yourself.

Watching your Course Bell

At one time, if you asked a real Stedman expert for a tip, he'd probably tell you to ***watch your course bell***. If you passed it coming out as you were going in, then you were going in slow. Otherwise you were going in quick.

That's alright if you know who your course bell is, but the chances are that you don't. If there are no calls, it's the bell that you dodged ***up*** with in the highest dodging position – i.e. 4-5 up in Doubles, 6-7 up in Triples, etc. So as long as you can remember to notice who your course bell is – and as long as you can keep that knowledge in your head all the way to 4-5 down – it's a good tip. But if you can't, or if you're affected by a call, it gets a bit mind-boggling for the ordinary ringer.

The "Tip for Stedman"

The *Ringing World Diary* describes a system known as *A Tip for Stedman*. It's a bit of a mouthful, and it can be difficult to wrap the brain around, but some ringers certainly use it. I shall quote it verbatim.

> *"If you arrive in 4-5 down without knowing whether to go in quick or slow, or knowing your course bell, note the bell you strike over at your first blow in fourths. If on leaving 4-5 your first blow in thirds is over this bell, make thirds and go in slow."*

This tip has stood the test of time, but it's nonetheless not wholly reliable because it depends on *other people* staying right. Even if the person you're taking most note of stays right, someone else may confuse you by ringing in the same place. And if the person you're taking note of goes wrong, you're in real trouble.

Nevertheless it's good ropesight practice and a lot of people are very keen on it. If you feel it's the right tip for you, then I wish you the best of luck in using it.

Taking Two Bells

And now for a less sophisticated method.

Whenever you go onto the front you'll find two other bells there. No matter whether you're quick or slow, your first two blows are over each of them in turn. Some ringers ring over those two bells and then look to see what position they're in. If they're in seconds place they know they're quick bell, but if they're still in thirds place they know they're slow bell.

Getting this right relies on a curious mixture of good and bad bell handling coupled with above average ropesight. It's essentially an unworkable system, and if you can nonetheless make it work, you're bringing into operation some quite advanced skills and talents which you would probably be better off employing on something more worthwhile.

The Crunch Method

And now for the least sophisticated system of all. Whilst few people openly admit to it, the ***Crunch Method*** is definitely the most popular. It is essentially this.

When ***in doubt***, go ***in quick***. If everything sounds good, lead right and carry on out quick. If a crunch occurs in seconds place, ***hold up one blow*** and then lead wrong at the start of your first whole turn. Then carry on with the slow work.

This may sound like a ***coarse ringer's*** tip, and I suppose it is, but it really does work. If you crunch in thirds place, it's because someone has forgotten to finish their last whole turn, and that *also* means that you must go in slow. So in essence, the tip is

Crunch means Slow.

It can, of course, put off the rest of the band, and you should try not to have to use it too often. But, when all else fails, it's as good a life-belt as any.

Staying Firm

And lastly, a strong word of advice to the well-brought-up ringer. ***When ringing Stedman, put all your natural politeness firmly behind you.***

No matter how much someone else wants to do your work, don't let them. If someone wants to pinch your lead, ***never*** say, "After you," and lead a blow later.

If someone wants you to carry on dodging when you should be going on to the front, ***never*** smile politely and accommodate them.

If three other people are crowding into the slow with you, ***never*** go up to 4-5 to give them a bit more room.

All those things are very polite but they invariably lead to disaster. Stick to your blue line as though bonded to it by super-glue and you'll be doing everyone a real favour. Such a favour, indeed, that with a little more practice you may all be able to move on to ringing touches. And *that* is what we shall be looking at next time.

Needless to say, this article produced a deluge of other patent tips and suggestions. Many were variations of the ones I'd written about, and others were combinations of two or more of them. They certainly all had merit, but it would take many pages to explain them all, and you would probably be left with your head spinning as much as mine was when I received them. Two, though, are definitely worth mentioning.

The first was sent me by a number of people and it really is a good one. Essentially it is a visual variation of the ***Taking Two Bells*** *method and it works like this.*

> As you come onto the front there are two bells below you. If one looks at you, you're quick bell. If neither looks at you, you're slow bell.

This undoubtedly works if both those bells are right. But if one of them isn't – and particularly if it has forgotten to finish its last whole turn – it doesn't. Although even then, you could use the ***Crunch Method*** *as a back-up.*

Interestingly, every one who told me of this method had discovered it for themselves. Indeed one ringer who wrote to The Ringing World *with it had named it after himself. Which goes to show how much private study and research goes on.*

The second tip is a variation of ***The Tip For Stedman*** *and was sent by Barbara Salmons of Horndean in Hampshire. She wrote,*

> "When you dodge 4-5 down, you are over three bells in turn at your fourths place blows, call them *a, b, c.* Observe the order in which you are over the first **two** (not just the first **one** as suggested in the Diary.) If, when going in after dodging, you meet these in the same order *(a-b)* you are going in slow, if in the reverse order *(b-a)* you are going in quick.

> "The advantage of the double observation is that you have twice as much data on which to base your decision, and two chances of picking up guidance.
>
> "When one of the bells – say *a* for argument's sake – is so far astray as to be unidentifiable, you still have half your signposts: if you can ring over *b* for your first blow in thirds, you must be quick bell: if you cannot, because he is much too far ahead of you, take him for a second blow in thirds and become slow bell.
>
> "If both *a* and *b* are at sea, and you cannot remember how to go in either, the collapse of the touch is imminent – which will solve your problem!"

That may sound rather complicated, but there is no doubt that it is the kind of belt and braces tip that many ringers are very much at home with. As with all tips, though, if you don't think it's for you, don't worry. Probably one of the others will do as well or better. At least, I hope one will. Because a good tip will make all the difference when you start on those terrible **Doubles Singles**.

20. Ringing Stedman

Doubles Singles

Above all else, the Stedman Doubles single is the ***bête noire*** of the experienced ringer. Many's the man who can ring Caters and Cinques with style and vigour but who can't get a Doubles single right to save his life.

And women ringers have trouble too.

Look around at the next District practice when the ringing master calls for a touch of Stedman Doubles. Suddenly, everyone is totally engrossed in the peal boards, or they're muttering, "No, no. I rang last time," or, "Well, I'll ring if you *really* want, but I'd rather *not* be affected by the singles."

Yet despite this, Doubles singles aren't particularly difficult, and there's no intrinsic reason why experienced ringers should have any trouble with them. But the problem is that the great majority of ringers get hustled past them and on to more complicated things before they've had any real chance of learning and practising them properly.

So I've written this chapter to try and prevent that from happening to *you*. And just to clear up any potential misunderstanding before we start, I stress that *there are no bobs in Stedman Doubles*, only singles.

The Unaffected Bells

As ever, the first thing to learn about the single is when you're ***not*** affected. So,

> You are ***not*** affected if
> you are ***on the front***.

If you're doing any part of the slow work or quick work, you need take no notice whatsoever of the calls. And that means that at any single you have a 60% chance of not being affected.

The Affected Bells

It follows from this that the only time you ***are*** affected is when you're dodging 4-5 up or 4-5 down, so there are only two new pieces of work to learn. We'll look at each of these pieces separately in a moment. But before that, we'll look at where the single is called, because there's a historical quirk to this which can catch you out.

Where the Single is Called

On the left is a picture of the eight changes that occur when one plain course is ending and another is beginning. And on the right is the same section but with a single called there.

23514
32154
31245
13254
12345
21354
23145
32415

Plain

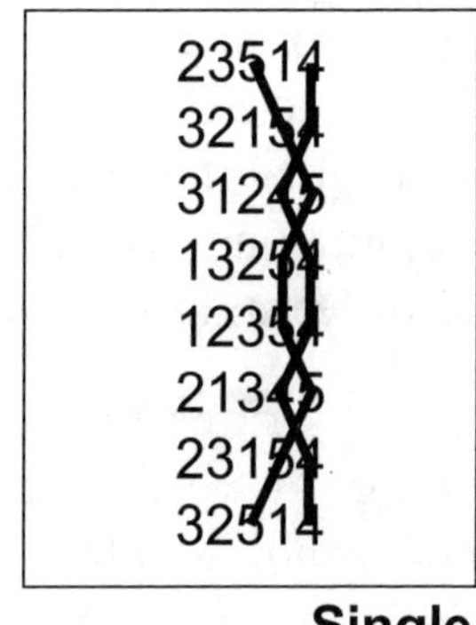

Single

You can see that the first three of the six changes during which Four and Five are together in 4-5, are exactly the same in both pictures. So the single takes effect at the ***fourth*** change when the treble is leading at backstroke.

Now, there's a universal rule which says that bobs and singles must be called in the change which gives exactly ***one whole pull's warning*** of their taking effect. You've probably noticed this in Plain Bob, Grandsire, and other methods, and it therefore follows that the Stedman Doubles single ***ought*** to be called at the ***second*** change of the six. And for want of anything better, we can call this place the ***conventional*** calling position.

But for various historical reasons – which date back to the time of Fabian Stedman himself – some people call the single at the ***first*** change of the six. And we can call *this* place the ***historical*** calling position.

I certainly don't blame you if you don't find this easy to understand, and if you're not very experienced at conducting and composing, it can indeed be confusing. So to help, here are those eight changes again but this time showing the two calling positions and the place that the single takes effect.

```
23514
32154  ← Historical calling position
31245  ← Conventional calling position
13254
12354  ← Where the Single takes effect
21345
23154
32514
```

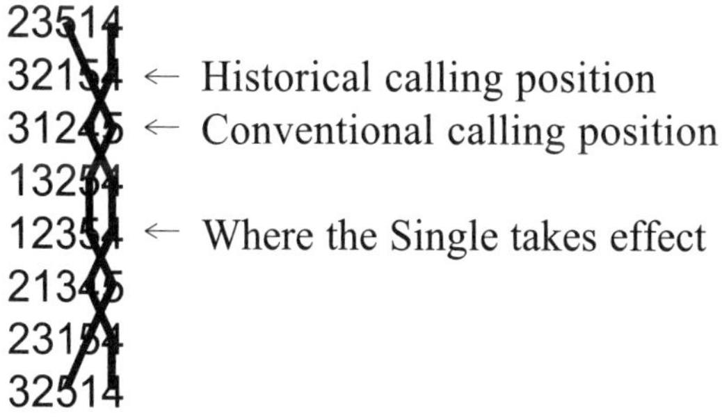

Which Way's Right?

So which way's right and which way's wrong?

Well, if I were to plump strongly for either I would be inundated with irate letters from supporters of the other. The truth is that there are some towers with a long and fixed tradition of using the ***historical*** calling position, and there are others with an equally solid tradition of using the ***conventional*** calling position. Difficulties normally only arise when the two cultures meet without either being aware of the other's existence. So the moral is that as long as you're prepared for variations, you'll be alright.

But having said that, even *I* can't sit on the fence completely. If your tower has a firm tradition of one way or the other, then well and good. But if your tower has no tradition – either because it hasn't rung Stedman in recent years or for some other reason – then I recommend you use the conventional position. Your fellow ringers will find it fits in better with their general ringing experience, and – dare I say it – the historical position is slowly but surely dying out.

The Cat's Ears

So much for that. But wherever the single is called, you've still got to learn what to do at it, and we'll look at the easier piece of work first. It's called ***cat's ears*** and the picture is on the right.

```
23514
32154 } Called around
31245 }     here
13254
12354
21345
23154
32514
```

Cat's Ears

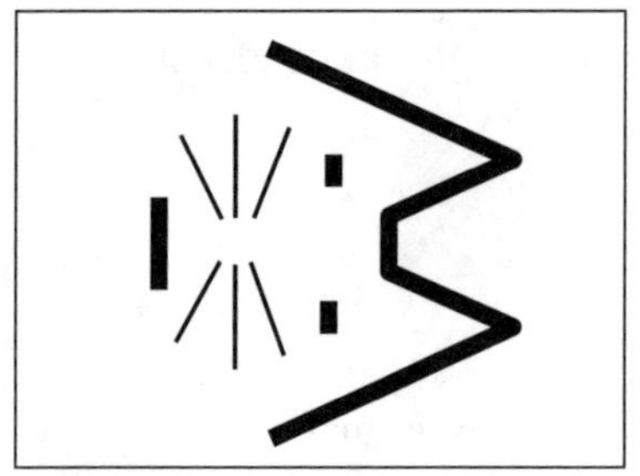

And in case you're wondering *why* it's called ***cat's ears*** you can turn this book on its side and look at the picture on the left.

It's not a very long piece of work, and there's not a lot to be said about it, but the rules for ringing it are

1. You do ***cat's ears*** if the single is called when you've just left the front and are starting to double dodge 4-5 up.

2. The first ear is at ***backstroke***, the second ear is at ***handstroke***, and the fourths between the ears is made ***right*** - i.e. handstroke-backstroke.

3. When you've finished cat's ears, you go back onto the front ***the same way that you came out***.

And I've emphasised the last bit because it's very, very important to remember and very, very easy to forget.

Cat's Ears Problems

Now you may think that compared to everything else we've looked at in Stedman, cat's ears shouldn't cause anyone much trouble. But for two reasons they often do. First, because the person working with you will frequently be all over the place and so making it very difficult for you. And second – and this is much more subtle – because the two blows in fourths are sometimes over the ***same*** bell and sometimes over ***different*** bells.

This is, of course, a ropesight problem, and those who don't suffer from it can't understand it at all. But those who *do* suffer from it, will often find cat's ears devastatingly difficult when they have to make fourths over the ***same*** bell.

Merely *knowing* that there are two different possibilities will be enough for most people, but if you want to be absolutely sure, the rule is,

> If you are cat's ears ***after quick***, you make fourths over the ***same*** bell.

But,

> If you are cat's ears ***after slow***, you make fourths over ***different*** bells.

The Coathangers

And now for the more difficult way of being affected. The most popular term for this is ***coathangers***, although ***castles*** runs a good second with a number of less favoured expressions such as ***bus tickets*** and – rather prosaically – ***the long work at the single*** coming along behind.

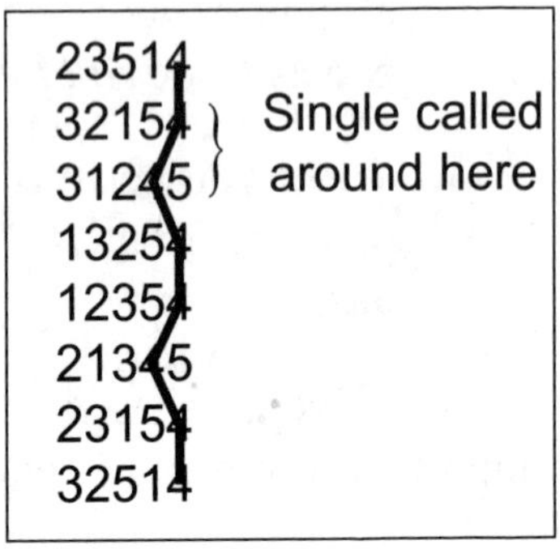

```
23514
32154 } Single called
31245 } around here
13254
12354
21345
23154
32514
```

Coathangers

I wonder if that looks like coathangers to you? I suspect not, and I shall explain why it's called **coathangers** in a moment. But the essential rules to remember are,

1. You do them when you have already double dodged 4-5 up and the single is called when you are just starting to dodge 4-5 down.
2. Instead of double dodging 4-5 down, you do one blow in fourths at ***backstroke***, two blows in fifths at ***handstroke*** and ***backstroke*** – both over the ***same*** bell – and one blow in fourths at ***handstroke***.
3. After that, you lie behind again – this time ***backstroke*** and ***handstroke*** – and ***then*** do the double dodge down.

4. And when you've finished all that, you go back onto the front ***the same way that you came out.***

A bit of a mouthful that, and you may feel that the picture was all you needed. Most people, though, find they need much more than the picture. My own view is that the truly important thing to remember is that ***you are doing no more than putting an extra section*** between your double dodge up and your double dodge down. That is the only piece that's different.

Why Coathangers are Difficult

So why do many ringers find Coathangers so appallingly difficult?

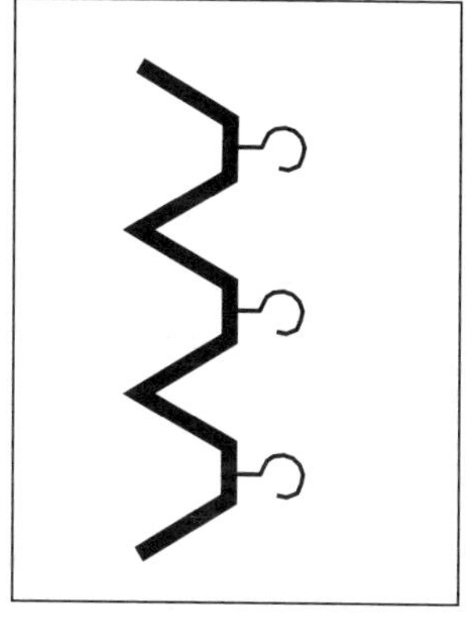

The trouble seems to be that they think of the single as being a much longer piece of work than it actually is. They regard the ***whole*** of their work on the back as something different produced by the call. Indeed, at one time ringers were encouraged to think just that, and that's where the term ***the long work at the single*** comes from. Even the term ***Coathangers*** arose through the unaffected work being added in to the affected work to make three coathangers like this. But if you just remember that the middle coathanger is the only thing that's different, you can't go wrong.

Getting the Practice

So now you know the whole of the theory about singles. But the trouble is that getting them right takes practice, and practice isn't easy to come by. Even if you ring touches fairly regularly, you may still find that you aren't often affected, and when eventually you *are* affected, you make a mess of it and then don't get another chance for weeks to come.

So to help you get the practice, I'm including two short touches especially designed for the treble ringer to ring cat's ears and coathangers several times over. The first touch is only 48 changes long and is **S P S P S P S P** – where **S** means single and **P** means plain.

This is cat's ears practice because the treble goes out quick, makes cat's ears and goes back in quick, over and over again.

The second touch is 96 changes long and is **(P S P P) x 4**. This is coathangers practice because the treble goes out quick, double dodges 4-5 up, does coathangers, double dodges 4-5 down, and goes back in quick, over and over again.

Persuade your tower captain – or, if your local band isn't strong enough, your local ringing master – to call these touches for you. After a couple of attempts you'll be so good at singles that you'll never be bothered by them again.

Next Time

And that's all I've got to say about Stedman Doubles. With luck and the chance to practise, you'll now be a real expert at it. Such an expert, indeed, that you'll be hankering for a go at Stedman *Triples*. And that's just as well, because Stedman Triples is what we shall be looking at next time.

This was another chapter which produced a large volume of tips, many of which were put forward with considerable fervour. Indeed, one or two ringers took me to task for even

***suggesting** that there was any alternative. And since some of these tips were distinctly intriguing, I wondered if there was rather more to them than was being put on paper.*

*The point is that most of us have ways of ringing that are so second nature that we aren't really fully aware of the extent of them. One gentleman from Scotland said that he counted his **up** dodges, "FOUR five FOUR five FOUR five," and his **down** dodges "FIVE four FIVE four FIVE four." When a single was called he swapped over in the middle, "...* like a soldier on the march changing step,*" and went, "FOUR five FOUR four FIVE four." This, he felt, was how all novices should learn singles.*

*I have to admit that I can't really see how this can help if you don't already know exactly what to do. But if you feel it will help **you**, try it.*

*A rather different approach was suggested by Pam Copson. She called coathangers **anti-cat's ears** because they are what needs to be done to fit round the cat's ears bell. You might like to try thinking of them that way too.*

What absolutely everybody agrees upon, though, is that where touches of Stedman Doubles are concerned, the course of true change ringing never does run smooth. So I expect you are thoroughly relieved that you can now put the whole wretched business behind you and move on to **Stedman Triples**.

21. Ringing Stedman

Triples

If you're one of those people who like to be absolutely sure about everything, you'll want to know at the outset that this is the last chapter. It's now ten weeks since we started looking at Stedman, and you may be feeling that it's time and past we moved on to Triples. But I've delayed this long because the majority of Stedman Doubles ringers don't even want to *try* triples.

By and large it's a matter of background. If you've already rung plenty of Grandsire Triples and Plain Bob Triples, the step up to *Stedman* Triples isn't so very big at all. But if you ring mainly on six bells – and only on eight at District meetings – the step up from Stedman Doubles can seem very big indeed. Indeed, it can seem *so* big that many Doubles ringers think it's well beyond them.

But it certainly *isn't* beyond them. And it certainly isn't beyond *you* either. This chapter has some hints on how to manage it.

The Theory

As ever, we'll start with the easiest bit – the theory. In fact most people find the theory so easy that I almost decided to leave it out. You probably know it already – as many Stedman Doubles ringers do – even if you've never attempted to put it into practice.

That's the way things are. Learning Stedman Doubles can be an enormous labour, but once you've learnt it, learning Stedman Triples takes only a very little bit extra. To recap, though, the Stedman Triples blue line is on the next page, and putting it into words, Stedman Triples is exactly the same as Stedman Doubles except that

Between your

double dodge ***4-5 up*** and your
double dodge ***4-5 down***

you put in a

double dodge 6-7 up and a
double dodge 6-7 down

And,

You do that between ***both*** sets of 4-5 dodging.

The Order of the Work

If you want to learn the order of the work as well – and, of course, I thoroughly recommend that you do – here it is. Rather interestingly, it's exactly the same as for Doubles,

quick work
dodging
slow work
dodging

but always remembering that in Triples, ***dodging*** is double dodge 4-5 up, double dodge 6-7 up, double dodge 6-7 down and double dodge 4-5 down.

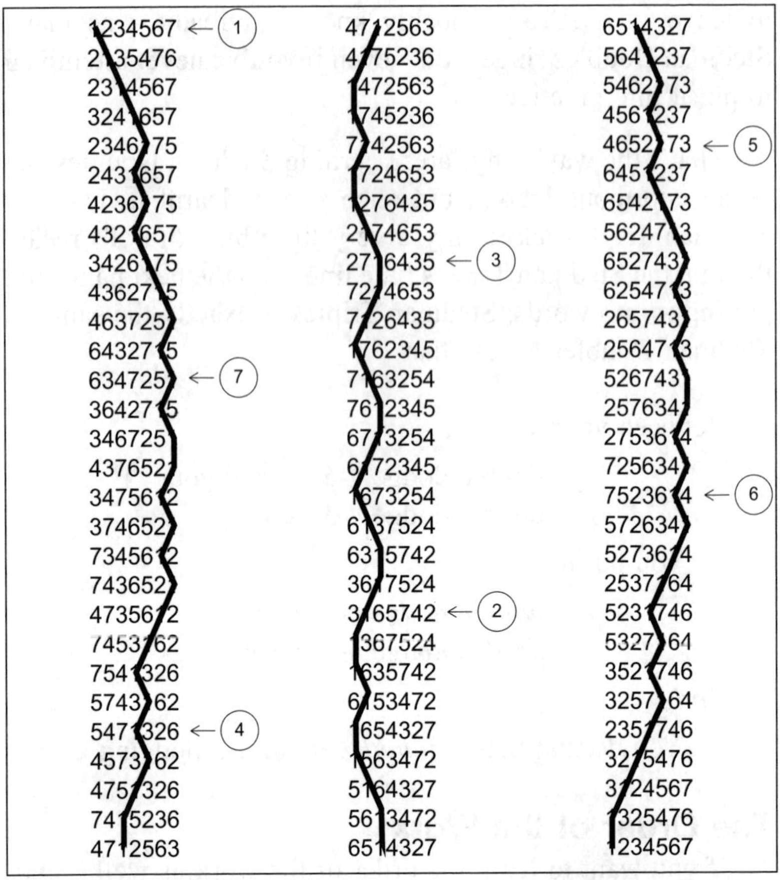

1234567 ← (1)	4712563	6514327
2135476	4175236	5641237
2314567	1472563	5462173
3241657	1745236	4561237
2346175	7142563	4652173 ← (5)
2431657	1724653	6451237
4236175	1276435	6542173
4321657	2174653	5624713
3426175	2716435 ← (3)	6527431
4362715	7214653	6254713
4637251	7126435	2657431
6432715	1762345	2564713
6347251 ← (7)	7163254	5267431
3642715	7612345	2576341
3467251	6713254	2753614
4376521	6172345	7256341
3475612	1673254	7523614 ← (6)
3746521	6137524	5726341
7345612	6315742	5273614
7436521	3617524	2537164
4735612	3165742 ← (2)	5231746
7453162	1367524	5327164
7541326	1635742	3521746
5743162	6153472	3257164
5471326 ← (4)	1654327	2351746
4573162	1563472	3215476
4751326	5164327	3124567
7415236	5613472	1325476
4712563	6514327	1234567

Stedman Triples

And that is all I'm going to say about the theory because, after Stedman Doubles, you shouldn't find it too hard.

The Dodging

But if the theory is easy, the practice certainly isn't, and like many things in ringing, it's the easiest looking bit that causes the most difficulty. The dodging.

In Chapters 16 and 18, I mentioned how important it is in Doubles to make sure that you are doing ***handstroke*** dodges and not ***backstroke*** ones. That is just as true in Triples. If you make a mistake in the slow you can easily find yourself dodging the wrong way round afterwards. But if you make a mental note to ensure that you always dodge the ***right*** way round, you'll be able to correct yourself at once.

In addition, though, in Triples it's not just the nature of the dodging that causes trouble but the ropesight as well. Due to the structure of the method, the bells sometimes come at you from quite unexpected directions.

With time and practice you get used to this, and you come to expect the unexpected. But in the meantime, if you can never seem to find the right bell to dodge with, the following tips may help.

The Dodging Tips

First, when you're dodging, each of your three blows in fifths is over the ***same*** bell. Similarly, each of your three blows in ***sixths*** is over the same bell and each of your three blows in ***sevenths*** is over the same bell.

For example, if you're dodging 6-7 up, each time you're in sixths you're over one bell, and each time you're in sevenths you're over another. So once you've found the right pair of bells, you must stick with them until the end of the double dodge.

Second, the great majority of Stedman ringers share the basic human need to be taken notice of. If *they* are dodging with *you*, they'll want *you* to know that *you* are dodging with *them*. So if you get confused, look around for someone nodding, winking or smiling at you. You'll then know to dodge with them.

If two – or, worse still, three or four – people are nodding, winking and smiling at you at the same time, you'll just have to do your best.

Third, since you have *three* attempts at each position, you can use the first two as ranging shots. By the third, you'll have worked out which bell you should be ringing over, and you can then move on to the next dodging position with confidence.

Fourth, in a plain course ***all*** of your six ***handstroke*** blows in sixths are over the same bell – i.e. for both sets of dodges in 6-7 up.

And fifth, in a plain course, ***all*** of your six ***backstroke*** blows in sixths are over the same bell – i.e. for both sets of dodges in 6-7 down.

Counting the Dodging

So much for finding the bells to ring over. But some people experience the most excruciating difficulty in *counting* the dodges correctly.

Perhaps you've had this trouble yourself. You doze off for a moment and wake up unsure of how many 4-5 up dodges you've done. For want of anything better, you assume you must have finished them, and you move on to 6-7.

A massive crunch occurs – together with a few groans and shouts – and you go red in the face and hot all over. In your embarrassment you loose track of where the 6-7 dodging started, and you again move on too soon.

Another crunch follows, and even louder groans, and you make absolutely sure you stay in 6-7 *down* long enough. Somehow, though, you stay there *too* long. Suddenly there are three of you dodging together, and the conductor is shouting, "***Get down***," rather fiercely.

Hurriedly you ***get down***. But you do it with such vigour that you shoot straight through 4-5 and arrive panting on the front, four blows early. The three people already there exhibit extreme surprise and consternation, and the touch fires out a few changes later.

Needless to say, it doesn't take many such nightmares to damage your confidence severely, and then the problem gets even worse. So if you have a counting problem yourself, mull over the following points.

1. There are ***not three*** dodges in each position, there are ***two***. It is true that you ring over each bell ***three times*** but that's because you do ***two dodges***. You pass through each position once and then go back to it twice. Being unclear about this is the biggest single problem in ringing Stedman Triples. Count the dodges, "Back once, back twice," as you do them.

2. ***Always count your dodges***. Or, at least, count them for the first ten years of your Stedman Triples career. You may find that after you've rung about 250,000 changes of Stedman Triples, your brain starts to count the dodges automatically. Until then, if you don't count your dodges you'll only have yourself to blame if you go wrong.

3. If in doubt, do an ***extra*** dodge. If everything sounds fine, then just continue as though you knew where you were all along. If everything ***doesn't*** sound fine – and you'll be able to tell by the crunch and the winces – move immediately onwards, counting, "Back once," at the next handstroke.

Getting Extra Practice

And if, despite everything, you still have tremendous dodging problems, ask your tower captain or District ringing master for extra dodging practice by way of a few courses of Cloister Triples. It's a simple extension of the Cloister Doubles which we looked at in Chapter 16, and you'll probably find the dodging in it rather easier than in Stedman because the ropesight is easier.

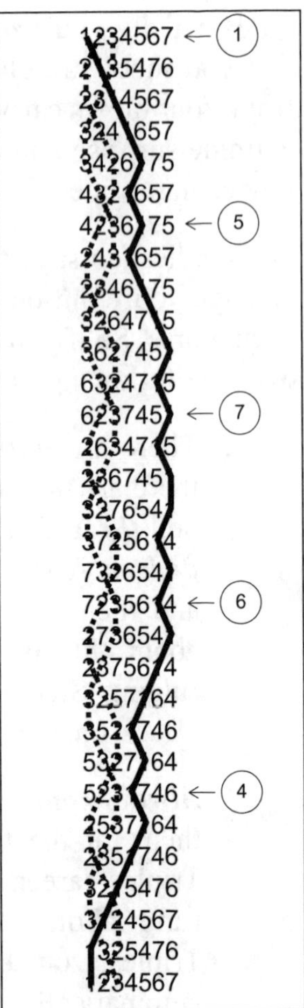

Cloister Triples

The Frontwork

And after all that hassle with the dodging, many people find the slow work a haven of peace and tranquillity in comparison. If you've rung the slow work a lot in Doubles, you won't have too much trouble with it in Triples. Ten of the blows are at lead so you should be able to get *them* right even if you can't always find the bells you should be ringing over in between.

As regards the ropesight, the main tip is to try not to ignore the back bells. And if you just can't find anyone to ring over, the chances are you should be looking at the Six or the Seven.

Bobs

And now for the bobs. And I'm afraid that all that work you put into learning Stedman Doubles singles is absolutely no use whatever to you here. The sad fact is that, in Triples, both the bobs ***and*** the singles are completely different. Bobs are rung far oftener than singles, though, so we'll do those first. And in case you find the picture of the kind on the right as difficult to make sense of as I do, here are the rules.

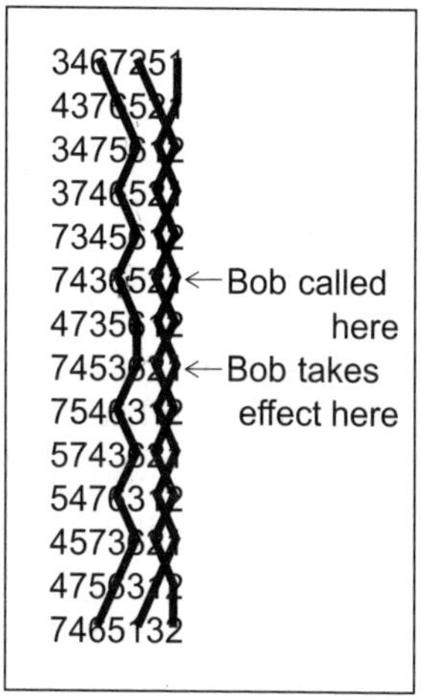

3467251
4376521
3475612
3746521
7345612
7436521 ← Bob called here
4735612
7453621 ← Bob takes effect here
7546312
5743621
5476312
4573621
4756312
7465132

Bob

First, if you are on the front or in 4-5 down when the bob is called, you are ***not*** affected.

Second, if you are double dodging 4-5 up when the bob is called, you

make fifths

and then,

double dodge 4-5 down as though you were ringing a plain course of Stedman Doubles.

Third, if you are double dodging in 6-7 up or 6-7 down when the bob is called, you

do ***three*** more dodges where you are – that's five in all –

and then

carry on going in the direction you were going anyway.

For example, if you're dodging 6-7 up, do ***three*** more dodges in 6-7 up and then double dodge 6-7 down.

> If you're dodging in 6-7 down, do three more dodges in 6-7 down and then double dodge 4-5 down.

And After

That may not sound too bad by itself, but bobs aren't always called in wide open spaces. Instead they have a rather gregarious habit of coming together in twos and fours – or even sevens and eights – and as a result you're often still dealing with the last bob when the next one is being called.

This in itself is rather tricky and we'll come to coping with it in a moment. But in addition, being affected in 6-7 affects the way you go onto the front.

Being affected in 4-5 up makes ***no*** difference to the way you go onto the front, because you make the bob and so effectively ring Stedman Doubles. So if you were going to go in slow before, you still go in slow now. But if you're called to do a bob in 6-7, that is ***not*** true. Instead,

> ***Each bob that affects you in 6-7 up or in 6-7 down, changes the way you must go onto the front.***

And I have given this rule a paragraph of bold, italicised type all to itself because it's so important.

For example, if you were going to go in slow and you get caught in 6-7 by ***one*** bob, you must go in quick instead. If you get caught by ***two*** bobs, you must go in slow just as you were going to anyway. If you get caught by ***three*** bobs, you must go in quick. And so on.

Because of this, some people remember the rule in the following way. An ***even*** number of bobs means you must go in the ***opposite*** way to the way you came out. And an ***odd*** number of bobs means you must go in the ***same*** way as the way you came out.

But rest assured that, despite your best endeavours, there will always be times when you have difficulty getting it right, and it is then that the tips we discussed in Chapter 19 will come into their own. If you use the ***feet*** method, remember always to move them at the very moment that the bob is called.

Counting the Dodges

Counting the dodges at the bobs can be a real problem too. After all, two and three is five – and three more makes eight – and counting eight dodges will tax the very keenest brain. Counting eleven or fourteen is even worse, so you must have a system for it.

The best system is not to count the total number at all but simply to count the ***extra*** three dodges after each bob. Even *that* can be difficult, though, because the last dodge of one block can merge very easily in your mind with the first dodge of the next, particularly if there are several bobs in a row.

To overcome this you must wait until each bob is called and then count, "Back once," at the next handstroke ***after that***. As long as you resist the temptation to start counting at the handstroke when the bob is called, you'll be alright.

Alternatively, you can remember that for each set of dodges – whether up or down – you must ring three times over the same bell in sixths place. If you've finished a set of three – and there is no further bob – it's time to move on.

Singles

And the very last thing to look at is the Triples single. By and large it is only the posh bands that ring singles, and even *they* don't ring very many, so you might ring Stedman Triples for years without ever having to cope with one. Nevertheless, they aren't very difficult, so you might as well learn them just in case.

Here is another of those rather confusing pictures, and as with a bob, the hard work all takes place near the back. But singles ***make no difference at all*** to the way you go on to the front. The rules are,

3467251
4376521
3475612
3746521
7345612
7436521 ← Single called here
4735612
7453612 ← Single takes effect
7546321
5743612
5476321
4573612
4756321
7465231

Single

First, if you are on the front or in 4-5 down when the single is called, you are ***not*** affected.

Second, if you are double dodging 4-5 up when the single is called, you

make fifths

and then

double dodge 4-5 down as though you were ringing a plain course of Stedman Doubles.

This is exactly the same work as you would do if a bob were called.

Third, if you are double dodging 6-7 ***up*** when the single is called, you lie behind in sevenths place as though no call had been made at all. The only difference is that ***both*** blows in sevenths place are ***over the same bell***.

Fourth, if you are double dodging 6-7 ***down*** when the single is called, you ***make two blows***

in sixths place – from back to hand – and then double dodge 6-7 ***up*** again ***with the same bell that you just dodged 6-7 down with***. This is the really tricky bit that most people have a great deal of trouble with. But if you learn it carefully – and you don't panic – you shouldn't find it too bad.

A Last Word

And that, you will be relieved to know, is that. If you've got this far, Stedman Caters and Cinques will require no more than a lot of practice, a cool nerve, and rather more opportunities than most ringers ever get.

Still, even if you never get past Stedman Triples, so what? As E.L.T. of Northamptonshire said at the outset, "An occasional touch of Stedman at a District practice and who could ask for more?"

Who indeed?

After this series appeared in The Ringing World *I got a number of very kind letters from people who had taken up Stedman Doubles after reading it. That was very nice, and the fact that they were really enjoying ringing it, was even nicer. But as time went by, several of them wrote again for a few tips on a plain course of Caters, and even Cinques. That too was nice because, as I said at the end of this chapter, for most ringers the opportunities for ten and twelve bell ringing are few and far between. So what* ***are*** *the tips?*

First, go for one of the middle bells as explained in Chapter 32. Second, the really difficult part of Stedman Caters is the dodging, so if you take the Four you'll be able to settle in by doing the slow work to begin with. After that,

4-5 up shouldn't be too bad, and that means that you'll have been ringing for at least a minute before the going gets tough.

Third, keep looking around ***all*** *the bells for your dodging partner, and don't get fixated with half the band. Remember that you are just as likely to have to dodge with the ringers next to you as those on the other side of the room.*

Fourth, the trickiest place to dodge in Stedman Caters is 6-7. It's a bit like being in the middle of the swimming pool while you're learning to swim. You're a long way from the front and a long way from the back and there's not much to hold on to. So if you want to secretly learn your 6-7 dodging partners before you start, do so.

Fifth, if the conductor calls any Caters bobs or singles, remember that they are exactly the same as Triples bobs and singles ***except*** *that they affect the bells in sevenths, eighths and ninths instead of fifths, sixths and sevenths. Similarly the Cinques bobs and singles affect the bells in ninths, tenths and elevenths. Only the multi-bell ropesight will be a problem. It's a good idea, though, to remind yourself about bobs before you start. Making fifths at a Cinques bob is an embarrassing give-away.*

And lastly, as with all ringing, go for your first course of caters with a band you know well if you possibly can. Get someone to stand behind you to help you with the ropesight if necessary. Try and be as relaxed as possible.

But whether you ever get to ring on ten or not, once you can manage Stedman Triples you're a pretty expert ringer. So expert, indeed, that this is as good a time as any to pause from method learning and look instead at some **General Matters**.

General Matters

22. Striking

Listening

I am worried that I don't strike very well. I am not sure what I do wrong, but I feel that people are uncomfortable when I ring with them. At Branch meetings conductors shout, "Listen to it," and, "Keep the leads in," and, "Push it on a bit," and although I don't know whether they mean me or not, I have the sad feeling that they probably do. I just want to be able to strike well enough to ring unnoticed in a normal band. Please help.

N.B.
Yorkshire

The trouble with striking is that the very word brings with it a whole pile of emotional baggage. To some it brings so much worry and fear that they won't read this chapter at all. To others it brings feelings of inadequacy and depression. To others it brings an irrational fury that bursts out in fits of aggression during ringing. And to others it brings superciliousness and an overwhelming desire to be firmly critical of everyone in sight.

But thankfully nowadays, all that is changing. Striking is a skill to be learnt and improved like any other. Most ringers, instructors, conductors and tower captains all look at it this way, and that is what these chapters are all about.

The Ideal

We'll begin with the ideal. ***Good*** striking is ***even*** striking. Not for us are the chords and rhythm variations of other musicians. Our aim is to space our bells evenly at all times except when we lead at handstroke. Apart from then, the interval between any pair of consecutively sounding bells should be exactly the same. And it should stay the same ***throughout*** a piece of ringing. It should be just as though we were doing it to a metronome.

But when we lead at handstroke, we must leave a double gap instead of a single one. We must leave a space big enough to fit in exactly one other bell. We leave no extra gap at backstroke but we do at handstroke, and this extra gap is called the ***open handstroke lead***.

I'm sure you knew that. But is it true?

Well, it's certainly what you want to strive for. But there are many who believe that the very best striking, particularly on heavy rings of ten or more, is *not* completely even. The variations, though, are extremely small and subtle, and no one will thank you if you leave a sizeable gap in your Bob Doubles for reasons of artistic interpretation.

In addition, until a few decades ago, many bands considered it right to leave a larger gap at backstroke when ringing the tenor behind, particularly when following the next biggest bell. Even now, many – if not most – ringers like a *slightly* larger gap there, and certainly, a quick blow is particularly disturbing.

The open handstroke lead is another source of variation. In the South West, of course, the call change ringers there don't have one at all, and the same is true of the method ringers around Barnsley. On the edge of the Peak District there used to be another centre of ***cartwheeling,*** as it is called, although it has almost died out there now. But even where an open handstroke lead *is* rung, it's a good deal more open in some places than others. A very large number of bands – and, indeed, striking competition judges too – like to leave slightly more than a one bell gap, and others like to leave slightly less. So if your own band leaves more – or less – please don't tell them I think they shouldn't.

Our Success

But whatever we're trying to do, are we successful at it?

Clearly not. ***No one*** has perfect striking. Neither you nor I nor the best ringer in the country has that. A precision machine marking our efforts would fault everyone one of us on every blow. But we nonetheless try to get as close as we can to the ideal.

And the better you get, the fewer the ringers who can tell your imperfections. It's like putting your striking through increasingly finer sieves. First, the newest learners can't tell, then the slightly more experienced can't tell, and so on. When you get to the stage of being acknowledged ***a good striker*** by the majority of ringers in your District, you're doing very well. If you go beyond that, even better.

The Accuracy

And that brings us to what level of inaccuracies ringers can detect. A 120 of Bob Doubles is rung in about four minutes, so each whole pull takes four seconds. In that four seconds, twelve bell notes sound and there is an open handstroke gap – making thirteen beats in all. So the space between two bells is about ·3 of a second. And that means that when you ring Bob Doubles, you want to place your bell exactly midway between two others that are themselves about ½ second apart.

Put like that it sounds impossible, particularly when you think that a bell is a huge and cumbersome musical instrument which you control with a rope from thirty feet away. Worse still, it doesn't sound until an amazing ***two seconds*** after the start of the physical action. Yet, impossible or not, most ringers can do it.

It seems that just about every ringer in the country can tell quite clearly if a bell is ⅓ of a second out and lands squarely on top of the bell in front or behind. Almost all can tell if someone is out by half that amount – ⅙ of a second – especially if they ring too close rather than too wide. If the rest of the ringing is good, most people will have no trouble noticing when someone is a ¼ of a gap out – that's about 1/13 of a second.

Remarkably, many ringers can detect a variation of 1/30 of a second in a good piece of ringing, and some can detect 1/50 of a second. Of course, if the ringing is a little ragged – or indeed, lumpy – small variations by one bell are masked by large variations by others, but overall, if you can get within 1/25 of a second, most people will think you are a good striker. There's still a long way to go after that, though, because the best strikers get very close to perfection indeed.

And if you doubt these seemingly remarkable figures, I can only say that tapes of computer produced ringing tested out on ordinary ringers, have proved them to be correct.

What it Takes

But now for the practicalities. Good striking requires two things – the knowledge of where your bell should sound, and the ability to put it there. Essentially, that is listening and handling, although there's a lot more to it than that. The two skills are very different and need to be learnt and practised separately as well as together. But in addition, there's one fundamental requirement. You must ***care***.

Good strikers are ***never*** complacent. They concentrate at all times and they agonize over every blow. At no time do they want to be even slightly out, even in a single change, and they really ***work*** at maintaining the highest possible standard. They don't manage it, but they definitely ***try***.

So the first rule is, be like them. For the moment, don't be the least bit dismayed if your striking is nowhere near the standard you'd like it to be. Don't even worry if it's awful. As long as you care, as long as you put the same concentration, the same hard work, and the same commitment into *your* striking that the best strikers put into theirs, in next to no time it'll get very much better.

Listening

And as regards listening, don't think that detecting what's going on, is beyond you. It isn't. It doesn't matter if you aren't musical, it doesn't matter if you're tone deaf, and it doesn't matter if you've got ***cloth ears*** – whatever *they* are. Most of all, it doesn't matter if you can't make head nor tail of what you hear at the moment. ***Anyone*** can develop or improve their listening skills as long as they're prepared to work at it.

One of the pities of ringing is that learners get very little help or instruction on listening. Striking criticism is common but listening tuition is rare. The result is that many people believe that it's an inherent skill of good ringers, and if they haven't got it to begin with, they never will. That, though, is nonsense. Like many other ringing skills, listening can come very slowly. But if you work at it, it'll come in the end.

Listening to What?

So what do you listen to? Learners are often told they must listen to their bell, but although people who say that, know what they mean, they aren't phrasing it very well. About ten years ago a lady wrote to me and said,

> "*For years people kept telling me to listen to my bell. I have now realised that I must listen to **all** the bells.*"

Quite! The skill you need to develop is being able to hear all the bells, both separately and as a group. One of the commonest reasons for being slow at backstroke is a determination to place the bell so far away from the others, that you can definitely hear it separately. Beware of this.

Listening Practice

For the best listening practice you need a teacher or helper – a mentor, as the modern parlance has it – someone to guide and advise you as you develop and expand your listening skills. It could be the tower captain but it could just as well be someone else – someone friendly, helpful and discreet.

To start with, listen to some rounds with them. Maybe outside the tower, maybe inside, but certainly without telling everyone else what you're doing. This is a private matter, and you don't want to offend anyone.

Listen very hard and tell your mentor what *you* think. Listen to the treble and listen to the tenor, and comment on those. Listen for anything that sounds wrong, even if you don't know what it is. Your mentor will be able to guide you towards identifying the problem. He or she will be able to tell you whether one bell is too quick or another is too slow, and he'll be able to assist where two errors add to the confusion. Even after one session, you'll notice a slight improvement in what you can recognise, and after several sessions, the quality of the rounds will be fairly clear to you.

After that, you can go on to call changes, then odd bell methods, and then even bell methods. Then you can go on to more bells, and so on. You can discuss your own striking too, both of you analysing how it was in each piece you rang. You can discuss your mentor's striking as well, and by now your listening awareness will be improving rapidly.

Learning Alone

But suppose you can't find a mentor? That will make it harder but by no means impossible. Set yourself to listen in just the same way, first to rounds, and then call changes, and so on. Listen to ringing cassettes and ringing on the radio too. The fundamental rule is to really ***listen***. Don't let your mind drift away as it does when you have the radio weather forecast on, and don't start chatting with other people sitting out. Force yourself to concentrate. And keep on concentrating even though in your early stages it seems as though you'll never make head nor tail of it. And as time goes by, these four exercises will help.

First, note carefully the open handstroke lead so that you can distinguish which change is which. Listening without being able to tell the changes apart is much more difficult.

Second, tap out and count through each change as it's being rung. When the bells fail to match your rhythmical tapping, something has gone wrong. Your counting tells you where.

Third, listen to some call changes or a method, and follow a bell through by ear. First the treble, then the biggest bell, then an inside bell. Count its place and listen to it sound. And as you hear it sound, judge it, ***right***, ***quick***, or ***slow***.

Fourth, try to recognise the *note* of the bell you are following. If you can do it a little, work at improving it. But if you can't do it at all, don't worry. Most ringers can't. Do, though, locate the bell by counting to it in the change. "One, two, three, ***four***, five, six," giving it a mental underlining as it sounds. Work on this skill especially.

All this will take a while, but don't be put off by that. It *is* possible to succeed, and you'll get there in the end. And when you do, you'll have successfully completed the first stage. You'll know just what your striking is like, and you'll be able to start thinking what to do about it. And what *that* is, is what we shall be looking at next time.

As you probably know, the extremely high standard of striking achieved by the call change ringers of the South West is legendary, and whilst in Devon one September, I joined in with a group of call change ringers in a village on the edge of Dartmoor. The ringing went on all evening and the striking was indeed excellent. But what was most interesting was the way the ringers not involved in each **peal** *– as a Devon call change sequence is called – wandered round the church in ones and twos listening. And they weren't listening in a vague or desultory way, they were listening hard and intently, and with knowledge and appreciation.*

That is surely why their standard is so high. They not only care but they work hard at developing and maintaining their listening skills. You too can do the same. And after that, your only problem will be **Handling**.

23. Striking

Handling

In Chapter 22 we talked about what good striking is and how to practise and improve your listening skills. This time we're looking at how to achieve the real thing.

Good Handling

When you first start to ring rounds, you don't handle very well. Even if you've had plenty of instruction and plenty of tied bell practice, you still have trouble keeping in place. But with time and effort you overcome that. You get to the stage when you no longer bump the stay at handstroke or come down too soon, and you can hold up or pull in just as you want to.

For the purposes of this chapter, that's good handling. It may not be classic and it may not be stylish, but it will suffice for most medium weight, easy going bells. For big bells and little bells, and for bells with peculiar problems, you'll need a much higher standard of handling, and you'll want to keep on working at it and improving it. But you can nonetheless strike perfectly well if your handling is average and you stick to the bells you can manage. Indeed, some of the greatest strikers have had the most peculiar styles.

So you would think that once you've got reasonable listening and handling, everything would all be alright. So why isn't it?

Anticipation

The first problem is the anticipation process. Once you've pulled your rope, there's nothing whatever you can do about where your bell is going to sound. If you pull too soon, you know it will go crunch. And two seconds later, it does.

But if you *do* pull too soon, it's quite likely because you didn't pull hard enough at the previous stroke. You didn't ***anticipate*** soon enough. It isn't that your handling skills aren't up to it, nor is it that you can't hear. It's simply that you didn't plan out your handling in advance.

We talked about this in Chapters 1 and 4. Make sure you plan out all your handling – particularly for your dodges – and make sure you always look ahead. As I said before, if you come across a dodge like a parked car on a bend, you're bound to have trouble with it. In addition, remember that you must place *both* strokes, not just your handstroke. Don't let your backstrokes follow your handstrokes like careless afterthoughts.

Feedback

But even when you put the bell where you intend to, it can still be wrong. You judge by eye how soon you should pull after the bell in front, and then two seconds later you hear the clip. You know you pulled too soon, so you know that next time you ring after that bell *at that stroke*, you must leave a bigger visual gap. Of course, that's not normally until at least ten changes later – and perhaps much longer – and, somehow, by then, you've forgotten. So you clip again, feel irritated again, and promise yourself that you'll get it right *next* time. And so on.

Most ringers strike by this continual feedback process – although we'll look at another way later. It can be frustrating but it's certainly effective, particularly on your own bells where you get to know the visual requirements very well.

The Twitch and the Doubt

But elsewhere, and on other occasions, things can be different. You really know when you should pull, and you're determined to pull then, but at the crucial moment you don't. Something takes you, and you pull at the wrong time.

Assuming you normally handle well enough, that is either ***the twitch*** or ***the doubt***. It is either an involuntary muscle spasm which makes you ring too soon or too late, or more likely, it's that at the last moment your confidence deserts you, and you pull when you didn't intend to.

The better your handling skills, the less you'll suffer from either of these. If you had the good fortune to learn and practise the handling and listening aspects of plain hunt and dodging ***before*** you started to struggle with ropesight, you will find it much easier. Your ropesight will be better, for one thing. But in addition, it will guide and assist your handling rather than directing it. Your handling will be more natural and rhythmical too. In particular, the handling imbalance between handstrokes and backstrokes will be more natural to you.

The point is that because of the open handstroke lead, you have to handle unevenly. You need to ring slower at hand than at back. So when you hunt down, you don't do it smoothly – as some people say – but in steps. You pull in much more sharply at back than at hand because there are fewer beats between handstroke and backstroke than there are between backstroke and handstroke.

The *ropesight-first* learners can take a long time to adjust to this because they're worrying more about who to follow than how to handle their bell. As a result they're generally slow in seconds place on the way down, and quick in fourths place on the way up. Of course, they're also out in other places too, but the irregularities of the other ringers striking often compensate more in those places.

But those who start plain hunt by learning the numbers beforehand, can give their whole attention to their handling and striking. And that helps both their striking ***and*** their ropesight. To them, the uneven handling becomes so completely second-nature that they don't notice it at all.

Atmosphere

And that brings us to atmosphere. You will ***always*** strike best in the right atmosphere – an atmosphere that's warm, friendly, supportive and relaxed, yet full of intense concentration. When the atmosphere is right, the twitch and the doubt diminish or disappear. Anticipative handling happens naturally, listening becomes very much easier, and remembering the visual quirks becomes quite straightforward.

Suddenly, you and everyone else are all striking to a far higher standard than you thought possible, and the world seems *good*. You all get better and better, and the less experienced ringers get *very much* better. Good striking *creates* good striking. You'll never strike better than in a band that's striking well.

So aim for the right atmosphere, and your problems will melt away.

Odd Struck Bells

But what about that dreaded ringing terror, the ***odd struck***

bell? An odd struck bell is a bell that strikes either sooner or later than you would expect, at either one or both strokes. So if you're ringing it and you leave the standard visual gap after the bell you're following, you strike too soon or too late.

A bell that strikes too soon is said to be ***quick*** – so if it strikes too soon at handstroke it is said to be ***quick at hand***. And a bell that strikes too late is said to be ***slow*** – so if it strikes too late at backstroke it is said to be ***slow at back***.

A bell may be quick at hand and slow at back, or slow at hand and quick at back, or it may even be quick or slow at both strokes. And since a quick bell needs to be pulled later, and a slow bell needs to be pulled sooner, the terminology can be very confusing until you get used to it.

Ringing an Odd Struck Bell

Some ringers revel in odd struck bells. They relish the fact that such bells ***separate the sheep from the goats*** and – by implication – put them in the sheep category. In fact, most odd struck bells can be corrected or improved with maintenance, so it's odd that so many people would rather have faulty equipment and poorer ringing, just so they can prove themselves to be sheep.

But you can't tell whether a bell is odd struck until you ring it, or see and hear it being rung. If you pull off in rounds, leave the normal visual gap, and then strike in the wrong place, your bell ***may*** be odd struck. Alternatively, the bell in front may be. It's not until you have to ring over another bell that you know which. Equally, you could strike perfectly after the bell in front because ***both*** bells are odd struck.

That all goes to show why odd struck bells are such a nightmare to visual ringers. You need to learn how much visual gap to leave for each bell – and it's not necessarily a lot easier for rhythm ringers either. If your bell is odd struck at one stroke, you need to pull your bell unevenly to compensate. So hunting up on a bell that's very slow at back is like doing an up dodge every whole pull. A down dodge on such a bell can feel like ringing rounds. A challenge, certainly, but definitely not conducive to good striking.

Listening

We talked about developing listening skills last time, but even when they're good, listening while ringing is very much harder. This is partly because you have difficulty with the timing difference between pull and sound, and partly because you can get too fixated on your own bell. It can also be because tenseness and worry stops you listening at all.

That is all to do with atmosphere again. And the better the atmosphere, the easier you'll find it to listen. But in addition, never be afraid to take part, over and over again, in really simple ringing, purely for listening and striking practice.

And really concentrate on your handling and striking during the initial rounds. That's what they're for. They're not an irrelevant add-on to pad things out while you think about your start; they're an essential preparatory process to good method ringing. The best conductors and the best bands have plenty of rounds beforehand because they want to produce as good as possible a base for launching into changes.

And if you were fortunate enough to get a mentor during the last chapter, bring him or her in again here. Discuss your striking with him after each touch. If you decide that you could hear what was wrong but couldn't do anything about it because the bell was too big or too small for you, take a different bell next time. But take the difficult bell for something simpler.

Uneven Sounds and Funny Tones

And lastly, another problem. The bell that ***sounds*** very different. Sometimes it's because it has a very odd tone, but more often it's because it ***shouts*** – i.e. it sounds very much louder, at one or both strokes, than the others.

The typical shouting bell is the one that you ring with your back to the belfry stairs door. Its sound comes down the stairs and though the door, and then blasts into the back of your head. Across the room it may sound much the same as the rest, but to you it sounds distinctly different. Somehow, wherever you put it, it sounds wrong. The sheer volume of sound fills up the space both in front and behind.

So the moral is, if you get one, just do your best. And if you can avoid getting one, that's even better. Simply accept that the problem is not of your making. Bells near a trap-door can be similarly difficult, as can bells that have their sound distorted by the sallies filling up the ceiling bosses.

Next Time

But even if all that's fine when you ring with a fairly proficient band, what about when you don't? What about when you have to cope with the rough and tumble of the real world? And what about all this ringing by rhythm business?

That is what we shall be looking at next time.

In the late eighties I received a most interesting letter from a lady in Cambridgeshire. Her problem was that she had always referred to ringing the tenor behind as ***bonking****, and she was now extremely embarrassed that a section of the tabloid press was using the word rather differently. Apparently, things had come to a head when she'd stepped* *down from the tenor box after a well struck touch of Stedman Triples, and announced, "**I really enjoy bonking**," only to have her statement received by a mixture of nervous tittering and bright red faces. She was therefore seeking my support that **bonking** was a completely proper ringing word.*

*Well, it has certainly been in use for a very long time. In Norfolk particularly, and in eastern England generally, a **bonker** was the local word for a large, strong man – **a great strapping fellow** as they used to say. So a **tenor bonker** was a big man, strong enough to manage a heavy and badly going tenor.*

In most towers, the tenor would always have been rung behind because the band would have rung no more than Grandsire, so a tenor bonker was normally a tenor behind ringer. It was no doubt a short step from there for people to suppose that he was called a bonker because he bonked, and to bonk therefore became a verb. The fact that bonk sounds rather like bong, probably helped.

Nowadays, the expression is a little condescending, but it has certainly been in one of the big selling beginner's book for many years. It has a long and honourable pedigree, and if you want to use it yourself, don't be inhibited from doing so. But of course, if you're going to ring tenor behind, make sure you ring it well. And that is one of the topics we look at in **Rhythm and Fitting In**.

24. Striking

Rhythm and Fitting In

Nothing in ringing raises stronger feelings than talk of striking. We've talked about listening and we've talked about handling. This time we're talking about the most apoplectic aspects of all – rhythm and fitting in.

Fitting In

Let's start with fitting in. Make no mistake, ***everybody*** fits in – and the very best strikers fit in just as much as anybody else. The difference is in *the way* they fit in.

This is how it works. A band of ringers catch hold and pull off. They try to pull off in perfect rounds, and they pay particular attention to this because a good pull off is so important. But however good they are, they rarely manage it. Some bells will be odd struck, and some people won't pull off quite as they would have wished. But most important of all, they're not all intending to leave the same gap.

And how could they? The gap hasn't been decided yet, and although they may have a good idea, they don't *know* what it's going to be. So they all listen to all the bells, and as the rounds continue, they come to a mutual accommodation. They're like a row of soldiers lining up on parade. They shuffle one way and the other until they're evenly spaced.

People used to say that the Two set the pace and everyone took the same gap as the Two, but, of course, it isn't that simple, particularly if the Two is the most inexperienced ringer. So quite simply, everyone fits in with everyone else.

When the method starts, the band often make further adjustments. If they hear that the back bell ringers can't keep up the pace, they slow down a little. If the ringing seems to be labouring, they may speed up. That's the mark of a good band. They hear the compass of the ringing as a whole and they adjust to it.

And that is the first essential of getting a good rhythm. It's not yours alone, it's everybody's. If you rang perfectly to your own rhythm and got to the end of the touch six changes earlier than everyone else, no one would think you anything but a complete buffoon. You must fit in to the other ringers' rhythm just as much as they fit in to yours.

And with Others

But what about fitting in when the band's much weaker?

Well, that's a very much more difficult question, although to a large extent exactly the same rules apply. Ringing is a team activity and you want to produce the best possible team result. You want to help maintain a good rhythm and compass, and that compass must be that of the band as a whole. But at the same time you want to avoid the crunches. There are no right or wrong answers, but you could try these suggestions.

First, if the bell in front of you rings too quick, ***never*** leave the normal gap. Ring in the spot you would have rung in anyway. There's nothing you can do to avoid the crunch, but if you ring in the right place, you'll help hold the rhythm for everyone else.

Second, if the bell in front of you rings too slow, make a decision based on all the circumstances. If the overall striking is very good, carry on as normal and clip him. If the bell is extremely slow – or lost – do the same. If it's a little slow, and the ringing is still settling down, wait and fit in. That's part of the shuffling and adjusting process.

Third, be very careful about clipping. If the rest of the band don't do it, you'll just have to fit in or become offset from them completely. Even the most fervent proponents of not waiting, still have to fit in with the ringing as a whole.

And last, if you're ringing rounds or call changes with a learner who is slow but roughly in place, ***definitely*** wait. They are still developing their listening skills, and a clear gap followed by the other bells correctly spaced, is much easier for them to pick out and adjust to than a gap followed by a crunch. Crunching on top of a learner, is a harsh and ineffective way of helping them improve.

Rhythm

And now for rhythm. And of course, you already *do* ring by rhythm. The early chapters of this book are full of tips about exactly that, because that is what correct handling is. It is simply pulling all your strokes by the correct amount so that you end up in just the right place both in that change and in the changes that follow.

And in that sense, rhythm and correct handling are essential to good ringing. The best ropesight in the world won't get you into the right place if you haven't pulled the right amount the stroke before. So if anyone asks you, "Do you ring by rhythm?" the answer is, "Yes."

But when most people talk about ringing by rhythm, they mean something more than that. They mean the kind of head down, powering on, ***time, tide and this ringer wait for no man***, approach.

The saddest example of this is the tenor behind ringer, looking at the floor, and ringing – as he has been told to – "with a steady beat." Often he is totally detached from everyone else, sometimes oscillating wildly, but normally just very slow. He rings the tenor ***behind*** rather than in sixths place.

But if you can do it properly, and you're ringing with a really good band, nothing could be better. It's like ringing with a simulator. You can settle down to some top class ringing that gets better and better. Indeed, peal ringers will tell you that that's why they ring peals. After a period – maybe 20 minutes, maybe an hour or so – the quality of the striking, good as it may have been before, can settle down into something quite excellent. The shuffling process is ended, the band has become as one, and everyone's rhythm is everyone else's.

But for most ringers most of the time, that simply isn't possible. So try and balance the two ways. Do all you can to hold a steady rhythm, but fit in when there's no alternative. And in addition – before, during and after – do everything you can to help everyone else. Quite possibly, *you* can give that tenor ringer the help and guidance no one else has.

And *that* is what we shall be looking at next time.

I get quite a few letters about striking, and I'm always grateful for these, particularly when they contain people's thoughts and experiences. One lady in particular wrote,

> Good striking when you're learning is like a miracle. When it happens it's like flying. It sounds wonderful, and you don't know what you've done, and you can't do it again. It is a mixture of everyone just getting it right – like everyone suddenly walking in step.

It's exactly that sort of insight that's so valuable to learners, and that makes it just the kind of thing we're going to think about sharing in **Helping Others**.

25. Striking

Helping Others

In the first three chapters we looked at how we can improve our own striking. But since ringing is a team effort, we want to help others improve theirs too. *We* want to help *them*, and we want *them* to help *us*. So how can we do that?

Moral Support

As I mentioned before, the most important thing in producing good striking is the creation of a relaxed and happy atmosphere. Do *your* bit towards making the ringing chamber a warm and contented place where everyone feels confident, secure and capable of giving their best.

Then, make it plain that you work hard at your own ringing – that you concentrate at all times, no matter who is ringing or what is being rung, and that you care about standards, the learners, and the band. Of course, you won't do that in a *speak out and shame the Devil* sort of way, but simply through your everyday actions and conversations.

And in addition, make it plain that you care about striking, and you care just as much, no matter how experienced or inexperienced you are. You know that there are many better strikers than you, but that doesn't stop you doing your best. You are always going to strike as well as you possibly can no matter what your limitations. *That* is what's important.

Detail

But what about more detailed help?

That's where things get more difficult. You may feel reticent about saying anything at all, and there's certainly nothing wrong in that. But even if you do feel reticent, it doesn't mean you've nothing to say. *Everyone* has something to contribute.

When you're struggling with Bob Doubles, you may feel a distinct novice. But to learners struggling with rounds, you're a real expert. Share your experience with them no matter what it is. Listen to what they have to say, and tell them what it was like for you. Tell them how you were helped or how you helped yourself, and let them know how you felt then and how you feel now. You'll give them confidence and support, and your closeness to their problems may help them in a way that others can't.

And the more experienced you are, the more you have to share. Always remember that most striking problems arise through ropesight, method and handling problems, and these are the things to look to help with first.

But it's when you start to call things, that all the head scratching over exactly *what* to share, really starts.

Those Comments

A conductor shouting, "Listen to it," is like a sign saying, "Beware falling rocks." You know there's a problem, but you have no real idea what you should do about it. You don't even know if the problem involves *you*. Quite likely the conductor doesn't either, and that's why he hasn't said anything more helpful. Shouting, "Listen to it," makes him sound knowledgeable, experienced and masterful without having to justify it with hard evidence.

To be fair, though, whilst I never use the comment myself, it probably does have its place in certain circumstances. A high class and experienced band can lapse temporarily from their normal standards due to tiredness, laziness or just plain boredom. Random slips and striking errors creep in. The conductor shouts, "Listen to it," to gee the whole band up to their usual form. He's not trying to guide or educate, he's simply trying to galvanise.

When

So what comments *should* you make?

First, there's the question of when. The middle of a touch is rarely a good time for any comments at all. There's a lot going on in everyone's minds, and anything you say isn't likely to be acted on even if it's understood. Indeed, it's quite likely to spook everyone into going wrong or striking worse still – particularly if you shout suddenly, or mutter so they can't hear.

The best time for comments is before and afterwards. If you know that someone has a particular problem, speak to them quietly beforehand. Say, "Don't forget to hold right up at back when you lead," or, "Keep the Five really close at hand because it's so odd struck." Say it in a friendly and personal way before you catch hold.

Afterwards you can say, "Those backstrokes were perfect," or, "That was very much better but you still need to hold up more," or, "That was a bit better, but you really need to hold up a ***very*** long way." And if you're the tower captain you might add, "We'll do some special practice later." Indeed, you *should* say these things. There's no point in guidance beforehand without feedback afterwards.

But don't get carried away. Keep your comments *few* and *brief*. You don't want a prolonged assessment and debriefing process that goes on for ages and embarrasses everybody. A little gentle and continuous improvement over a long period, produces the best results.

And Others

Of course, a comment while you're ringing *may* be appropriate, particularly during the rounds at the beginning. But you must be sure it's going to work. You don't want to disrupt the ringer's concentration or equanimity. Say it in a gentle and supportive manner, and at the right moment.

For example, if in the middle of a touch you hear someone leading very quickly, don't say something just after they've led. Wait until they're in thirds place on the way down and then say, "Can you lead much slower, please," or something like that. And when they've led, give a nod of approval, or say, "That was much better," or, "Splendid!" or, "Even slower, please." Don't leave them in doubt.

Similarly, you might say to someone, "Leave much more room over the big bells," or, "Hold the tenor off at backstroke."

Be very careful, though, with someone who may take offence, particularly a loyal, long serving local. As I've said before, ringing with someone whose striking is poor is like ringing with someone whose trousers are undone. *You* would rather they were not undone and *they* would rather they were not undone. But shouting at them about it in front of everyone will only cause embarrassment.

Be like the Lord Chamberlain who, seeing the King's trousers were undone, announced, "Gentlemen, we will all adjust our dress." Comments like, "Can we all keep our leads tight at backstroke," or, "I think we need to hold the little bells up to give the tenor a chance," can be extremely effective.

The Stranger

But even then, there are two overriding rules. First, never say anything that you aren't completely sure is true. If you notice that the tenor has clipped you at backstroke, ***don't*** say, "Ring slower at backstroke, tenor," unless you're sure he's clipping most of the bells most of the time. If you notice the Four leading slow at handstroke as he takes you off, ***don't*** say, "Keep the handstrokes tight, Four," unless you're sure he has a general problem.

The tenor's tower captain may have spent months getting him to get his backstrokes in, and the Four's tower captain may have spent years stopping him from rushing his handstroke leads. A casual and ill-considered comment could set them back disastrously.

And the second rule is, be very careful about saying anything at all to someone you don't know well. They come with a whole host of experiences, problems and special peculiarities of which you know nothing. As any good doctor will tell you, ***don't*** give a snap diagnosis without the full case history.

And Lastly

And after all that, you may well have got to the end of a touch without saying anything at all. You may have said nothing before, nothing during, and nothing after. Or at least, ***almost*** nothing after. Because whatever else happens, there's one thing you ***must*** say.

"Well done," or, "That really was O.K," or, "That was a big improvement," or, "I really enjoyed that." Anything that shows you paid attention to the ringing and give your approval to the band's efforts. More than anything else, *that* is what will ensure even better striking *next time.*

During the time that I was writing regularly for The Ringing World, *a friend used to keep asking me what I was going to write about next. "Ropesight," I would say, or, "Call changes," and he would shake his head sadly and say, "Oh dear,* ***that's*** *going to be controversial."*

It didn't seem to matter what the subject was. Slipping wheel, ringing half-muffled, ringing teas, all got the same mournful shake of the head. But when I said I was going to write about striking, he was so shocked that for several seconds he was completely unable to speak. Discussing striking, he felt, was like discussing ***Law and Order****. Anyone who discussed it sensibly was likely to be vehemently attacked by people with deep-seated but irrational prejudices.*

Bravely, though, I took no notice. And fortunately, the great majority of ringers responded in the same level headed and constructive fashion that ringers respond to everything. All the same, it was a relief to move on to something totally non-controversial ...

26. A Small Technicality

I wonder if you could tell me about *Place Notation.* A couple of young chaps in our Branch are always talking about it, but when I asked one of them to explain it to me, he lost me during the second sentence. If you could give me a *simple* explanation, I would be very grateful.

I.A.
Oxfordshire

I'd better let on at the outset that, for many, ***place notation*** is definitely on the dry side of ringing. It's all to do with how methods are constructed, and if you aren't interested in that in the slightest, now's the time to turn to another chapter and read about something else instead. But if you're even a *little bit* interested, stick with it, and you might end up finding it as fascinating as I do.

The Basics

We'll start at the beginning. In all methods, bells move about. They hunt up, they hunt down and they dodge, and sometimes they make places as well. They lead and they lie, and they also make ***internal*** places such as seconds in Plain Bob and thirds in Grandsire.

And it's probably no secret to you that it's where those places are made that causes each method to be what it is.

Plain hunt on six, for example, starts like this.

```
123456
 x x x
214365
 I x x I
241635
 x x x
426153
 I x x I
462513
```

To get from the first change to the second, all the bells cross over in pairs. Then the bells in the first and sixth place lie still while the inside bells cross over in pairs. Then all six cross over in pairs again, and so on until you get back to rounds.

Bob Minor starts off exactly the same as plain hunt on six. But at the very end, when the bells would get back to rounds if first and sixths place were made, first and ***seconds*** place are made instead.

```
315264
 x x x
132546
I I x x
135264
```

So in general, when you go from one change to the next, either all the bells cross over, or some bells make places, and those that don't, cross over in pairs.

A Method

And since what makes a method what it is, is the places that are made in it, if we had a shorthand way of expressing where those places are, we could use it to describe the method without having to write out all the changes. And that is exactly what place notation is. Here are the first twelve changes of Bob Minor, and written next to them are the places made when going from one change to the next.

```
123456
 x x x     None
214365
I x x I    1,6
241635
 x x x     None
426153
I x x I    1,6
462513
 x x x     None
645231
I x x I    1,6
654321
 x x x     None
563412
I x x I    1,6
536142
 x x x     None
351624
I x x I    1,6
315264
 x x x     None
132546
I I x x    1,2
135264
```

The numbers on the right are not the bells that make the places, but the places that are actually made.

Shorter Still

Now, that list of places is shorter than writing out all the changes, but we'd like it shorter still. So where no places are made, instead of writing ***none*** we write x, and we also look for repetition.

The main repetition is that every section in which the treble goes all the way out to the back and down to the front again – every ***lead***, as we call it – is identical. Identical, that is, from the place notation point of view. The ***changes*** aren't identical but the ***places*** are. Indeed, it's those identical places that result in all the bells having the same blue line. Of course, you *could* invent something in which the sections *weren't* identical, but we wouldn't call that a method, and people wouldn't want to ring it.

If you're a bit doubtful about this, check it out with a few methods in this book, and when you are happy with it, you can see that Bob Minor can be completely described by the place notation of one lead,

x 1,6 x 1,6 x 1,6 x 1,6 x 1,6 x 1,2

And Even Shorter

Pretty good eh? But we can get it even shorter. In almost all the methods commonly rung, each ***lead*** is symmetrical. Symmetrical, that is, if you ignore the places made at the end when the treble leads. So you only have to give half the main place notation, and then add on those final places. Bob Minor now becomes,

x 1,6 x 1,6 x 1,6   l.e. 1,2

Not much shorter for Bob Minor, but a good deal shorter for very long methods such as Surprise Major or Maximus. ***l.e.*** stands for ***lead end*** but you'll also see ***l.h.*** for ***lead head***, which effectively means the same thing. It's the places made when the treble leads full at the end of the lead.

And we can get it even shorter by missing out the commas between the two places, although we still pronounce 16 as ***one six***, not ***sixteen***.

Of course, all sorts of places might be made. For example St Clement's Minor is,

x 16 x 36 x 36   l.e. 12

And Cambridge Surprise Minor is,

x 36 x 14 x 12 x 36 x 14 x 56   l.e. 12

This is longer because each lead is longer, but all place notations follow the same rule. Since the methods are symmetrical, you need to reverse the place notation to get the second half of the lead. So a full lead of St Clement's Minor is,

x 16 x 36 x 36 x 36 x 16 x 12

Pivot Point (at the middle 36) — l.e (at 12)

And a full lead of Cambridge Minor, squeezed up to fit on one line, is,

x 36 x 14 x 12 x 36 x 14 x 56 x 14 x 36 x 12 x 14 x 36 x 12

Pivot Point (at 56) — l.e. (at 12)

Bobs

Bobs can be expressed in place notation in the same way as the method. Most bobs are simply 14 at the lead end instead of 12 or 16, but there are a few other bobs as well. People may tell you that a particular method ***has a fourths place bob***, and when they do, they mean that the place notation of the bob is 14.

Major and Upwards

Place notation is equally useful on Major and upwards, although when you get to Royal and above, ten is abbreviated to 0, eleven to E and twelve to T.

Unfortunately, when first and last place are made, ***and internal places are made as well***, the first and last place occasionally get missed off. So 1258, which occurs in Cambridge Major, is sometimes written simply as 25. This is a bit difficult to begin with but you get used to it in time.

Some Practice

If you want some practice in writing out methods from place notation, try these.

x 16 x 14 l.e.12 – Little Bob Minor
x 14 x 36 x 16 l.e.16 – Double Court Minor

And for a really exciting test, try the Double Darrowby place notation on page 417.

Not all methods, of course, need lots of x's in them. Elsewhere in this book we look at the difference between ***forward*** methods – where most places are made from handstroke to backstroke – and ***backward*** methods – where they're not. A forward, even-bell method has an x every other change, but a backward one doesn't. So London Surprise Minor – a notoriously difficult backward method – goes,

36 x 36 . 14 x 12 x 36 . 14 x 14 . 36 l.e. 12

And the dots show where one notation stops and the next starts.

Oddities

All methods and principles, including the rare asymmetric ones, can be described by place notation in some way or other. So Stedman Doubles, which repeats itself every 12 changes, could be written,

3.1.5.3.1.3.1.3.5.1.3.1

although most technicians would prefer to start the block two changes later at what is known as the ***six end***.

Double methods are particularly interesting. In a double method the blue line reflects vertically as well as horizontally. So even if you turn it upside down, back to front, or both, it still looks the same. And the reason for this is that its place notation is ***rotationally symmetric*** – what a lovely expression – *within* each half lead, whilst the notation *at* the half lead is symmetrical to the notation at the lead end.

So the place notation for the double method, Double Oxford Minor, is,

x 14 x 36 x 56 l.e. 12.

The 36 is an upside down 14, the x's are all symmetrical with each other, and the 56 at the half lead is an upside down version of the 12 at the lead end.

Double methods make more sense when you get more used to them, but have a look at the blue line of Double Oxford on page 91 to see what happens in practice.

Ringing by Place Notation

And lastly, a radically different thought. Some ringers ***ring*** by place notation, particularly when they're ringing handbells. They don't remember – or even know – the blue line at all. They simply remember the places.

You can see that a place notation is a lot easier to remember than a blue line because a blue line that would take you a month to learn, can be replaced by a short string of numbers. But how do those ringers do it?

Well, they always know what position they're in. If they're in an ***odd*** position, and they're ***above*** an ***even*** place in the next notation, they move up. Similarly, if they're in an ***even*** position above an ***odd*** place. Otherwise, they move down. And they do this for every blow until someone says, "That's all." In addition, they have to look ahead to the coming notation as well, because that's what good striking requires.

Does this leave you gasping at the very thought? Certainly it does most people. It's an extremely difficult thing to do, and even those who can manage it, don't normally bother because they find that ringing by blue lines is much more fun. So I won't go into any more detail. It's one of those little ringing mysteries that you could comfortably pass your whole ringing career knowing absolutely *nothing* about.

On a ringing course a couple of years ago I gave a short talk on how to ring by place notation. By the end, several people were quite incensed. "But that's not real ringing!" they said. "They don't know the blue lines. They're not ringing properly at all."

Perhaps you think that too. For most of us, blue lines are such an essential feature of ringing, that they're part of the life, tradition and colour of it all. But a place notation ringer gets as much pleasure and challenge from his own system as we do from ours; and as I explained earlier, for 250 years all ringers rang without any blue lines at all, yet they were just as intensely interested as we are.

How fascinating it would be to go back 300 years and ask those early method ringers for their views on blue lines. It would give us a real insight into alternative ways of ringing. Their views on other modern matters would be interesting too. What would they think, for example, about ball bearings, sallies, ringing Associations and sixteen-bell towers. And no doubt they'd also have strong views on **Method Names**.

27. What's in a Name

Please help me with two questions. The first is, how can I get a method named after my tower? – or even me? – and the second is, what do all the words like *Surprise*, *Court*, etc mean?

Adam
The Midlands

The very first methods to be named weren't really methods at all but call change sequences. ***The Twenty All Over*** was a late sixteenth century sequence of 20 call changes, still regularly rung today, and initially the name was probably more a description than anything else. Similarly, ***The Cambridge Eight and Forty*** was a 48 change sequence from – presumably – Cambridge.

But many of the early method names were decidedly strange. In the late seventeenth century you could ring ***The Wild Goose Chase***, ***Blunderbus***, ***The Parasite***, ***Topsie-Turvie***, ***The Whirligigge***, ***Jack-on-both-Sides*** and ***My Honey***, and people apparently did. Naming methods after yourself was alright too. Stedman, after all, named ***Stedman***. And later on, Samuel Francis named ***Francis Genius***, which still appears in books of methods today even though no one rings it.

Societies named methods after themselves too. The *Union Scholars* named ***Union*** and the *London Scholars* named ***The***

London Scholars Pleasure, though thankfully the eighteenth century *Beardless Club* didn't follow suit.

But by and large, after the first flush of foolishness, ringers settled down to naming methods after places. Often they were the places where the methods were first rung or invented – Kent, Oxford, Cambridge, Yorkshire, Pudsey, etc – although not always. Some methods, particularly Doubles, are named after saints, and some other methods – such as ***Primrose Surprise*** – still retain their original flower names. Not many of the very old bizarre names are with us now, although we still ring ***Antelope*** – but in a rather different form – ***Orpheus*** and, of course, ***Grandsire***.

Nowadays there are so many new methods being rung all the time that place names are getting in short supply. So ringers sometimes look elsewhere. There's now a whole set of methods named after chemical elements – ***Argon Surprise Major***, for example.

What's Available

But what about *you* naming a method?

Well, the first thing to do is find one that no one else has named already. All the symmetrical plain doubles methods have long since been taken, as have all the symmetrical plain minor methods with no more than two blows in any one place. There are still a heap of Doubles variations available – see Chapter 12 – but they're being used up fast, and besides, they aren't *real* methods. So the field is narrowing.

If you have a band that can manage it, there are still a good few ***Treble Bob***, ***Delight*** and ***Surprise*** Minor methods left – see later for definitions – and there are also enough un-named Surprise Major methods to last everybody for the next few centuries at least. Indeed, Roger Bailey of the

Central Council Methods Committee has calculated that there are about 64 trillion of them. Of course, the Surprise Royal and Maximus possibilities are absolutely inexhaustible.

Does that help, though? Naming some obscure Surprise Major method after your six bell tower, isn't likely to be much fun. After all, you could only ring it on outings, if then, and hardly anyone else would even get to hear of it. Better instead to invent either a ***Treble Place*** Doubles method or a five or six-bell ***principle***. Go for something that your band can ring but that's also fun, musical, challenging – but not ***too*** challenging – and guaranteed to sweep the world with its popularity.

Fabian Stedman (1677) did it, James Barham (1772) did it, Sir Arthur Heywood (1887) almost did it, and Gabriel Lindoff (1908) sort of did it. Don't be put off that the most recent of these was Gabriel Lindoff a century ago, and that even *he* could only manage it with ***Erin***, a plagiarised Stedman look-alike. *You* could be the Fabian Stedman of the 21st century.

The Rules

Explaining how to invent the wonder method would take several chapters to itself. And besides, if I really knew how to do it, I would have done it already. But the basic rules for methods – as laid down by the *Central Council* – are,

1. All the working bells must do the same work in the plain course.

2. There must be more working bells than hunt bells.

3. No bell can make more than four consecutive blows in one place.

4. No change may be repeated in the plain course.

And in addition, most people want methods to be symmetrical and, except in Doubles, to have no more than ***two*** consecutive blows in any one place.

Naming It

But once you've invented the method, what then? First, make sure no one else has already named it. Contact the *Central Council Methods Committee* – details in *The Ringing World Diary* – and ask, or interrogate the *Central Council* website. ***Don't*** rely on an old list. Not only might your method have been rung and named since, but it might have been rung and named under its ***extension*** – i.e. rung and named on more bells. This is a real minefield, and checking with the *Methods Committee* is the only sure way. Equally, check that your proposed name hasn't been used already.

But once you know the field is clear, get on and ring it. Naming a method isn't like naming a ship. You don't get the vicar's wife to break a bottle of sparkling wine over the tenor or anything like that. You simply ring an extent of the new method or you ring it in a peal.

If you ring it in a peal – and it can be a multi-method peal – the details will appear in *The Ringing World* anyway. But if you ring it to a 120 of Doubles or a 720 of Minor, send a letter up detailing the place notation, the date of ringing, and the name. If someone rang the same method the night before and gave it a different name, you're scuppered. But that doesn't happen often.

Of course, you could say, "To hell with rules," and carry on calling your method what you wanted. But, somehow, that wouldn't be very satisfying.

The Other Bits

And now for those bits before and after the name – ***Surprise***, ***Treble Bob*** and such. They began as descriptive expressions to aid clarity, and then they got formally defined and required by the *Central Council*. After that, some of them went back to being just descriptive again. But required or not, everyone adds one or two to any new method name.

Plain A method in which the treble plain hunts.

Principle A method in which there is no hunt bell and all the bells do the whole of the work.

Bob As in Plain Bob and Little Bob – A plain method with some dodging in it

Little A method in which the treble doesn't get all the way to the back but turns round sooner.

Place As in Shipway's Place and Winchendon Place – A plain method without any dodging. It just has places and hunting.

Pleasure No meaning at all. The people who invented pleasure methods obviously thought they were fun.

Court As in Double Court – An obsolete classification for a plain method in which ***court places*** are made. ***Court places*** used to mean a number of things, but for most people nowadays they are a simple set of places made round the treble, normally without any dodges either side.

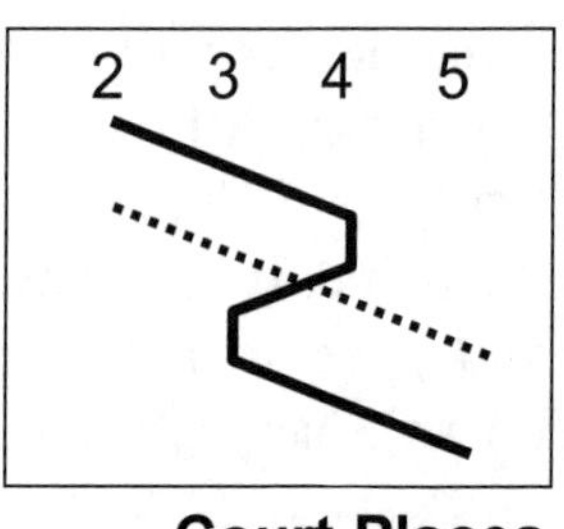

Court Places

Imperial Another obsolete classification for a method in which ***imperial places*** are made – such as Canterbury or Reverse Canterbury.

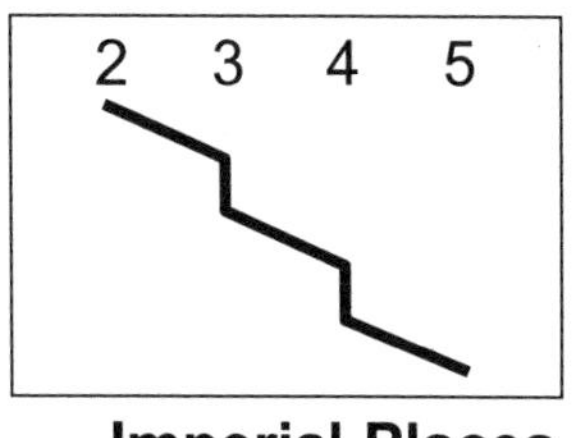

Imperial Places

College A method in which a pair of bells stay dodging together in 1-2 after the treble has left them – such as St Clement's. This is yet another obsolete term.

Slow Course A plain method in which the bell in seconds place at the lead end gets back to seconds place again at the following lead end, but doesn't plain hunt – for example, Slapton Slow Course Doubles. Interestingly, the method formerly named Stedman Slow Course wasn't a slow course method at all.

12345
21435
24153
42513
42531
42351
42315
24135
21453
12543
12453

Slapton

Treble Dodging A method in which the treble, treble bobs. These methods are sub-divided – see next.

Surprise A treble dodging method with an ***internal*** place made every time the treble passes from one dodging position to another – although not including the lead end or half lead. So in Minor, when the treble passes through 2-3, fourths must be made, and when it passes through 4-5, thirds must be made. In Major, there are more possibilities, but the place must always be internal.

Treble Bob A treble dodging method in which ***no*** internal places are made when the treble passes from one dodging position to another.

Delight A treble dodging method that is neither Surprise nor Treble Bob. That means that in Minor,

either Fourths is made when the treble passes through 2-3, and only first and sixths are made when the treble passes through 4-5 – a ***fourths place Delight***.

or Thirds is made when the treble passes through 4-5 and only first and sixths are made when the treble passes through 2-3 – a ***thirds place Delight***.

Once again, there are more possibilities on higher numbers. In fact, ***Delight*** used to mean a method with an internal place at ***all but one*** cross-sections. All but two was ***Exercise***, all but three was ***Pas-alla-tria***, and all but four was ***Pas-alla-tessera***. Extraordinary!

Treble Place In strictness, a method in which the treble makes a place somewhere but still rings a symmetrical path and rings the same number of blows in each position. Often – but not always – it's a Doubles method in which the treble invariably dodges in 1-2 and 4-5 but makes thirds in between. Like this.

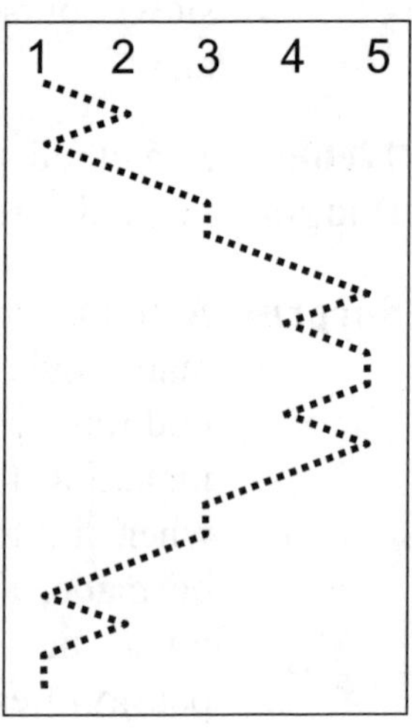

Alliance A method in which the treble has a symmetrical path but doesn't ring the same number of blows in each position. For example, in ***Yaxley Alliance Minor*** the treble plain hunts apart from dodging in 5-6 up and 5-6 down. Alliance methods can be spliced with Little Methods to produce extents.

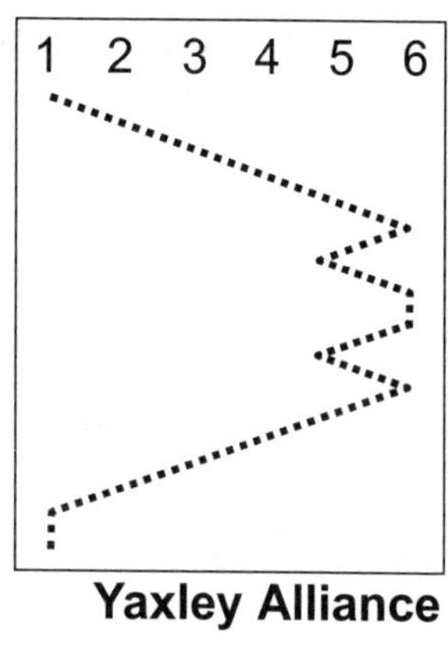

Yaxley Alliance

At one time, methods where the treble dodged everywhere but 1-2 were called ***Special Alliance***.

Hybrid A method in which the treble's path is not symmetrical. Normal people don't ring these.

Double A method for which the place notation is rotationally symmetric – see page 237. This makes the blue line the same both upside down and back to front. The ***Double*** part goes in front of the name.

Single A method corresponding to a plain ***Double*** method but with no internal places below the treble. Once again, ***Single*** goes in front of the name.

Reverse A method which is another method upside down.

Extension

And lastly, if you want to ring your new minor method on eight or more, you will need to work out what its ***extension*** is. If you think you can just fiddle with it to produce something that seems sensible, ***beware***. Method extension is an absolute minefield that few ringers understand.

The most obvious extensions ***may*** not fit the rules, and once again, a check with the *Methods Committee* ***before*** you ring your extension to a peal, may save you buckets of tears and irritation afterwards. I'm not entirely convinced that we need all these rules, but I absolutely guarantee that the *Methods Committee* are not only extremely knowledgeable, they are the nicest and most helpful people possible.

I often get asked about method extension, the commonest question being, "Why isn't **this** *an extension of* **that**; *it looks alright to me?"*

The simple answer is always that the rules say it isn't. For 350 years there were no rules on method extension and nobody minded much. Everyone knew that Bob Major was an extension of Bob Minor – and Grandsire Triples was an extension of Grandsire Doubles – and that was more or less that. But the more complex that methods became, the more difficult it was for people to agree what a proper extension was, and there was always a heap of alternatives. Some ringers became very upset when they saw one method named as the extension of another when they didn't think it was much like it at all, and long discussions took place at the Central Council.

So to do away with these problems, between 1949 and 1953 the Methods Committee *drew up some extension rules. They knew they wouldn't please everybody and they also knew they didn't cover every reasonable possibility, but they were nonetheless an extremely good first attempt. Those rules have been modified and improved upon bit by bit ever since, and although they don't produce perfection, they're probably the best that can be done in the circumstances.*

But are they necessary?

In my view they aren't. If different people come up with different extensions of the same method, so what? They can be called No 1, No 2, etc, and everyone can ring whichever one they like best.

This happened with London Royal. Lots of people wanted an extension of London Major but no one knew what it should be. A band in Stepney rang one possibility in 1907, a band in Brighton rang another in 1926, and a band in Beddington rang a third in 1933. To a layman they all look pretty reasonable, although none of them would pass the current rules.

They are now known as London Royal No 1, London Royal No 2 and London Royal No 3, and although No 3 came last, that is the version that everybody rings today. I see no problem in this, and in 1992 I proposed at the Central Council *annual meeting that the* Methods Committee *consider abolishing the extension rules. My motion was defeated by a significant margin – although with substantial abstentions – but afterwards several members told me that they thought my proposal made perfect sense.*

"So why didn't you vote for it?" I asked.

"Because I don't really understand it all," they replied, "so I suppose that what we've got, must be right."

Hmm!

Fortunately, though, compared to most activities, ringing doesn't have many rules at all. Certainly, rules didn't come into it when I received a most intriguing letter from a 10 year old Wiltshire boy ...

28. E'en Eternity

Please tell me what method I can ask my tower captain to ring so that I can hear a change that has never been rung before. Please also tell me how many unrung changes there are left.

Peter (aged 10)
Wiltshire

What a thoroughly intriguing question! The very first person to muse in print on the total number of changes was Richard Duckworth in 1668, but the famous Fabian Stedman soon followed suit. In his book, *Campanalogia*, published in 1677, he devoted 17 pages to the issue – although it being what used to be called an ***octavo*** book – that's about 10cm by 15cm – those pages were only quite small. Still, he not only tells us how many changes can be rung on twelve bells, but he goes on to point out that writing them all out at 1,440 changes to the sheet would take 665 reams of paper – that's 332,500 sheets in all – although he doesn't tell us the size.

Helpfully, he then adds that as paper cost five shillings a ream, that would be £166 and 5 shillings worth. A man of detail without doubt – although by my calculation he was one shilling and five pence out.

The Possibilities

So how many changes are there?

You can easily see that on two bells there are two - **12** and **21**. On three, there are six, because for each of **12** and **21**, you can take the Three and put it before, between or behind.

312 1**3**2 12**3**, **3**21 2**3**1 21**3**

So that's 3 x 2 ways which is six.

On four, there are four places you can put the Four into each of the six changes on three. If we look at just one of those six changes, 312, we would get

4312
3**4**12
31**4**2
312**4**

And since there are six changes on three, there are 4 x 6 changes on four, and that comes to 24.

And carrying on like this, we can quickly work out that the total changes on all numbers of bells are as follows.

On 2 : 2x1 = 2
On 3 : 3x2x1 = 6
On 4 : 4x3x2x1 = 24
On 5 : 5x4x3x2x1 = 120
On 6 : 6x5x4x3x2x1 = 720
On 7 : 7x6x5x4x3x2x1 = 5,040
On 8 : 8x7x6x5x4x3x2x1 = 40,320
On 9 : 9x8x7x6x5x4x3x2x1 = 362,880
On 10 : 10x9x8x7x6x5x4x3x2x1 = 3,628,800
On 11 : 11x10x9x8x7x6x5x4x3x2x1 = 39,916,800
On 12 : 12x11x10x9x8x7x6x5x4x3x2x1 = 479,001,600
On 14 : 14x13x12x11x10x9x8x7x6x5x4x3x2x1 = 87,178,291,200
On 16 : 16x15x14x ..... x5x4x3x2x1 = 20,922,789,888,000

And I'll stop there as sixteen is the most in any U.K. ring of tower bells at the moment.

The Unrung

So which of them haven't been rung?

Certainly, all the 120 changes on five get rung a great many times every day of the week. Similarly, the 720 changes on six are rung every time a band rings a quarter peal of Minor. And since every full peal of Triples must include all the 5,040 changes on seven, they've all been rung a good bit too.

The 40,320 changes on eight are less clear. On three occasions – twice in tower in 1761 and 1963, and once on handbells in 1977 – a peal of all those changes has been rung. On the last two occasions, at least, the bands were extremely good, and it is most unlikely that either of them crunched up more than a few of those 40,320 changes. Still, it is *just possible* that they both crunched up the same change and that no other band has rung it properly either. But since we'll never know, if you're looking for an unrung change, you'd do best to start by looking on nine or ten.

On Nine and Ten

Now, here we have a problem. There aren't really all that many changes on nine, and they could easily be rung in about nine days or so. A peal of that length with relays of ringers would probably be possible, yet no one has ever attempted it. I once thought of organising an attempt myself – although not actually ringing in it – and I enquired of the secretary of the *Central Council* if he thought that body would accept it. "You will have to ring it first, and then the Council will consider it," he replied. Hmm!

So in the absence of such a peal, there *may* be some

unrung nine bell changes although no one can say what they are. Similarly with the ten bell changes. I could provide a list of changes that can't have been rung often, but ***never*** is another matter.

Of course, the nine bell changes I'm talking about here are those with a ***cover*** – that is with the tenor following on at the end. If you were looking for an unrung nine bell change ***without*** a cover, there are probably quite a lot, but most ringers don't really approve of ringing on nine that way.

Eleven and Twelve

But once we get to twelve we're on fairly safe ground. Fabian Stedman calculated with remarkable – but inaccurate – precision that the extent on twelve would take 75 years, 12 lunar months, one week and three days – although this may have been a misprint of Richard Duckworth's earlier estimate of exactly two lunar months less. And although the best estimate is now down to rather less than 34 years, it's still a very long time.

The first twelve bell ringing took place towards the end of the 1600s, and although today there are over 100 twelve bell towers, there used to be rather fewer. But even if an average of 40 towers had all rung solidly for two hours a week for 300 years – which, of course, they couldn't have – that would still only amount to 142 years' ringing. But as at least 80% of this would have been Cinques and ringing up and down, the number of years' worth of ringing with the tenor away from twelfths place, would have been about 26.

And all that means that even if no change had ever been rung twice, at least 13% of the possible changes have yet to be rung – although, since the same methods and touches tend to get rung over and over again, the true figure is probably well over 50% if not over 90%.

So what methods are likely to produce unrung changes?

Well, probably none of those already rung are likely to have them in their plain course, although it may be that one or two are lurking there. On the other hand, most changes can be rung in touches of most methods if you go on ringing long enough. Indeed, any twelve bell change can be got to in a touch of Bob Maximus in a few hours' ringing.

But here is the amazing thing. Although so many twelve bell changes have yet to be rung, every twelve bell change in existence can be got to from rounds in a maximum of 66 call changes, and that could be less than fifteen minutes ringing. So to ring an unrung change, stick to call changes.

An Unrung Change

And now for a concrete suggestion. I'm not certain, of course, because no one could be, but here is a change which I strongly suspect has never been rung before. It is a change that's most unlikely to crop up either in a plain course or touch of anything, or in a set of call changes.

T981237564E0

(where 0 means 10, E means 11 and T means 12)

Ring it soon, though, because once it appears in print, someone else is bound to ring it just for the hell of it.

And Upwards

And just so as you know, here are a few modern figures that Fabian Stedman would have revelled in. The extent on 14 would take about 6,000 years and the extent on 16 about 1½ million years as long as the ringers really pushed it along. Of course, handbell peals are rung on even higher numbers nowadays, and on 18, even a really brisk extent would take

450 million years. A good round estimate for a 20 bell extent would be two hundred thousand million years.

You can imagine the umpires' report in *The Ringing World*. To have the best chance of success the band would need to have started when the universe came into existence at the time of the big bang. Assuming a 19 part peal – Plain Bob would probably be safest – they would only have got to the first part-end by the time the sun started to form. Life on earth would appear a third of the way through the second part – by which time the ringing should have settled down to a good rhythm – and human beings would evolve a handful of courses later. Once ringing was invented, a few people might go along to watch.

From here on it's conjecture, but the best estimates are that the sun would go nova at the beginning of the third part, and the ringing would go on by starlight only. With several parts still to go, though, the Universe would implode again. Time would come to an end, and the peal would be lost.

George Herbert, the seventeenth century hymn writer, clearly knew it. If you're going to do it with the extent on twenty, **e'en eternity's too short to extol Thee**.

And did Peter ring his change first? Of course, I don't know, particularly as he hasn't got as far as ringing on twelve yet. But I did send him a fairly long list of other possibilities as well, so he should be first with one of them. I'm sure you'll understand, though, that for the time being, both he and I are keeping them ***very*** *secret.*

Triples and More

29. Plain Bob Triples, Major and Upwards

Yes, we're back to Plain Bob again, and since we've already had six chapters on it, you may well think there's not a lot more to be said. But your first course of Bob Triples – or Bob Major – always feels such an important step, that you'd probably like a few more pages on exactly that.

The Method

So overleaf are two charts. They set out the order of the work of Plain Bob from Minimus to Maximus, and from Doubles to Cinques. And just to make it clear, 0, E and T stand for ten, eleven and twelve respectively.

Nowadays, of course, you might also ring Plain Bob on thirteen, fourteen, fifteen and sixteen – normally known as ***Sextuples***, ***Fourteen***, ***Septuples*** and ***Sixteen***, although people are becoming more inclined just to say ***Thirteen*** and ***Fifteen***. But for practical purposes, Maximus is the limit. You can see that each step follows quite naturally from the one before, with an extra *up* dodge and an extra *down* dodge in each new position. You'll probably find that, whatever number you're looking at, learning the method is no problem to you.

The Calls

Learning the bobs and singles will probably be no

Plain Bob

Order of the Work

Minimus	Minor	Major	Royal	Maximus
3-4 down	3-4 down	3-4 down	3-4 down	3-4 down
↓	5-6 down	5-6 down	5-6 down	5-6 down
↓	↓	7-8 down	7-8 down	7-8 down
↓	↓	↓	9-0 down	9-0 down
↓	↓	↓	↓	E-T down
↓	↓	↓	↓	E-T up
↓	↓	↓	9-0 up	9-0 up
↓	↓	7-8 up	7-8 up	7-8 up
↓	5-6 up	5-6 up	5-6 up	5-6 up
3-4 up	3-4 up	3-4 up	3-4 up	3-4 up
Seconds	Seconds	Seconds	Seconds	Seconds

Doubles	Triples	Caters	Cinques
3-4 down	3-4 down	3-4 down	3-4 down
↓	5-6 down	5-6 down	5-6 down
↓	↓	7-8 down	7-8 down
↓	↓	↓	9-0 down
4 Blows Behind	4 Blows Behind	4 Blows Behind	4 Blows Behind
↓	↓	↓	9-0 up
↓	↓	7-8 up	7-8 up
↓	5-6 up	5-6 up	5-6 up
3-4 up	3-4 up	3-4 up	3-4 up
Seconds	Seconds	Seconds	Seconds

problem either. They're exactly the same as the bobs and singles in Bob Minor, and only the bells which would have dodged 3-4 up, 3-4 down, or made seconds, are affected. If you're dodging in 5-6 or above, you're unaffected.

Always pay careful attention to the calls, though. On the higher numbers you can go so long without being affected, that when you *are* affected, you take no notice.

Passing the Treble

But if learning the method is easy, ringing it certainly isn't. Ropesight on the extra bells is the big problem, and although knowing where you pass the treble will certainly help, the fact that there's a whole new set of passing positions for each stage, makes learning them difficult. Remembering which set is which can be a problem too.

Fortunately, many passing positions are the same for all stages. For example, when the treble takes you off, you make seconds, and when you pass the treble in 2-3 after leading, you dodge 3-4 up. Learn these at the outset and then learn the others as you go along. Essentially, they get nearer to the *middle* of the change as you get nearer to the *middle* of the course, and they get nearer to the *ends* of the change as you get nearer to the *ends* of the course – assuming you think of making seconds as the starting point.

On Triples you may particularly want to remember that you pass the treble in 4-5 before *and after* making long sevenths.

Other Tips

And now for some other tips to keep you afloat in your early attempts.

First, choose the best possible bell. You want a medium weight, well behaved and correctly struck bell with a good view of all the others. For example, the Four may be better than the Two because its view may be clearer and it may be easier to handle. If you take the Two, make sure you don't spend all your time looking left and never noticing the treble at all.

Second, check carefully which bell you've got and what your start is. Don't get confused by all the ropes and then set off in the wrong direction. That's devastating.

Third, know your course bell and after bell even if you know no others. Nothing is more settling for your rhythm and ropesight than the certainty of knowing who to ring over just before and after leading.

Fourth, be prepared to hold up for longer. If you have rarely rung on eight before, you may try to ring much too fast. Wait for everyone else.

Fifth, be prepared to ring closer. Although the ringing is slower, the bells strike closer together. Don't leave big gaps.

Sixth, stay relaxed. Plain courses of Bob Triples and Major take a long time and touches take even longer. Being as relaxed as possible before you start – and *staying* relaxed – will really help you last out.

And lastly, enjoy it. You're in the big league now, ringing with all those other bells and managing it. Concentrate on the method, concentrate on your handling, and concentrate on your striking. But above all, ignore the butterflies in your tummy and tell yourself, positively and firmly, that you are most definitely ***having fun***.

If you only ring them rarely, Bob Triples and Bob Major remain a real treat. You can dust them off every now and again for years on end, and always enjoy them. But if you have the rare good fortune to ring with an eight-bell band that can manage them without the slightest difficulty, familiarity sets in.

> "Bob Major," *someone once wrote to me*, "is like a Christmas toy soon put away. It looks so good in the shops and you long for it so much, yet you so quickly grow tired of it. Much as you must have it, you are soon putting it by."

So if ***you*** *find the pleasures of Plain Bob waning, don't put it by* ***too*** *readily. Keep on working hard at it, and keep on ringing it as well as you possibly can. That will not only make it more fun for you, but it will be really important to those ringing with you who are new to it. But at the same time, apply your developing eight bell skills to the eight bell alternatives. In two chapters' time we will look at some other Major methods, but for real interest, don't just start on those. Make sure you also get a firm grasp of* **The Classic Triples**.

30. The Classic Triples

I tried, and failed, to learn all the Doubles methods, and I tried, and failed, to learn all the Minor methods. I stand now at the edge of trying to learn all the Triples methods. What am I to do? There must be thousands.

J.D.
London

Fortunately, there aren't thousands. Or, at least, not that anybody rings, there aren't. Although over 100 Doubles methods are regularly rung, only a handful of Triples are. Doubles ringers may go for variety, but Triples ringers go for ***the classics***.

Bob Triples

Bob Triples, or to give it its full name, ***Plain Bob Triples***, is something we looked at in the last chapter. It's popular, enjoyable and very widely rung, and it's essential learning for any aspiring Triples ringer. But regrettably, the discerning Triples connoisseur doesn't rank it among the ***great*** Triples methods.

It's not so much that its warm and comfortable homeliness is looked down upon, nor is it that it's despised for its ease of learning. It's more that it can't produce the range and quality of music that the others produce. And in addition, there's an element of snobbery that goes back a long time.

Posh ringers have always been encouraged to look down on Triples methods with four blows behind, and for a very long time they were also encouraged to look down on Triples methods that weren't ***true Triples*** methods. A ***true*** Triples method is a method in which all the changes are ***triple*** changes. But when the treble leads in Bob Triples, only ***two*** pairs of bells swap over, so that is only a ***double*** change.

But whatever other ringers may think about it, you and I are going to go on ringing and enjoying Bob Triples nonetheless.

Grandsire Triples

Grandsire Triples, on the other hand, is *unquestionably* a classic. It is enjoyable, challenging and musical, and it has a long and honourable tradition. Like Grandsire Doubles it has an extra hunt bell in addition to the treble, and the order of the work, starting on the Three, goes

thirds
4-5 down
6-7 down
6-7 up
4-5 up.

A thorough study of that, coupled with the picture on the next page and the *Tip for Grandsire Bobs* in Chapter 8, will fully equip you with a complete theoretical knowledge. Thereafter it's just practice. Work hard at it, though, even if you find it difficult to begin with. It really will repay the effort.

Stedman Triples

Stedman is a method – or as the purists call it, a ***principle*** – about which I could write whole chapters. Indeed, I already have done. It's ***the*** classic Triples method above all others, and people have dedicated their lives to exploring its

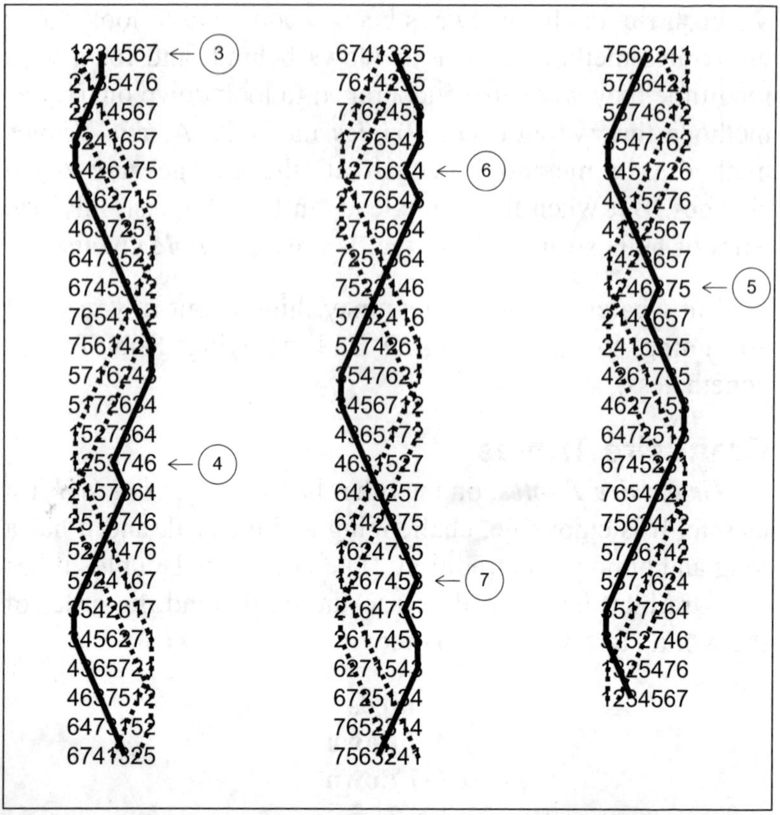

1234567 ← 3	6741325	7563241
2135476	7614235	5736421
2314567	7162453	5374612
3241657	1726543	3547162
3426175	1275634 ← 6	3451726
4362715	2176543	4315276
4637251	2715634	4132567
6473521	7251364	1423657
6745312	7523146	1246375 ← 5
7654132	5732416	2143657
7561423	5374261	2416375
5716243	3547621	4261735
5172634	3456712	4627153
1527364	4365172	6472513
1253746 ← 4	4631527	6745231
2157364	6413257	7654321
2513746	6142375	7563412
5231476	1624735	5736142
5324167	1267453 ← 7	5371624
3542617	2164735	3517264
3456271	2617453	3152746
4365721	6271543	1325476
4637512	6725134	1234567
6473152	7652314	
6741325	7563241	

Grandsire Triples

mysteries. For many ringers it's the ultimate ringing experience and one they never tire of.

No matter how long it takes you, I really do recommend that you aim to master it, and I guarantee that you'll have no regrets. The Stedman chapters start at Chapter 16, and the Triples details are in Chapter 21.

Oxford Bob Triples

Oxford Bob Triples – also known as ***Single Oxford Bob Triples*** – is another genuine classic. Easier than Stedman but more taxing than Grandsire, it was first pealed in 1788 and

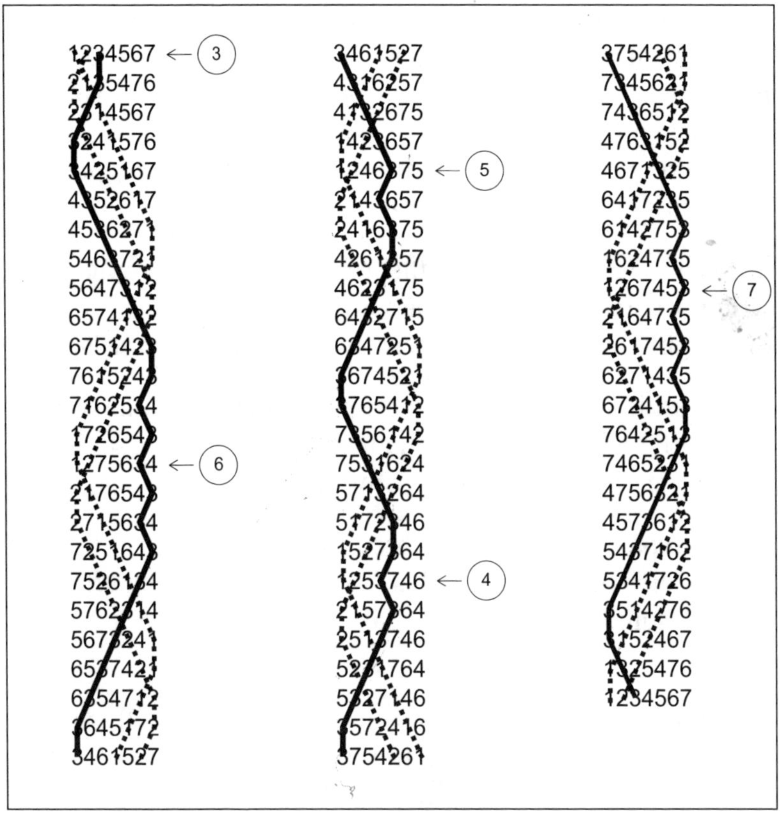

1234567 ← (3)
2135476
2314567
3241576
3425167
4352617
4536271
5463721
5647312
6574132
6751423
7615243
7162534
1726543
1275634 ← (6)
2176543
2715634
7251643
7526134
5762314
5673241
6537421
6354712
3645172
3461527

3461527
4316257
4132675
1423657
1246375 ← (5)
2143657
2416375
4261357
4623175
6432715
6347251
3674521
3765412
7356142
7531624
5713264
5172346
1527364
1253746 ← (4)
2157364
2513746
5231764
5327146
3572416
3754261

3754261
7345621
7436512
4763152
4671325
6417235
6142753
1624735
1267453 ← (7)
2164735
2617453
6271435
6724153
7642513
7465231
4756321
4573612
5437162
5347126
3541276
3152467
1325476
1234567

Oxford Bob Triples

was hugely popular from the late nineteenth century to the First World War. In many places it's been rung steadily ever since, and it has undergone a substantial resurgence recently.

Like Grandsire, it has two hunt bells, and the order of the work, starting on the Three, goes

thirds
3 dodges 6-7 down
4-5 up, fifths
fifths, 4-5 down
3 dodges 6-7 up.

Many ringers think of it as Grandsire Doubles on the front and triple dodging on the back. They ring Grandsire Doubles ***unless*** by the time they get to ***fourths*** place on the way up, they haven't passed the treble. ***Then*** they go out to 6-7 and either dodge up or down, depending on whether they pass the treble in 4-5 or 5-6.

That sounds alright in theory, but a lot of people get it wrong in practice, and it's better by far to learn the blue line thoroughly. All the same, there are four major hazards.

First, it's ever so easy to miss the fifths after the 4-5 up, especially when, as often happens, the bells in 6-7 stop dodging early and accommodate you.

Second, counting up to three for your dodges in 6-7 can be *very* difficult. Try really hard not to stop dodging after two even if someone forgets to make fifths and barges in with you.

Third, trying to dodge 6-7 up with the hunt bell is a real temptation. If you pass the treble in 5-6, ***lie behind*** before dodging down.

Fourth, remember to keep hunting when you're hunt bell. ***Don't*** dodge 6-7 down.

The Calls

The bob will look quite familiar to you. The bells in 6-7 are unaffected, while the bells below 6-7 ring a Grandsire Doubles bob. The truly difficult thing is remembering to make fifths after double dodging 4-5 up.

Similarly, most people ring a single that's exactly the same as a normal Grandsire single – sometimes called a ***common*** Grandsire single – and, once again, the bells in 6-7 are unaffected. But for rather complex reasons, it isn't

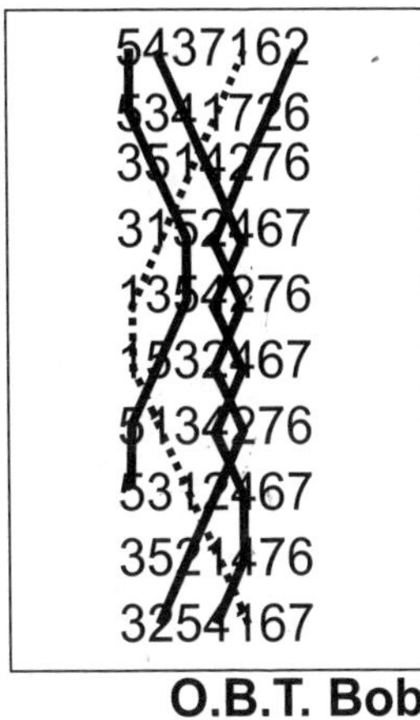

O.B.T. Bob

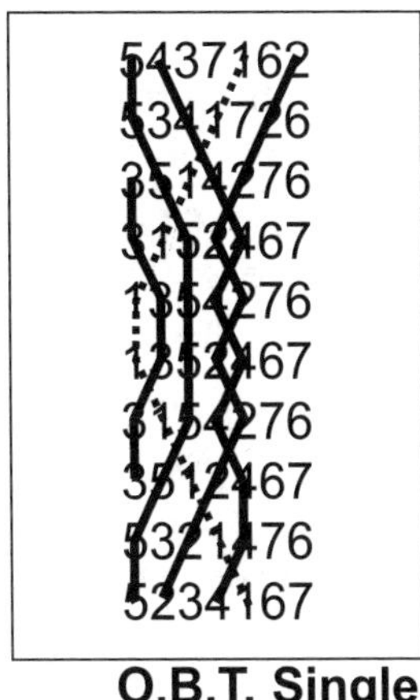

O.B.T. Single

possible to ring all 5,040 different changes unless you use a different kind of single called an ***in-course single***. Don't bother to learn these until you know you're going to ring one.

Erin

Erin Triples is a junior classic. Invented at the beginning of the 20th century by the great Irish resident ringer, Gabriel Lindoff – who very properly named it after the country he was living in – it's a short course, Stedman look-alike. On the picture overleaf I've drawn the blue line through the Seven so that you can see the whole of the frontwork undivided.

If you can ring Stedman, the dodging will be no trouble to you. Indeed, it should be a lot easier because you meet the other bells in the normal plain bob coursing order. On the front there is ***no quick work*** but there's a slow work which goes

thirds
lead and dodge
thirds
dodge and lead
thirds and out to 4-5.

Traditionally, the lead and dodge was called ***two and a penny***, and the dodge and lead was called ***one and tuppence*** or ***one and two***. Of course, these expressions mean nothing at all to anyone not old enough to remember pre-decimal currency, but bizarre though it may seem, they can be extremely helpful to those that do.

A useful tip is that all the thirds are made *right* – i.e. handstroke-backstroke – and all the leads are made *wrong* – i.e. backstroke-handstroke. Bobs and singles are exactly the same as Stedman bobs and singles.

Watch out for the starts, though. Unlike Stedman, the method begins at a ***six-end***, so there's no initial dodge. Instead, the Seven lies behind and the Five and Six move on a position before dodging. The Three goes straight to 4-5 up, and the Four goes straight into the frontwork.

The starts for the One and Two are the most difficult of all, and if you're going to ring either, you'd do best to study the picture beforehand. It's astonishingly easy to find yourself caught out when the conductor calls ***Go***.

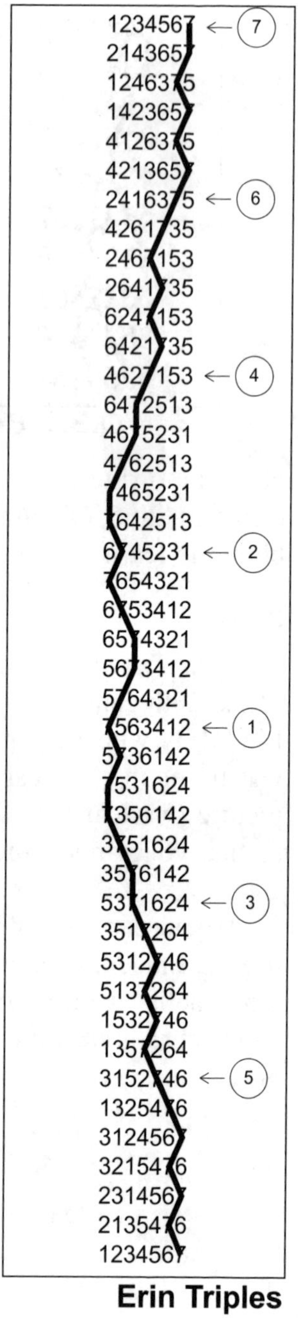

1234567 ← (7)
2143657
1246375
1423657
4126375
4213657
2416375 ← (6)
4261735
2467153
2641735
6247153
6421735
4627153 ← (4)
6472513
4675231
4762513
7465231
7642513
6745231 ← (2)
7654321
6753412
6574321
5673412
5764321
7563412 ← (1)
5736142
7531624
7356142
3751624
3576142
5371624 ← (3)
3517264
5312746
5137264
1532746
1357264
3152746 ← (5)
1325476
3124567
3215476
2314567
2135476
1234567

Erin Triples

Incidentally, Erin is one of the few methods that can be started with a bob. So if the conductor calls, "Bob, Go Erin," the first few changes should be,

```
1234567
2143576
1245367
1423576
4125367
     etc.
```

Hopefully, though, if he's going to start that way, he'll warn you in advance.

The Other True Triples

And lastly, some almost forgotten classics. There are in fact eleven ***regular true triples*** methods in which the treble and Two both plain hunt throughout the plain course, and they were held in considerable esteem in years gone by. We've already looked at Grandsire and Oxford Bob, but there are also,

Reverse Grandsire
Double Grandsire
Single Court
Double Court
Double Oxford
St Clement's
College
Hereward
and **London**.

Of these last nine, the only one still rung at all commonly is St Clement's, and I have included a picture overleaf. It's fun, challenging and musical, and not all that difficult to learn once you can ring St Clement's Minor. You might try some

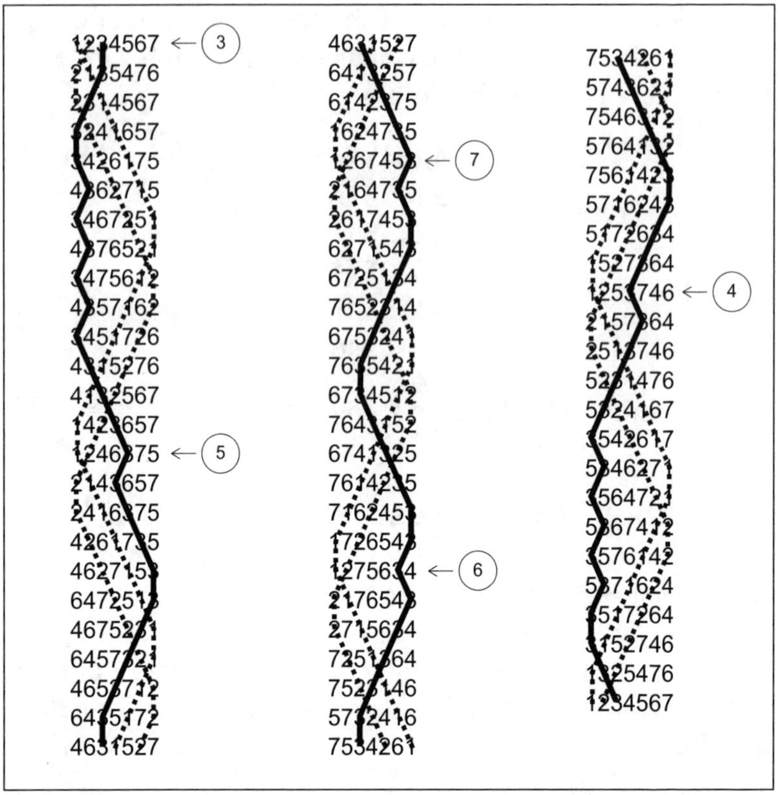

1234567 ← 3	4631527	7534261
2135476	6413257	5743621
2314567	6142375	7546312
3241657	1624735	5764132
3426175	1267453 ← 7	7561423
4362715	2164735	5716243
3467251	2617453	5172634
4376521	6271543	1527364
3475612	6725134	1253746 ← 4
4357162	7652314	2157364
3451726	6753241	2513746
4315276	7635421	5231476
4132567	6734512	5324167
1423657	7643152	3542617
1246375 ← 5	6741325	5346271
2143657	7614235	3564721
2416375	7162453	5367412
4261735	1726543	3576142
4627153	1275634 ← 6	5371624
6472513	2176543	3517264
4675231	2715634	3152746
6457321	7251364	1325476
4653712	7521346	1234567
6435172	5712436	
4631527	7534261	

St Clement's Triples

of the others too if you can find a band to ring them with you. Indeed, people have been known to learn all eleven and then splice them all together. And that ***is*** a thought to conjure with.

I learnt recently that the fish and chip shops in Fife sell red puddings to eat with chips. They are rather like white puddings or black puddings – a sort of sausage – and they are cut in half lengthways before being battered and fried. You can buy two halves and chips – ***a pudding supper*** *– or one half and chips –* ***a half-pudding supper****. National tastes come and go, but in Fife they still enjoy their red puddings.*

How splendid this is, and yet it's just an example. Fish and chip shops throughout the country still reflect local tastes and traditions that a hundred years of conformity have completely failed to eradicate. And it's exactly the same with method ringing. No matter what methods appear in print, local bands continue to ring only what they enjoy most. And quite right too.

So if you normally ring ***St Nicholas Triples*** *before popping into the* Jolly Fryer *for mushy pea fritters and gravy, please don't be at all put off that St Nicholas wasn't in the last chapter. It's just as good a method as the others but there simply isn't enough space to include them all. And the same thing goes for* **The Basic Major**.

31. The Basic Major

There are quite a lot of booklets to guide you into Doubles and Minor methods but not many at all to guide you into Major methods. I ring Bob Major occasionally, and I should be grateful if you would guide me into the rest.

E.J.
South Wales

By far and away the biggest problem with ringing the basic Major is the seven other bells. Simply finding your way through all those ropes is the real trouble, and I gave some tips on that in Chapter 29. But now that you can manage Bob Major, you're definitely ready for a crack at the alternatives.

Little Bob Major

First, try ***Little Bob Major***. Since the treble only hunts up to fourths place and back, the plain course is a mere 56 changes long. And that means that, as long as there are no bobs, you only have to last out for about two minutes. Touches are fun too, though, because they can be packed with bobs and singles yet still be over in next to no time.

As you can see from the picture opposite, you always ***treble bob*** above fourths place and you always make seconds over the treble. In addition, you also always dodge in 3-4 ***unless*** you meet the treble there.

Bobs are the same as Bob Major bobs, so you are unaffected in 5-6 and 7-8, and you run in, run out and make the bob, just as in Plain Bob. Beware, though, that if you run out at a bob, you ***hunt all the way to 5-6*** even though when you get to 3-4 the treble isn't there. ***Don't*** dodge in 3-4 up. This is a major elephant pit to be very wary of.

Singles are the same as Bob Major too. Once again, though, be careful not to dodge in 3-4 up after making reverse thirds.

Without doubt, Little Bob is musical, challenging and fun. Try it and enjoy it.

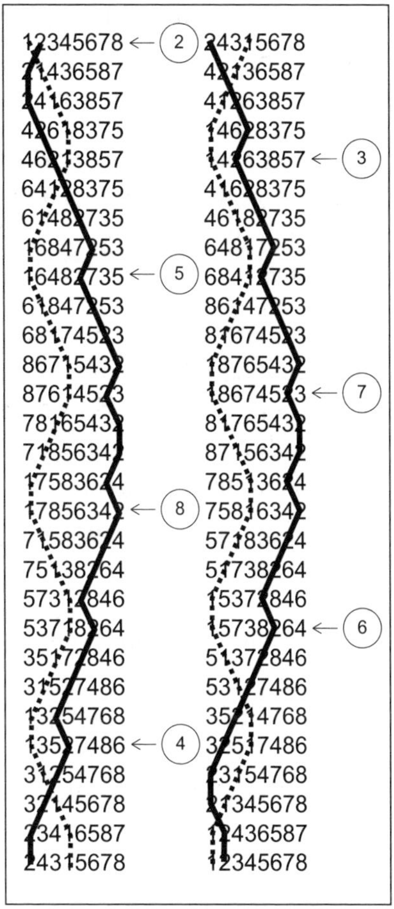

12345678	← (2)	24315678	
21436587		42136587	
24163857		41263857	
42618375		14628375	
46213857		14263857	← (3)
64128375		41628375	
61482735		46182735	
16847253		64817253	
16482735	← (5)	68412735	
61847253		86147253	
68174523		81674523	
86715432		18765432	
87614523		18674523	← (7)
78165432		81765432	
71856342		87156342	
17583624		78513624	
17856342	← (8)	75816342	
71583624		57183624	
75138264		51738264	
57312846		15372846	
53718264		15738264	← (6)
35172846		51372846	
31527486		53127486	
13254768		35214768	
13527486	← (4)	32517486	
31254768		23154768	
32145678		21345678	
23416587		12436587	
24315678		12345678	

Little Bob Major

Plain and Little

And once you can ring Plain Bob and Little Bob, you can ring them spliced together. ***Plain and Little*** – normally pronounced ***Plain-'n-Little*** as though it were only one word – is another of those classic combinations that are at the shallow end of multi-method ringing. The change of method takes place just after the dodge at the lead end, so deciding what comes next is no problem.

If you change from ***Little*** to ***Plain***, you simply do what your next Bob Major work will be. So, for example, if you're dodging 5-6 Down when ***Plain*** is called, your next work is 7-8 Down. If you're making seconds when ***Plain*** is called, your next work is 3-4 Down.

If you change from ***Plain*** to ***Little***, you simply switch to the rules on the previous page. You treble bob in 5-6 and 7-8, and you dodge – ***or not*** – in 3-4, according to where you meet the treble.

Fortunately, both Plain Bob and Little Bob start off the same way, and that means you always have a couple of whole pulls to change gear. So don't panic and immediately do an extra dodge or anything like that. Just change gently to the rules of the new method.

And incidentally, ***Plain and Little*** is good on six as well.

Kent

And now ***Kent***, and there are so few methods in the basic Major repertoire, that Kent ranks number three even though it's a good deal more difficult than Little Bob. Once you can ring Kent Minor, though, *learning* Kent Major will be no problem because to all intents and purposes it's identical.

The Kent Minor rules on pages 131 onwards apply in their entirety to Major. There is the slow work – which is exactly the same as Minor but goes on for a little bit longer. There is the treble bobbing – ***except*** that you never dodge in 1-2 unless you meet the treble there. And there are the Kent places in 3-4 whenever the treble is below you. It's only the extra bells that will cause you any problem.

Even the ropesight isn't too bad, because you always dodge with the same bells in the same places ***except*** when the treble's there instead. Indeed, many people ring Kent Major entirely by numbers. The picture – writ small, I'm afraid – is opposite.

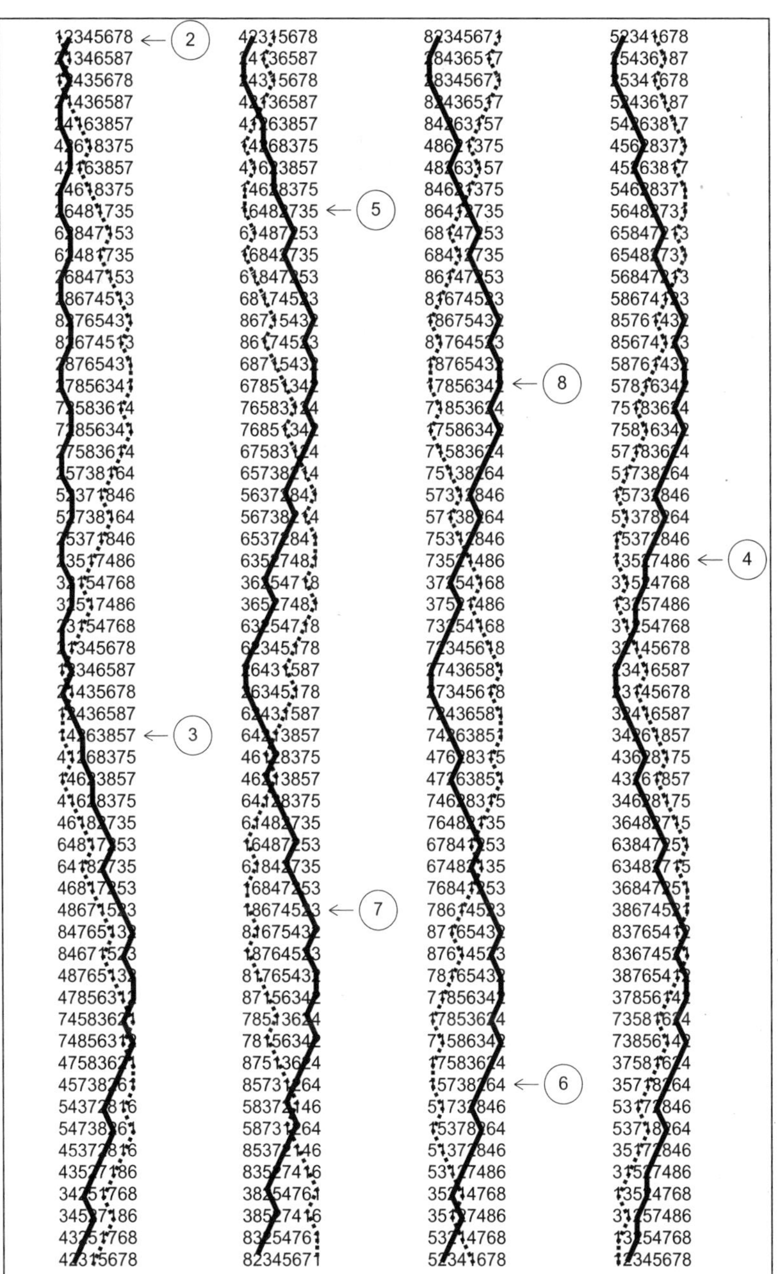

Kent Treble Bob Major

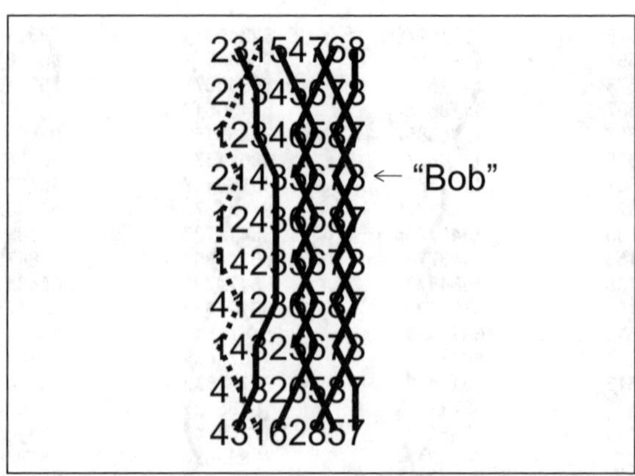

Kent Major Bob

The bobs are like Kent Minor bobs. So the bells in 5-6 ***and*** the bells in 7-8, end up doing three dodges – that’s the normal one plus two extra for the bob. There are no singles.

Because a plain course goes on for so long – about 8½ minutes – there often isn’t time to ring a whole course of it – and indeed, some ringers impolitely call it ***Graveyard Surprise*** because it’s so interminable. So instead, people normally ring a three lead touch with a bob every lead. That only lasts about 4 minutes and is traditionally known – very reasonably – as ***Three leads of Kent***.

At each bob the Five, Six, Seven and Eight do the extra dodges and so get back to where they started, and only the Two, Three and Four ring the slow work. And since Kent is rung so much more often in three leads than plain courses, if you want to get the chance of ringing the method at all, you really do need to learn the bobs before you start.

Oxford

Oxford Treble Bob Major has exactly the same relationship to Kent Major that Oxford Minor has to Kent Minor. It’s only in the 3-4 places that there’s any difference.

It's rung by itself very much less often than Kent – though see below for spliced – and when it *is* rung, it's normally only rung in three leads. If you think you might get to ring it somewhere, recap on the rules in Chapter 14.

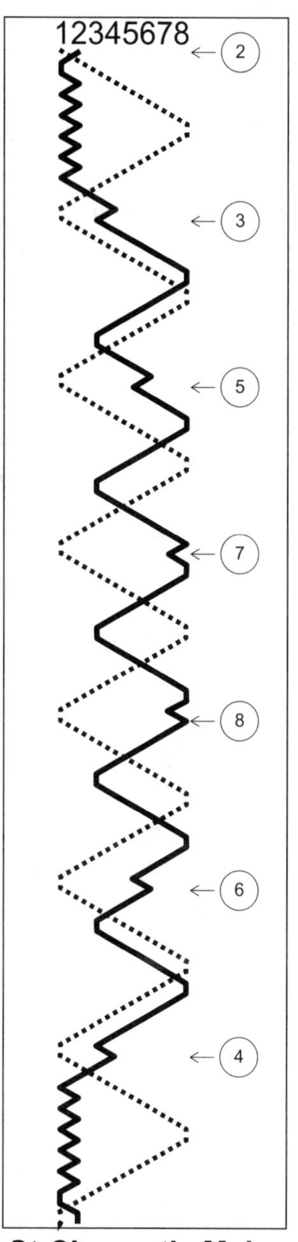

St Clement's Major

Kent and Oxford

But even though Oxford isn't rung much by itself, it *is* sometimes rung with Kent. Time was, when ***Kent and Oxford*** Major was rung widely and frequently, and although it isn't really rung frequently any more, it's still rung in a lot of places. Chapter 15 applies in exactly the same way to Major as it does to Minor, so if you feel like a taste of yesteryear, bone up on it and give it a go.

St Clement's

St Clement's Major is the sort of method that gets rung now and again, often as a special method at District practices. The blue line is on the right, and if you can ring St Clement's Minor, you'll certainly want to ring Major some time. Very few people, though, develop a long term affection for it. The really hard part is counting up to five when dodging on the front. Calls are as in Minor.

Double Norwich

And the last method in the basic Major repertoire is a *true* classic. ***Double Norwich*** – or to give it its full name, ***Double Norwich Court Bob Major*** – is the zenith of the basic Major. It dates back to the middle of the eighteenth century – when it was first rung, reasonably enough, in Norwich – and it has remained perennially popular ever since. Now less frequently rung than it used to be – largely because so many people go wrong in it – it's still a must for the complete Major ringer.

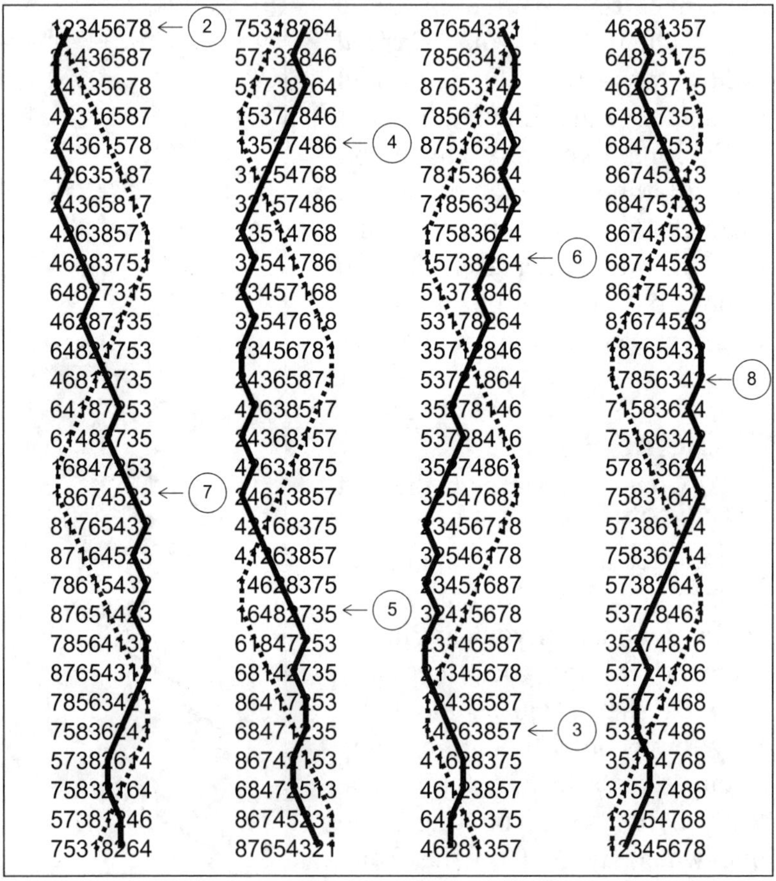

12345678 ← 2	75318264	87654321	46281357
21436587	57132846	78563412	64823175
24135678	51738264	87653142	46283715
42316587	15372846	78561324	64827351
24361578	13527486 ← 4	87516342	68472531
42635187	31254768	78153624	86745213
24365817	32157486	71856342	68475123
42638571	23514768	17583624	86741532
46283751	32541786	15738264 ← 6	68714523
64827315	23457168	51372846	86175432
46287135	32547618	53178264	81674523
64821753	23456781	35712846	18765432
46812735	24365871	53721864	17856342 ← 8
64187253	42638517	35278146	71583624
61482735	24368157	53728416	75186342
16847253	42631875	35274861	57813624
18674523 ← 7	24613857	32547681	75831642
81765432	42168375	23456718	57386124
87164523	41263857	32546178	75836214
78615432	14628375	23451687	57382641
87651423	16482735 ← 5	32415678	53728461
78564132	61847253	23146587	35274816
87654312	68142735	21345678	53724186
78563421	86417253	12436587	35271468
75836241	68471235	14263857 ← 3	53217486
57382614	86742153	41628375	35124768
75832164	68472513	46123857	31527486
57381246	86745231	64218375	13254768
75318264	87654321	46281357	12345678

Double Norwich Court Bob Major

Double Norwich is a ***double*** method – which, as explained on page 92, means that the blue line is the same upside down and back to front, as well as forwards and back. You can see that there is a lot of double dodging on the front and back, and you can also see that when going from the back to the front – or vice versa – you either treble bob or you do a set of places.

The places can be either in 3-4 or 5-6, and they can be either ***place, place, dodge*** or ***dodge, place, place***. None of which sounds very helpful at first reading, but it's certainly the basis that most people use for ringing it. They make use of the method's doubleness and they remember the phrase,

First, ***treble bob***, ***last***, ***near***, ***full***, ***far***.

And the individual parts mean,

First: When you arrive at the back or the front, you lie or lead ***first*** before double dodging.

Treble bob: Dodge 3-4 and 5-6 on the way up, or 5-6 and 3-4 on the way down.

Last: When you arrive at the back or the front, you double dodge to begin with, and then lie or lead ***last*** before going away.

Near: Do a set of places ***near*** where you have just come from. So if you've come from the back, the places are in 5-6. If you've come from the front, they're in 3-4.
Near places always go ***place***, ***place***, ***dodge*** and not the other way round.

Full: When you arrive at the back or front, you double dodge ***before*** and ***after*** lying or leading.

Far: Do a set of places ***farthest*** from where you have just come. So if you've come from the back, the places are in 3-4. If you've come from the front, they're in 5-6.
Far places always go ***dodge***, ***place***, ***place***.

And if all that sounds a terrible puzzle to you, I can certainly see why. But you will probably become as attached to it as most Double Norwich ringers are. Study it with the picture to see what's happening, and remember that it applies just as much whether you are going up or going down. So you ring ***first***, ***treble bob***, ***last***, ***near***, ***full***, ***far*** to get you halfway, and then you ring it a second time to get you back again.

Watching for the treble can be a big help too. The only time you don't double dodge on the front or back, is when the treble stops you. So, if in doubt, double dodge in 1-2 and 7-8, both up ***and*** down, unless you meet the treble there.

In addition, you always pass the treble just before and after your ***full*** work, and it always passes through the middle of your places. The only other time you meet it is in 4-5 while you're doing the ***treble bob***.

Bobs and Singles

The bob is a ***sixths place bob*** which makes it very different from any bob we've looked at so far. The rules are,

> The bell doing ***treble bob up*** makes ***sixths*** and does ***treble bob down***.
>
> The bells ***dodging in 7-8*** do ***three more dodges*** – making five in all – and then scratch their heads about what to do next.
>
> And the other bells are all unaffected.

D. Norwich Bob	D. Norwich Single
35271468	35271468
53217486	53217486
35124768	35124768
31527486	31527486
13254768	13254768
12345786	12345768
21437568	21437586
24135786	24135768
42317568	42317586
24371586	24371568

D. Norwich Bob **D. Norwich Single**

In fact, if you get caught in 7-8, do ***far*** places after dodging ***down***, and ***near*** places after dodging ***up***.

The single looks even worse. But it's not too bad once you've studied it. The bells not affected at a bob are not affected at a single either, and the bell doing ***full*** work on the back is also unaffected, although it dodges both up ***and*** down with ***the same*** bell.

The bell doing treble bob up makes sixths, as at a bob. But the bell which has just finished ***first*** work behind, makes ***sevenths*** and does ***last*** work behind.

Needless to say, touches are fraught with danger and touches with singles in are rung extremely rarely. Prior consent of anyone affected by a single, is definitely necessary.

A Last Word

And after all that, you can see why people have such trouble with it. If you're going to ring Double Norwich in the traditional way, study it long and hard in advance. But if you already ring Surprise Minor by ***place bells***, try learning

Double Norwich the same way. It may not be so colourful, and it may not be so traditional, but it will certainly be easier. What's more, you will be able to catch hold in the comforting knowledge that you will be ringing at least ***ten times*** more reliably than anyone else.

Of course, one of the reasons why the basic Major repertoire is so small, is that the Surprise Major repertoire is so big. Surprise is seen as so desirable by many ringers, that they don't want to dally on the way. For them, Major ringing goes from Plain Bob to Kent to Cambridge, and even Kent gets missed out at a pinch. All of which is rather a pity because they miss out on so much of the richness of Triples and Major on the way.

I've got nothing against Surprise Major, of course. It's certainly a lot of fun, and you can read about it in Chapters 42 to 44. But don't feel you have to move on to Surprise if you don't want to. You can just stick with what you enjoy at the moment or you can even miss out Surprise entirely and go straight on to ringing **On Ten and Twelve**.

32. On Ten and Twelve

In a moment of madness I went to a Twelve. It was a meeting, and there were lots of ropes and lots of people, and they all looked very severe – including everyone I knew – and I was really nervous. I had studied hard – really I had – but it was a real disaster.

I started on the treble to Grandsire Cinques but couldn't control it despite having rung Grandsire Triples inside for ages. Then I tried Plain Hunt Cinques on the Four, and that would have been O.K. except some old man stood behind me telling me every blow. I got home really fed up. But insanity is still with me, and I'm going again. Please give me some clues.

Sarah
The North

Doubt it not, in your ***moment of madness*** you took the ***big*** step. No matter how good you are on eight, ringing on ten and twelve is a whole new world. But hang on in there and it *will* be worth it.

The Nerves

Many tens and most twelves seem expressly designed to overwhelm you with nervousness. They are big and austere, with long draughts, icy corners, aged and darkened peal boards, and a forbidding air of ***history***. Just walking into them and seeing all the ropes is bad enough, but seeing the other ringers is the clincher. They're either as nervous as you are – and that's most of them, including the District ringing master who's terrified the ringing is going to be awful – or they're sublimely confident. The nervous ones will make you feel even more nervous, and the confident ones will make you feel inadequate. Oh dear!

Still, don't let it get you down. Go up to the most nervous ringer present – probably huddled in a corner miles away – and in a hushed whisper engage him or her in a little mutual worrying. That should make you *both* feel a lot better.

The Bells

And then there's the bells themselves. A lot of tens and twelves aren't easy to control. The back bells are heavy, the front ones are light, and the ceiling is a long way up. Quite often they handle a little differently too. But difficult or not, all twelves share one problem. There's a big weight range between the treble and the tenor.

So here's the first tip. ***Don't take the treble to Cinques as an easy option***. The front two or three bells are almost never easy to handle without practice, and to hunt up on them, you need to stand a moment at every blow, both at handstroke and backstroke. You also need to leave very large visual gaps after the big bells if you're going to strike in the right place. In addition, a very large bell may have to pull ***before*** you in order to strike after you, and that can be very confusing indeed for your ropesight. And if your bell comes down too soon – or, worse still, bumps the stay – you can be out of place, and out of control, in next to no time.

Similarly, ***don't take a large bell until you've had a lot of experience***. The back bells are extremely important to the rhythm and they may need to be pulled at the same time as –

or even before – the little ones, in order to strike accurately after them. They are much harder to control too.

And that leaves the middle ones. For preference go for the Five or Six. The striking is easier, the handling is easier, and the ropesight is easier, and any errors you *do* make will be much less noticeable to everyone else. You are already a method ringer and you've learnt the method on ten or twelve. Your chances of ringing well inside are far higher than your chances of ringing well on the treble. Go for it.

The Handling Problems

Of course, you'll take every opportunity to ring call changes too. Only the real expert is in a position to turn down handling and striking practice. Work your way round to the very big bells and to the very small ones. Give your total concentration to getting your handling and your striking as smooth and accurate as possible. Pay particular attention to the variations between what it looks like and what it sounds like. Being really at home with a bell in call changes will make it ever so much easier to ring the same bell to methods.

And when you ring a little bell, remember this overwhelmingly important fact.

> ***The weight of the rope of a light bell significantly affects its handling*.**

And that's so important that I've given it a paragraph of bold italicised type all to itself.

The point is that when you pull the handstroke, you have to pull hard enough to get the bell to go round ***and*** the rope to go up. Indeed, it needs to go up at least nine feet if not more. The longer the draught, the heavier the rope, and the more the pull required. A light bell with a long draught requires a very significant pull just to get the rope to go up.

But at backstroke, the reverse is true. All the rope comes back down again and gives the bell a hefty pull in the process. So at backstroke you need do no more than guide the rope down.

I often demonstrate this by setting a very light bell at backstroke and then just tipping it off the balance by pulling the tail end with one finger. The bell travels right round and goes over the balance at handstroke without any pull at all. Indeed, I often have to catch the sally quite firmly to protect the stay. But when I tip the bell off the balance at handstroke, it gets nowhere near the balance at backstroke. It just comes straight back down again.

So the moral is, pull ***firmly*** at ***handstroke*** and ***gently*** at ***backstroke***. Getting this wrong is what causes so many people to get completely out of control on the front bells of tens and twelves – and, indeed, smaller rings too.

And in case you're wondering, the heavier the bell, the smaller the effect of the rope. The mathematics are rather complicated, but you can see that the weight of the rope on a tenor is not a lot more than the weight of the rope on the treble even though the weight of the bell is a great many times more.

Incidentally, don't let anyone con you into believing that only men and boys can ring heavy bells. That is absolute nonsense. Women and girls can ring them every bit as well – or indeed, better – as long as they get the practice.

The Methods

And now for the methods. We haven't mentioned them yet, but with the basic ones you're unlikely to have any problem.

The chart for Plain Bob is on page 260, and with Grandsire, extra dodges get added on as the bells increase in exactly the same way. See Chapter 8, though, to get the bobs right.

With Stedman, extra sets of ***double*** dodges are added on at each stage. So in Caters the two sets of dodging are

double dodge 4-5 up
double dodge 6-7 up
double dodge 8-9 up
double dodge 8-9 down
double dodge 6-7 down
double dodge 4-5 down.

And in Cinques you add in a double dodge 10-11 up and a double dodge 10-11 down between your double 8-9 up and your double 8-9 down. And you can find more about Stedman Caters and Cinques on pages 199 and 200.

Little Bob and Kent Royal and Maximus follow exactly the same rules as Minor and Major – although remember that when you treble bob, you dodge in 9-10 and 11-12 as well.

Surprise Royal and Maximus are rather more difficult, and it would take a good bit of this book to explain them all. But for when you get to them, here's a tip. Cambridge Royal and Maximus are relatively straightforward to ***learn*** after Cambridge Major, but Yorkshire Royal and Maximus are far easier to ***ring*** because the ropesight is much easier. The ringing will probably be of a higher quality too. So learn Yorkshire Royal at the same time as learning Cambridge Royal, and choose it for preference whenever possible.

The Ropesight

But if the methods are fairly easy, the ropesight is another matter, and while your multi-bell ropesight is improving, it's just as well not to put too much strain on it. So many people ring on ten and twelve by learning the numbers.

Take Bob Maximus, for example. In a plain course the bells follow each other round in the order **2,4,6,8,0,T,E,9,7, 5,3**, and this is what is known as the ***coursing order***. So if you're ringing the Six, once you've led, you hunt up over **8,0,T,E,9,7,5,3,2,4**, and then you hunt down over them again in the same order.

Of course, somewhere you have to dodge – but you know where that will be – and somewhere else you have to pass the treble – but you learn that as well. A whole course of Bob Maximus is then yours for the asking without the slightest trouble. Similarly, in Grandsire Cinques the bells follow each other in the order **3,4,6,8,0,E,9,7,5** with, of course, the treble ***and*** Two popping in at intervals.

Bobs would be a problem except that in Bob Maximus they normally only affect the front bells. So you can use your ropesight on the front six and then follow **8,0,T,E,9,7** until you get back to the front six again. Grandsire is a bit more difficult, but **8,0,E,9,7** normally remain in a block even though they sometimes change their relative positions.

Courses of Kent and Little Bob follow the Plain Bob rules, although in Kent you have to take the slow bell out of the coursing order and replace it with the treble. Stedman, though, is a real problem. You need a very sharp brain indeed to ring *that* by numbers. Still, you do at least get three goes at each dodging position, so after two ranging shots, you should be right before it's time to move on.

And Lastly

And when you can do it – when you can ring Cinques and Maximus with skill and confidence – do give a hand to those coming up behind. The "old man" who told you every blow in plain hunt, may not have been very helpful, but he certainly had the right idea. A little moral support goes a ***long*** way.

Many years ago I lived in a town with a ten and a twelve. I was tower captain at the ten but from time to time I used to ring at the twelve as well. One day I was sitting next to an elderly ringer there during a touch of Cambridge Minor.

"Ah," he said, "I admire you young chaps with that ***fancy*** *stuff. When I was your age we had a hard time from the old boys but they never taught us anything* ***fancy****."*

"But your Stedman Cinques is superb," I replied.

"Ah, Stedman, yes," he said, "but nothing ***fancy****. When it comes to* ***fancy*** *ringing, we never had the opportunity."*

I believe there are far fewer Stedman Cinques ringers like that nowadays but there are nonetheless a great many people who vastly underestimate their capabilities – people who believe that Surprise ringing is only achievable by a talented and dedicated few. Indeed, I kept meeting so many ringers who felt it was way beyond them, that I decided that the time had come to do something about it. So late one September in a mellow and autumnal mood, I set to and wrote **The Social Ringer's Surprise Minor**.

Surprise Minor

33. A Plain Course of Cambridge

When the nights start drawing in and the trees take on autumnal tints, a young ringer's fancy lightly turns to thoughts of learning a new method.

And perhaps older ringers' fancies turn that way too.

Now is the time, with the winter stretching before you, to make a determined effort to become a ***surprise ringer***. To join that special group that always has the good fortune to take part in the best ringing at District practices. And if you always thought that Surprise ringing was beyond you, then sit quietly back and ease your way into it with this series.

We won't be looking at anything very complicated, nor will we be aiming at the heights of peal ringing. Instead, we'll be looking at ***social*** ringing – at how to get by at local and District practices – and at how to get good enough to ring Surprise for Sunday services. Dedicated Surprise ringers may read this series if they wish, but above all, it is ***the social ringer's*** Surprise Minor.

The First Step

So we'll start with the very first step in social Surprise ringing – Cambridge Minor. Cambridge is the first step because it's rung many times more often than all the other Surprise methods put together. Once you can ring a plain course of Cambridge, you can miss out all the other methods and still call yourself a ***surprise ringer*** if you want to – and many people do.

But Cambridge is also the first step because, in learning it, you acquire the skills which set you firmly on the road to all the other Surprise methods. It's a down-payment for later which will amply repay the effort involved. When you've got past Cambridge Minor, nothing will ever seem so difficult again.

How to Learn it

So how *do* you learn it?

Well, a difficult method – and Cambridge certainly *is* a difficult method – is much too much of a mouthful to be learnt as one long piece. Even if you ultimately managed it, it would take you a very long time, and it wouldn't help you much with your *next* difficult method either. So you must divide it up.

The experts divide up the difficult methods into ***place bells***, but until you *are* an expert that isn't a particularly easy way of doing it. If you would like to know what ***place bells*** are all about, they're explained in Chapter 40 at the start of *The Novices Guide to Ringing Spliced Surprise*. But as this is the ***social*** ringer's guide, we aren't going to divide Cambridge into place bells here, we're going to divide it up ***naturally***.

Dividing it Naturally

Take a look at the blue line on the page opposite. You can see that there are various chunks which naturally separate themselves off from the rest and which hang together in a

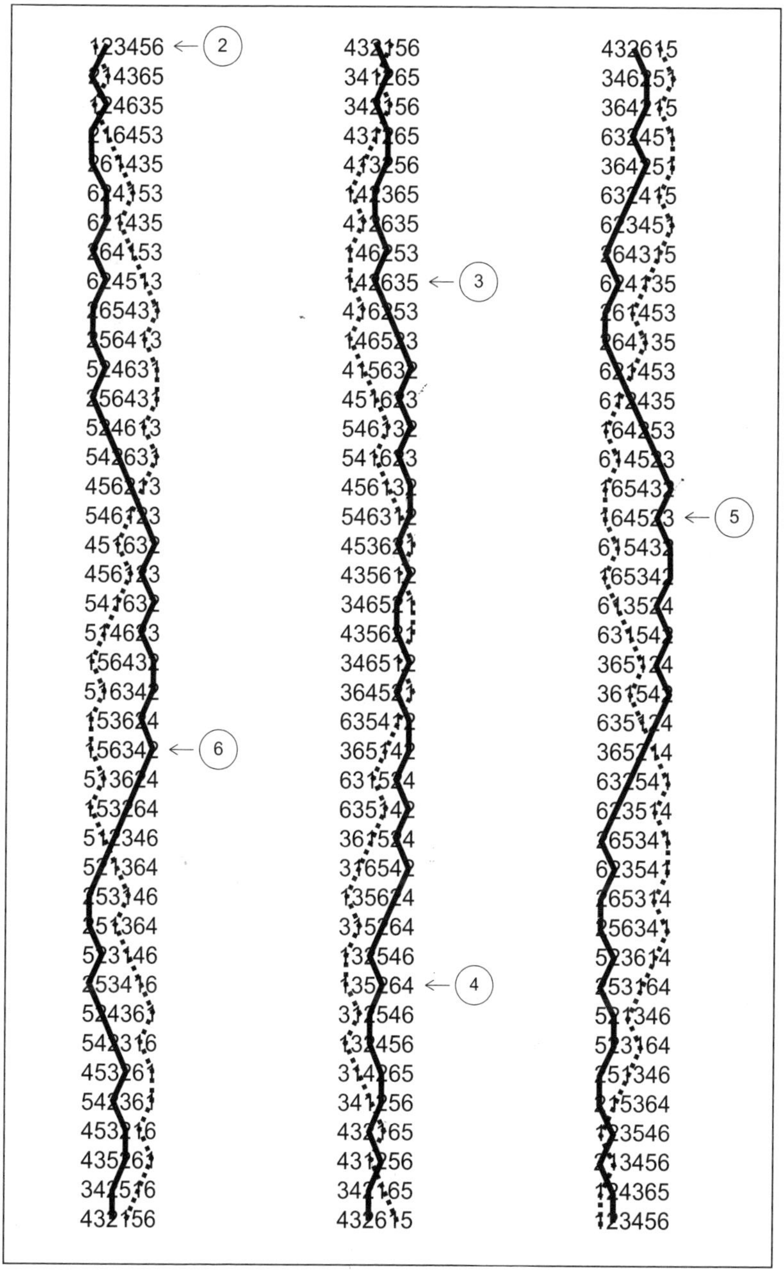

123456 ← 2
214365
124635
216453
261435
624153
621435
264153
624513
265431
256413
524631
256431
524613
542631
456213
546123
451632
456123
541632
514623
156432
516342
153624
156342 ← 6
513624
153264
512346
521364
253146
251364
523146
253416
524361
542316
453261
542361
453216
435261
342516
432156

432156
341265
342156
431265
413256
142365
412635
146253
142635 ← 3
416253
146523
415632
451623
546132
541623
456132
546312
453621
435612
346521
435621
346512
364521
635412
365142
631524
635142
361524
316542
135624
315264
132546
135264 ← 4
312546
132456
314265
341256
432165
431256
342165
432615

432615
346251
364215
632451
364251
632415
623451
264315
624135
261453
264135
621453
612435
164253
614523
165432
164523 ← 5
615432
165342
613524
631542
365124
361542
635124
365214
632541
623514
265341
623541
265314
256341
523614
253164
521346
523164
251346
215364
123546
213456
124365
123456

Cambridge Surprise Minor

sensible sort of way. Over the years these chunks have acquired their own names. The easiest chunk of all is called ***backwork*** and – rather sensibly – most of it is on the back. It's also known as ***thirds place bell*** because it is what the Three does at the beginning of a plain course.

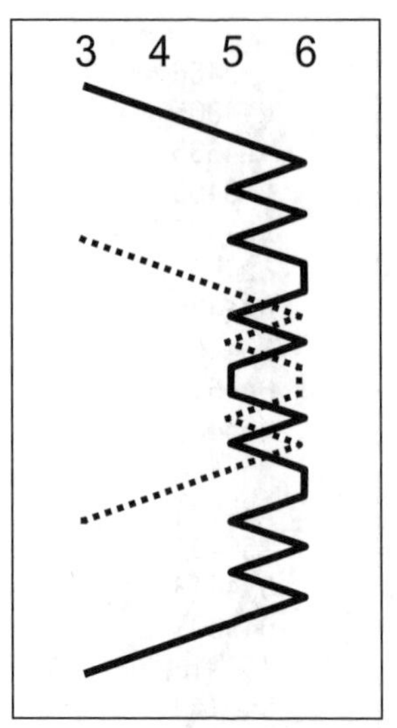

Backwork

The next easiest chunk is called ***frontwork*** and this – equally sensibly – occurs on the front. It's often further divided into ***the first half of the frontwork*** – the piece *before* you make seconds over the treble – and ***the second half of the frontwork*** – the piece *after* you've made seconds over the treble. You may find that from the ropesight point of view, it's the simplest bit because in much of it you're leading.

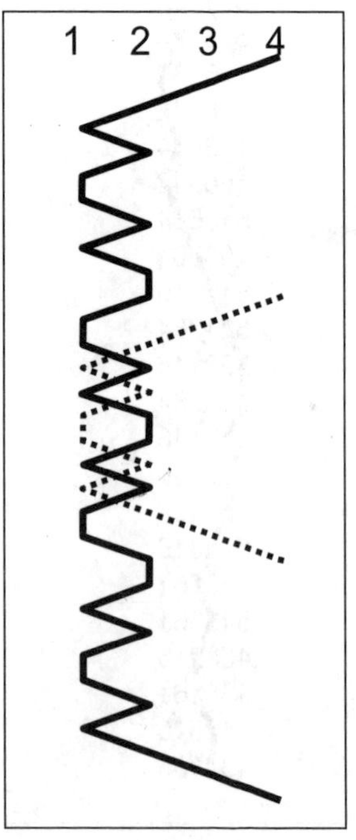

Frontwork

The last and most difficult chunk is called ***Cambridge places***, and it – or rather, they – occur in 3-4. The places in the first picture on the next page are called Cambridge places ***up*** because you do them while you're on your way ***up*** to the back. And the places in the second picture are called Cambridge places ***down*** because you do them while you're on your way ***down*** to the front.

You can see that they are identical to each other except that they are each the opposite way round – just as an up dodge is the same as a down dodge but the opposite way round.

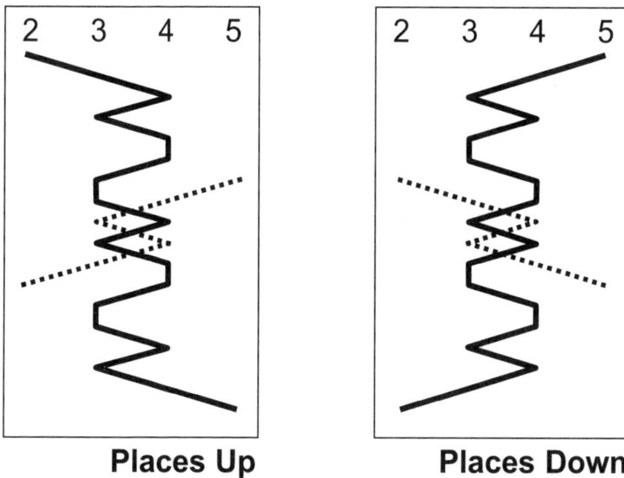

Places Up Places Down

Learning the Pieces of Work

When you've had a good look at these ***pieces of work***, try learning them. Learn each one as a thing in itself, a blue line all of its own, quite separate from the rest of the method. You must learn them all thoroughly, of course, but don't be in too much of a hurry about it.

Take your time. Most people find that a little learning every now and again is much more digestible – and much more enjoyable – than one long brain-befuddling session. Best of all, learn the different pieces at different sittings. That way you're less likely to confuse them.

The Order of the Work

And when you've learnt the named pieces of work, you're nearly there. All that's left is to join them all together. And you do that by learning the ***order of the work***.

And since the order of the work is circular you can start it from any bell. I've written it out here as though you were starting on the Six because that doesn't split the frontwork, but lots of people learn it from the Two.

Lead and dodge
Cambridge places up
backwork
Cambridge places down
dodge and lead
one and two on the back
frontwork
two and one on the back

That's still a bit of a mouthful but it's definitely learnable. It consists of only eight phrases, three of which are the reverses of three of the others. You don't need to remember anything more complex than that because each time you get to a big chunk – like the backwork – you put a separate piece of pre-knowledge into operation.

Nevertheless, you must learn the order of the work ***very, very*** thoroughly. Keep on repeating it to yourself and your friends until you – and they – are well and truly fed up with it.

The Extras

And when you've learnt the pieces of work and the order of the work, you're ready to ring the method. A cool nerve and a razor-sharp brain will get you faultlessly by without you knowing anything else at all. If, though – like the rest of us – you're just a normal ringer, a few extras will really help. You don't need to learn these extras before you have a go at your first plain course, but it's definitely useful to add them to your knowledge bit by bit as the method becomes clearer to you. They are

The places where you dodge with, ring over and/or pass the treble,

***The places where you dodge with your* course bell,**

And,

***The places where you dodge with your* after bell.**

The last two are less important, but a knowledge of where you pass the treble can be *very useful indeed* as we shall see later.

The Starts

And finally, you *must* learn the starts of *all* the bells whether you think you might ring them sometime or not. That way, you'll never catch hold and then have to whisper to the person next to you,

"Psst! Where do I begin?"

At the beginning of this article I suggested that people didn't immediately start learning Cambridge by place bells, and I still think that's correct. But there are times when place bells ***are*** *helpful, and I explained why in another article which appears in this book as Chapter 40.*

Some time afterwards, though, whilst on holiday in Somerset, I called in at a ring of six on their practice night. I had never met any of the band before, and as ringers do, I introduced myself by my christian name. After about half an hour the tower captain decided that with my help the band could ring a course of Cambridge, and they set to for some last minute revision. After a few moments of silence a heated exchange developed about how they should be learning it.

*"Well," said one of them positively, "**Coleman** says you should learn it by place bells."*

*"Oh no Coleman doesn't!" said someone else. "**Coleman** says you **shouldn't** learn it by place bells."*

*They went at this vigorously for a couple of minutes while I stood there aghast, hoping desperately for a change of subject. Eventually someone turned to me and asked the inevitable question, "What do **you** say?"*

*Sheepishly, I had to admit that I **was*** Coleman *and that, depending on the circumstances, I recommended both. No one seemed very comfortable with this reply, and they went back to their* Ringing World Diaries *in an embarrassed silence.*

Fortunately, by the end of the plain course everyone was back to normal again, and a thoroughly enjoyable evening continued. Indeed, a little later they were even kind enough to ask me about our next subject, **A Touch of Cambridge**.

34. A Touch of Cambridge

I contemplated starting this chapter with the words, "Following Chapter 33 you have now rung a plain course of Cambridge Minor," but the chances are, of course, that you haven't.

Quite likely you never found the time to learn it. Probably Aunt Jane called unexpectedly, or something like that. But even if you learnt it most assiduously, it's extremely unlikely that you've had the ***opportunity*** to ring it.

Perhaps there has been no District meeting since you learnt it, or perhaps there has, but you couldn't get to it. Perhaps you got to the meeting but they didn't ring Surprise, or perhaps they rang it but left you out.

Learning Surprise is like that. You can swot something up for months on end without getting the chance to practise it, and then when you eventually *do* get the chance, you've forgotten it. It can be frustrating and upsetting, and I fully understand what a difficult business it all is.

But nonetheless, there's nothing like a little homework for helping to make the best of any opportunities that *do* occur. So this week, whether you've yet rung a plain course of Cambridge or not, we're going to think about a touch.

The Plain Course

The first step towards ringing a touch of Cambridge is being able to ring a plain course really well. You need to be able to recite swiftly and unhesitatingly

> ***the order of the work,***
>
> ***the pieces of work,***
>
> ***the points at which you pass the treble,***

and,

> ***the starts on each bell.***

The Bells Not Affected

Next, you must learn the ***un***affected positions. There are two of them but I'm putting them in a single block to make them easier to remember.

> ***If a bob is called when you're about to dodge 5-6 up or 5-6 down, you are not affected.***

Do memorise the unaffected positions very carefully. It can be very tempting – and totally devastating – to force yourself to be affected by a bob merely because you aren't absolutely sure whether you're affected or not.

The Affected Bells

And lastly, you must learn the affected work. There are three ways of being affected by a bob, and you must learn each of them carefully and separately. They are:

> If a bob is called when you're ***dodging 1-2 up*** with the treble in the middle of the frontwork, you must ***run out*** and do the whole of the ***backwork***.

> If a bob is called when you've just finished doing the ***backwork***, you must ***run in***, dodge 1-2 down with the treble, and do the ***second half of the frontwork***.

Not surprisingly, ***running in*** is the exact reverse of ***running out***, but there are two points to be careful of. First, in addition to everything else you're holding in your mind, remember that it's the treble that you take from lead. And second, don't forget to *dodge* with it when you *have* taken it from lead.

> And lastly, if a bob is called when you're making thirds at the end of the ***Cambridge places up***, miss off the last dodge, ***make fourths*** instead, and ring ***Cambridge places down*** omitting the first dodge.

This is the most difficult way of being affected.

A Useful Tip

So much for that. But no matter how well you do your homework, you may still find that you can't manage to ring your places down properly after making the bob. If that happens to you, there's a seemingly odd tip which is surprisingly useful.

> When you make thirds immediately after making fourths at the bob, the ***first*** of those two blows is over the treble.

Nine out of ten ringers look the wrong way at this blow during their early efforts at Cambridge touches. Normally they latch on to the bell ringing in fifths place, and so go instantly to the back. Understandably, this makes the rest of the places difficult.

At a Single

Singles in Surprise methods are fairly common these days, so you might as well learn them now rather than later. The rules are,

> ***Three*** bells are ***not*** affected.
>
> > The bell dodging 5-6 up,
> >
> > The bell dodging 5-6 down,
> >
> > And the bell making seconds in the middle of its frontwork.
>
> ***The bell*** doing its Cambridge places up, makes fourths and finishes its Cambridge places down, exactly as at a bob ***except*** that both its blows in fourths are over the same bell.
>
> ***The bell*** which has just done its backwork, makes two blows in thirds and does its backwork all over again.
>
> > It does ***not*** dodge in 3-4 at all,
> >
> > It does ***not*** get to the front,
>
> And,
>
> > Its two blows in thirds are over the ***same*** bell.

Another Useful Tip

And lastly, another useful tip.

By far the commonest mistake in a touch of Cambridge is going down to the front too soon after making the bob. Somehow, having made all those places up, it seems like much too much of a good thing to make all those places down as well, so you miss off the last bit.

To avoid this mistake, note carefully when you're dodging 3-4 down with the treble. Then concentrate on doing another thirds, fourths, dodge 3-4 ***after that***.

From time to time people ask me where I get the titles for my articles from, and that was particularly so with this series since it was called The Social Ringer's Surprise Minor.

"But why the ***Social*** *Ringer's Surprise Minor?" I was asked by a well known peal ringer at an Association A.G.M. "What* **is** *a social ringer?"*

I tried to explain that the title was simply intended to convey the right atmosphere.

"Yes," he said, "but ***I'm*** *a social ringer – particularly in the pub after a good peal – and you didn't write the series for me."*

"That's the point," I said. "If I'd just called it Surprise Minor you might have read it by mistake thinking it was very technical, and the ringers who would have enjoyed it, might not have read it for the same reason. This way, those who were interested, knew it was for them."

He went away still scratching his head, and I wondered if I had indeed got it wrong. So in case you're wondering too, to my mind a social ringer is a bit like you and me. The sort of ringer who rings on Sundays and practice nights, and perhaps at District practices as well, and who enjoys the whole business but who doesn't see him or herself as quite so dedicated as some other ringers. Just the sort of ringer, indeed, who might like a little help with that essential Cambridge problem – **Treble Trouble**.

35. Treble Trouble

From time to time, when I'm answering readers' letters or doing talks or training sessions, I emphasise how useful it is to know where you pass the treble. But since hardly anyone seems to take much notice, I can only assume they regard it as some kind of harmless eccentricity. But undeterred by previous failure, I'm now going to make yet another attempt to convert the unconverted – to show that a knowledge of where you pass the treble really is useful. And hopefully, at the same time, I'll provide a little help about how to use that knowledge in Cambridge Minor.

The Set-Up

And breaking new ground, this chapter is in the form of a quiz. If you get to the end of it and find you've correctly answered all the questions entirely without the aid of a blue line, you're a genuine Cambridge expert. Indeed, you needn't have read the chapter at all. But even if you need to look at the blue line for all ten questions, you'll still be acquiring a whole heap of really useful knowledge.

So here are the questions, and in keeping with all the best quizzes, they get more difficult as you go on.

The Questions

1. When do you dodge 3-4 up with the treble?

2. When do you pass the treble in 2-3 on the way down?

3. When do you pass the treble in 4-5 on the way up?

4. When do you dodge with the treble in 5-6?

5. You are completely lost when the conductor shouts, "***Dodge in 1-2 with the treble now***."

   What do you do next?

6. You are momentarily confused when the treble ringer hisses at you, "***Make thirds now. Over me at backstroke***."

   Where must you be?

7. You are dodging 5-6 down but not sure where you are in the method. The person you are dodging with says, "***And now go straight down to the front***."

   How will the place you pass the treble tell you what to do next?

8. During a general jumble whilst the treble is panicking, you get your Cambridge places up in a twist. "***Lead now, treble***," yells the conductor.

   What must *you* do?

9. In the heat of the moment the up and down dodges in your backwork get horribly confused. No one seems to be fitting in with you no matter how hard you try to fit in with them. "***Bob***," says the conductor urbanely, completely unaware of your plight.

   What should *you* do?

10. What is the most outlandish situation you can think of where a knowledge of your own position in relation to the treble would be helpful?

Why You Need to Know

So how did you do? Hopefully, in answering the questions you'll have found that a knowledge of where you pass the treble helps you in four ways.

First, it eases the pressure on your ropesight because you have fewer bells to worry about. No matter how good your ropesight is in plain methods, it will be severely tested when you start ringing Surprise.

Second, it provides way-markers to let you know that you are still following the right path. This creates increased confidence, and increased confidence creates improved concentration. Improved concentration results in fewer mistakes, and fewer mistakes results in increased confidence, and so on.

Third, it enables you to pick yourself up after a momentary mental lapse. When you wake up with a start and think, "Where am I?" you can continue for a moment on autopilot until you meet the treble again.

Fourth, it provides you with an opportunity to get yourself right in a seemingly hopeless situation. All the scenarios in questions 5 to 9 are just the sort of disasters that occur in real life. Conductors often provide singularly unhelpful snippets of information, not because they're trying to tease, but because it's the best they can do in the heat of the moment. A knowledge of where you pass the treble enables you to turn these snippets into genuinely helpful contributions.

Noticing the Treble

"That's all very well," you may say, "but when I'm lost I'm much too tense to ***notice*** when I'm ringing over the treble."

Well, I understand that. And it's certainly a very real problem. But it's a problem you can overcome, and to do so, you need to do two things. First, take particular note of which bell is the treble ***before*** you start the method. You must tell yourself several times that "***that*** bell ***there***" is the treble and that ***Bartholomew*** is ringing it.

Second, you need to concentrate hard on noticing the places where you ring over the treble when you *aren't* panicking. It will then be much easier to notice them when the going gets tough.

The Answers

And just in case you thought you had to wait until next week for the answers – or read them upside down on the back page – here they are.

1. **In the middle of Cambridge places up**.

   It may help to remember that *all* the 3-4 dodges in the places *up*, are *up* dodges, and *all* the 3-4 dodges in the places *down*, are *down* dodges.

2. **On the way to the lead and dodge before doing the Cambridge places up**.

   The commonest mistake in Cambridge is trying to put in an extra 3-4 down when you should be passing the treble in 2-3.

3. **On the way to the two and one on the back**.

   At your first dodge you ring over the treble a *second* time at backstroke.

4. **During the backwork**.

   Both the 5-6 up dodge with the treble *and* the 5-6 down dodge with the treble occur here.

5. **You must be in the middle of your frontwork.**

You don't know, though, whether to dodge up or down. If you can't see what the treble is doing, try dodging *down* with it first. If that seems right, lead and carry on as normal. If there's a crunch and the treble looks annoyed, make seconds over him immediately and then do the second half of the frontwork.

6. This is a difficult one which few people could answer without a little thought. **Clearly you are doing Cambridge places**, but which lot? and whereabouts are you in them?

Well, since you're in thirds place over the treble at backstroke, the treble itself must be in seconds place at backstroke. The only times it's in seconds place at backstroke are,

> When it's going from thirds to seconds on its way to its 1-2 down dodge,

And,

> When it's actually dodging 1-2 down before leading full.

But since *you* are making thirds, the treble can't have been in thirds place at handstroke at the same time, so that rules out the first option. Accordingly, the treble must be dodging 1-2 down, and that means that *you* must be making the last lot of thirds in your places up.

And all that means that the full answer is that at the next whole pull you will dodge 3-4 up and then go out to the backwork.

7. Another tricky one. **There are three possibilities.**

    a. You pass the treble in 4-5. In which case you do your frontwork.

    b. You pass the treble in 2-3. In which case you lead and dodge, and do Cambridge places up.

    c. You get to thirds place but ***still don't meet the treble***. And if that happens you must start Cambridge places down.

    In this last case, of course, the person who told you to go ***straight down*** to the front was wrong. But, then conductors often are wrong in Surprise because it's so complicated. You have been lucky that he was skilled enough to tell you as much as he did, so rather than give him a telling off afterwards, just try to avoid making the same mistake next time.

8. **Quite simply, you dodge 3-4 up and go out to the backwork.**

    While the touch is still in progress, ***never***, ***never*** try to think about what you've just done wrong. Wait until the touch finishes before you do that. While you're still ringing put all your troubles behind you and concentrate on staying right. You've been thrown a life belt and it is up to you to hang on to it. As the cowboy gamblers' song puts it, "***There'll be time enough for counting, when the dealing's done***."

9. You have learnt that, if a bob is called at the end of your backwork, you run in, dodge with the treble in 1-2, and finish your frontwork. So, once again you put the murky past behind you and do just that.

Mind you, you shouldn't have ***been*** trying to fit in with everyone else, especially as they were trying to fit in with you. It's clearly not a strong band, and all of them – including the conductor – are trying to take their early steps in the method. The very best thing you can do, is be the rock on which they can rely.

10. And lastly, an open question. But don't just dismiss it as a joke. The more you ponder on it, the greater your knowledge of Cambridge will become. And if you think of a funny answer, please write in with it. When you're ringing something as complicated as Cambridge, a little light relief before and after is ***very*** welcome.

Needless to say I received a sizable number of answers to question 10, ranging from the complex and the bizarre to the just plain smutty. I was tempted to include a selection of the smutty sort here, but I wouldn't like to embarrass anybody, least of all me. Interestingly, most of the sensible – or, at least, fairly sensible – answers related to getting right again after some traumatic non-ringing incident, such as a ringer being stung by a wasp or the tower being struck by lightning. The fact that the writers all assumed they'd still be ringing after such appalling disasters, quite took my breath away.

The moral of it all, of course, is that a detailed knowledge of your own position relative to the treble, really does help, and it helps, not only in Cambridge, but also in all other Surprise methods. So please keep it just as much in mind as we move on to **Beverley and Surfleet**.

36. Beverley & Surfleet

We spent three chapters on our first Surprise method, and now we're moving on to our second. Or, to be more exact, our second and third. Fortunately, the social Surprise repertoire has very few methods in it, so there's not a great deal left to learn. But although everyone agrees that Cambridge is the *first* method to learn, there's no universal agreement as to which should come next. So we're going on to Beverley and Surfleet now because, in many ways, they require the least amount of *extra* learning.

Why Learn Them

People ring Beverley and Surfleet for a number of reasons. They're rather similar to Cambridge, they're rather similar to each other, and most important of all, *other people* ring them.

There are many, many Surprise methods which you might ring – and a good few of them are a good bit nicer than Beverley and Surfleet – but there's no point in learning them because hardly anybody rings them. Beverley and Surfleet, on the other hand, are standard methods for the social ringer. They're likely to be rung at any practice where something a little more complex than Cambridge is looked for.

The Similarities with Cambridge

Starting, as ever, at the shallow end, let's look at the ways in which Beverley and Surfleet are the ***same*** as Cambridge. There are three of them.

First, ***above the treble*** Beverley and Surfleet are identical to Cambridge.

This means that whenever you pass the treble on the way up to the back, you start ringing exactly the same work as you would have rung if you'd been ringing Cambridge. And you continue ringing that work until you pass the treble on your way back down to the front again.

And since all that seems a bit of a tangle when you're first told it, let's look at an example. The blue lines of both Beverley and Surfleet are on the next double page so you can compare them while reading the next few paragraphs.

Suppose you are ringing Beverley. Having passed the treble in 4-5 on the way up, you do two dodges in 5-6 up, one dodge in 5-6 down, and then go back down and pass the treble in 2-3. That's exactly the same work that you would have done if you had passed the treble in 4-5 on the way up when ringing Cambridge or Surfleet.

You can check for yourself that a similar rule applies ***whenever*** you pass the treble on the way up. And when you've done that, you'll know what people mean when they say that ***Beverley and Surfleet are Cambridge above the treble***.

There are two other similarities between Beverley, Surfleet and Cambridge which really stem from this but which most people like to remember separately.

First, both of the new methods have a ***backwork*** – or ***thirds place bell*** – which is identical to the backwork in Cambridge. And second, and most importantly, the bobs and singles affect you in exactly the same way in all three methods.

The Order of the Work

And now for the differences. The blue lines over the page may help, but better still are the orders of the work down below. To show how similar they are I've placed them side by side with the different sections in bold type.

You can see that there's rather more to both of them than there is to Cambridge, but much of it you already know. The trouble is, though, that the new bits really are quite tricky.

The Orders of the Work

(Starting on the Six)

Beverley	Surfleet
Stedman whole turn	Stedman whole turn
Double dodge 1-2 up	**Seconds, lead**
Thirds	Thirds
Finish Cambridge places up	Finish Cambridge places up
Backwork	Backwork
Start Cambridge places down	Start Cambridge places down
Thirds	Thirds
Double dodge 1-2 down	**Lead, seconds**
Stedman whole turn	Stedman whole turn
One and two on the back	One and two on the back
Fourths	Fourths
Thirds, fourths	**Double dodge 3-4 down**
London frontwork	London frontwork
Fourths, thirds	**Double dodge 3-4 up**
Fourths	Fourths
Two and one on the back	Two and one on the back

123456 ← 2	432156	432615
214365	341265	423651
124635	342156	246315
216453	431265	426351
261435	413256	243651
624153	142365	423615
621435	412635	246351
264153	146253	264315
624513	142635 ← 3	624135
642531	416253	261453
465213	146523	264135
645231	415632	621453
462531	451623	612435
642513	546132	164253
465231	541623	614523
456213	456132	165432
546123	546312	164523 ← 5
451632	564321	615432
456123	653412	165342
541632	563421	613524
514623	654321	631542
156432	564312	365124
516342	653421	361542
153624	635412	635124
156342 ← 6	365142	365214
513624	631524	356241
153264	635142	532614
512346	361524	352641
521364	316542	536241
253146	135624	356214
251364	315264	532641
523146	132546	523614
253416	135264 ← 4	253164
235461	312546	521346
324516	132456	523164
234561	314265	251346
325461	341256	215364
235416	432165	123546
324561	431256	213456
342516	342165	124365
432156	432615	123456

Beverley Surprise Minor

123456 ← 2	432156	432615
214365	341265	423651
124635	342156	246315
216453	431265	243651
261435	413256	426351
624153	142365	423615
621435	412635	246351
264153	146253	264315
624513	142635 ← 3	624135
642531	416253	261453
465213	146523	264135
462531	415632	621453
645231	451623	612435
642513	546132	164253
465231	541623	614523
456213	456132	165432
546123	546312	164523 ← 5
451632	564321	615432
456123	653412	165342
541632	654321	613524
514623	563421	631542
156432	564312	365124
516342	653421	361542
153624	635412	635124
156342 ← 6	365142	365214
513624	631524	356241
153264	635142	532614
512346	361524	536241
521364	316542	352641
253146	135624	356214
251364	315264	532641
523146	132546	523614
253416	135264 ← 4	253164
235461	312546	521346
324516	132456	523164
325461	314265	251346
234561	341256	215364
235416	432165	123546
324561	431256	213456
342516	342165	124365
432156	432615	123456

Surfleet Surprise Minor

The Rights and Wrongs

When you ring Cambridge, all the places are made from handstroke to backstroke, all the dodges are a step back at backstroke, and all the plain hunting is done at the same stroke as in Plain Bob. So we say that the places are made ***right***, the dodges are ***right*** dodges, the hunting is ***forward*** hunting, and Cambridge is a ***forward*** method.

But in Beverley and Surfleet some of the places are made from backstroke to handstroke, some of the dodges are a step back at handstroke, and some of the plain hunting is at the ***opposite*** stroke to Plain Bob. So we say that those places are made ***wrong***, those dodges are ***wrong*** dodges, that hunting is ***backward*** hunting, and Beverley and Surfleet are partially ***backward*** methods.

At first sight you might think that this ***wrongness*** shouldn't make much difference, but to most people it makes an enormous amount of difference. It makes the methods more difficult to ring because they feel less natural, and it makes the ropesight more difficult to manage because the other bells behave oddly. It also makes a small slip much less easy to correct.

The thought processes which make backward methods more difficult are very intriguing. They're rather complicated and largely subconscious, and they vary from person to person. Certainly, many years of ringing nothing but forward methods has a lot to do with it. But suffice it to say, that if you find Beverley and Surfleet very much harder than Cambridge, you share that problem with most other ringers.

The Tricky Bits

So now let's look at the tricky bits in detail. One of them has its own name. It's called ***London frontwork*** and it occurs in both methods around where you make seconds over the treble. It is called London frontwork because it's on the front and you also come across it in ***London***.

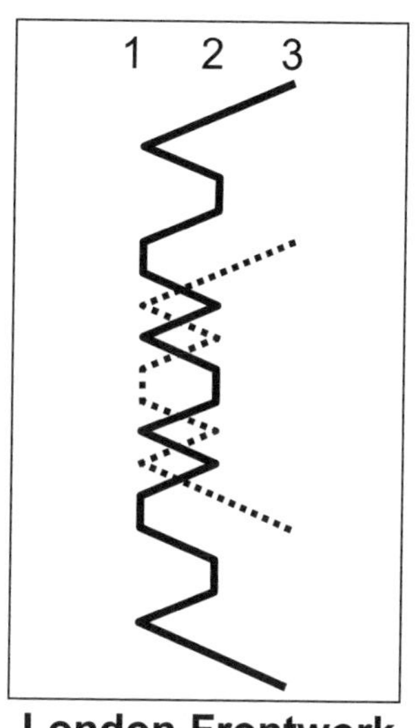

London Frontwork

At first sight it looks quite easy. After all, it's shorter then Cambridge frontwork and the middle bit isn't a lot different. But the trouble lies with the point leads at the beginning and end. Somehow, it can be particularly difficult to get these right, so if you have problems yourself, the following tips may help.

First, concentrate really hard on doing exactly one blow at lead and no more. Don't lapse into autopilot and put in a second blow without thinking.

Second, remember that the point blow at the beginning is at ***backstroke*** whilst the point blow at the end is at ***handstroke***. If you expect to do them both at the same stroke, you'll have real trouble.

The Funny Frontworks

The other new bits don't have their own names but that doesn't make them any easier. Two occur on the front, with different versions for each method.

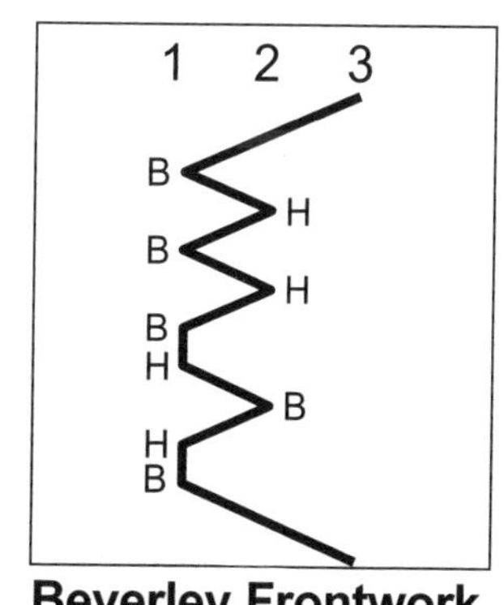

Beverley Frontwork

Think of the Beverley version as a double dodge followed by a Stedman whole turn, with the dodges being ***wrong*** dodges. I've put little "H"s and "B"s next to the diagram to show which stroke each blow is at.

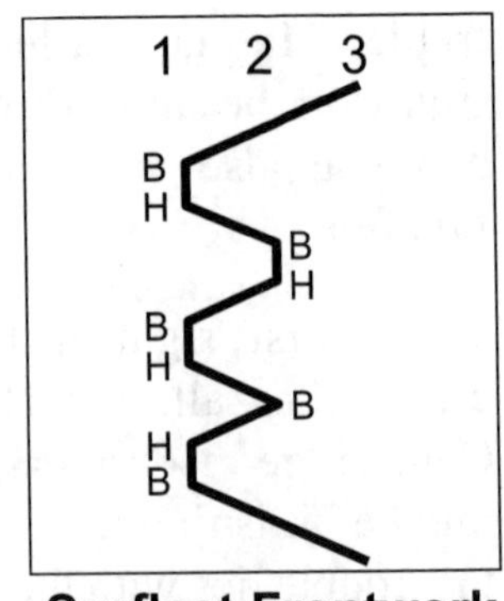

Surfleet Frontwork

Think of the Surfleet version as, lead, seconds, followed by a Stedman whole turn. And since both the lead and seconds are made ***wrong***, I've put little "H"s and "B"s in this picture too.

The Middle Works

And the last new pieces come in 3-4, sandwiched between the London frontwork and the *two and one on the back*. The Beverley version is on the left, and the Surfleet version is on the right, and once again I have included "H"s and "B"s.

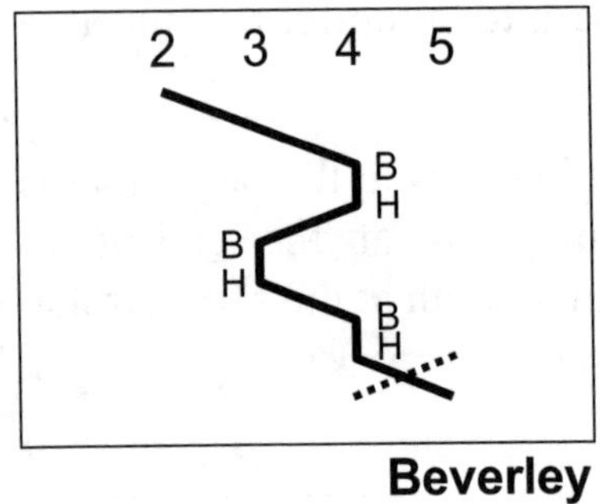

Beverley

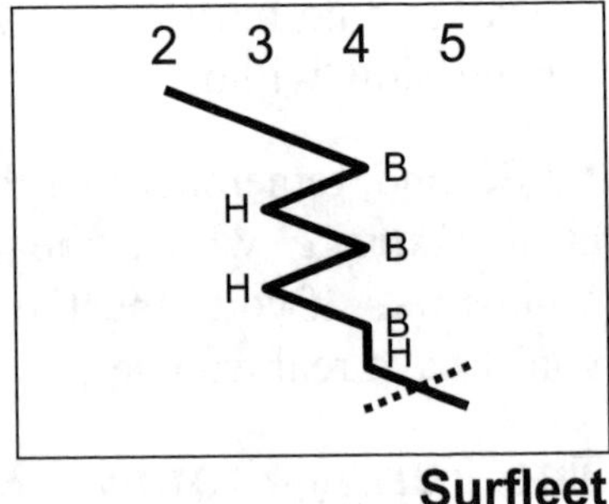

Surfleet

They're both deceptively treacherous. Not only can you have trouble making the places wrong and getting the dodges correct, but you can also find yourself sorely tempted to do everything in 4-5 instead of 3-4. Beware.

Remembering Which is Which

And lastly, even when you've learnt Beverley and Surfleet thoroughly, there's still the terrible problem of remembering which is which. But as you can see, in the parts where the two methods differ, Beverley is dodges on the front and places in the middle, whilst Surfleet is places on the front and dodges in the middle. Most people find that remembering which is which is a constant nightmare, but those who can manage it, swear by the following expression.

Beverley has **B**umps on the front.

In the first three editions of this book, I mentioned in the last chapter that Beverley and Surfleet were in The Ringing World Diary. *I've taken that out now, though, because nowadays Beverley isn't. A couple of years back, a small but vociferous group of ringers argued volubly that many of the commonly rung Surprise methods lacked merit – whatever that meant – and that people only rang them because they were in the Diary. "Change the Diary," they said, "and everyone will ring the new methods instead."*

So Beverley went out and Chester went in. But did that result in ringers changing from the one to the other?

Apparently not. As good a measure as any is the number of quarter peals rung, and an analysis of these shows that Beverley quarters are still being rung at more than ten times the rate of Chester quarters. The other new Diary methods are rung even less often, and several have only been rung once to a quarter in the last year – all by the same band.

In fact, over the past 200 years there have been quite a few occasions when ringers have been vigorously told by a small minority that they should be ringing something different, but invariably they've taken no notice. The popularity of different methods has certainly changed over the decades – and a very interesting subject of study that is too – but it's always been a gradual thing. It's never been a matter of what appears in print, but simply a response to how people feel in some way. Indeed, many methods have survived for hundreds of years with no written information at all, whilst others have been promoted vigorously in print but have remained virtually unrung.

So I'm pleased to say that the social ringers surprise minor repertoire is still just the same as when I wrote the original articles over twenty years ago. Certainly, I believe Beverley and Surfleet are rung less now then than they were then – and Norwich is rung more – but not enough to change the order of the chapters round. In another twenty years time, though, who knows?

37. Norwich

This week, as a little light relief between the rigours of Beverley and the horrors of London, we're looking at Norwich. In many ways Norwich is easier than Beverley and Surfleet, and you might feel we should have looked at it last time. Quite probably you're right. But traditionally, Surprise ringers have been encouraged to learn Beverley and Surfleet before Norwich, and who am I to defy tradition.

Why Learn it

Like the other methods in the social Surprise repertoire, Norwich Minor is rung at meetings and practices throughout the country as a step up from Cambridge. It's a pleasant and musical method, and once you've learnt Cambridge, it will come fairly easily to you. Not only is it enjoyable to ring and nice to listen to, but it gives you the opportunity to take part in the higher quality of ringing with which it's normally associated.

When Learning it

Unlike Beverley and Surfleet, all the places and dodges in Norwich are made ***right*** – i.e. hand-back – and all the hunting is ***forward*** hunting. All the dodges are ***backstroke*** dodges too. This makes it much easier to learn and ring than Beverley and Surfleet, and indeed, some people find it easier than Cambridge. The blue line is on the next page, and the

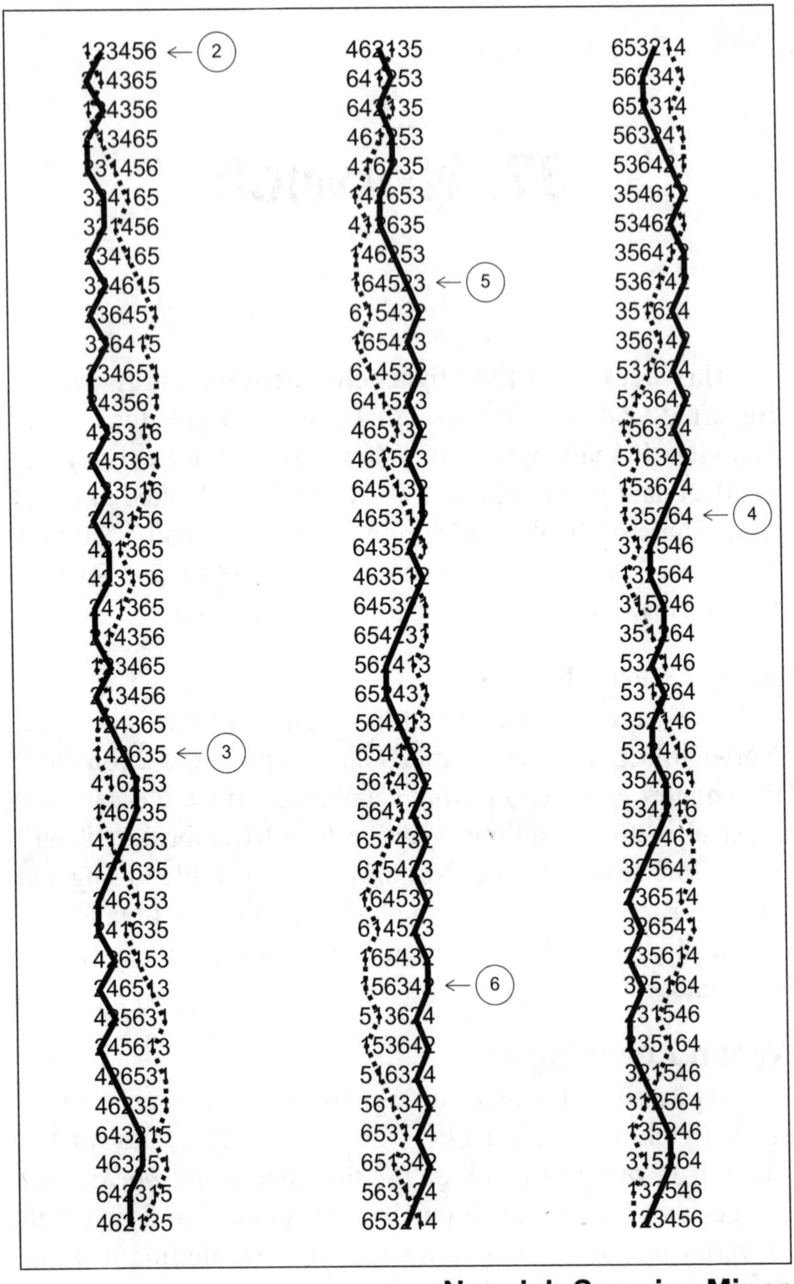

123456 ← (2)	462135	653214
214365	641253	562341
124356	642135	652314
213465	461253	563241
231456	416235	536421
324165	142653	354612
321456	412635	534621
234165	146253	356412
324615	164523 ← (5)	536142
236451	615432	351624
326415	165423	356142
234651	614532	531624
243561	641523	513642
425316	465132	156324
245361	461523	516342
423516	645132	153624
243156	465312	135264 ← (4)
421365	643521	312546
423156	463512	132564
241365	645321	315246
214356	654231	351264
123465	562413	532146
213456	652431	531264
124365	564213	352146
142635 ← (3)	654123	532416
416253	561432	354261
146235	564123	534216
412653	651432	352461
421635	615423	325641
246153	164532	236514
241635	614523	326541
426153	165432	235614
246513	156342 ← (6)	325164
425631	513624	231546
245613	153642	235164
426531	516324	321546
462351	561342	312564
643215	653124	135246
463251	651342	315264
642315	563124	132546
462135	653214	123456

Norwich Surprise Minor

order of the work – starting on the Two – is

Frontwork
fourths
lead and double dodge
places up
three and one
thirds
three and three
thirds
one and three
places down
double dodge and lead
fourths

and back to seconds place.

You'll see that I have referred to ***places up*** and ***places down***, but these aren't *Cambridge* places up and *Cambridge* places down. Instead they're the same as Cambridge places except that the dodges at each end are missed off. The ***up*** form is on the left and the down form is on the right.

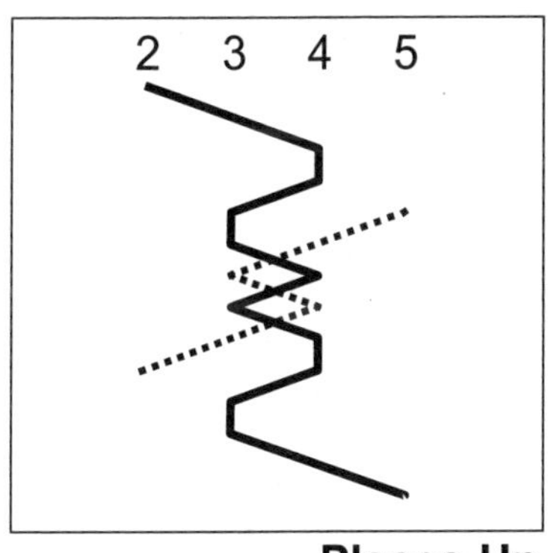

Places Up

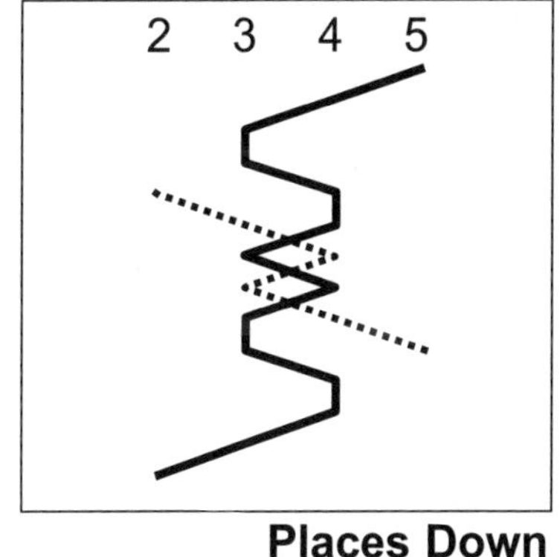

Places Down

You wouldn't normally refer to these places as ***Norwich places*** – although a few ringers do – you'd just call them, ***places***. In different methods there are lots of different pieces of work called ***places***, and which places you do depends on which method you're ringing. Indeed, in some methods there are more than one kind of places. But even so, most places are just called ***places***.

I've also referred to ***frontwork***, although once again, it isn't ***Cambridge frontwork*** and nor, for that matter, is it ***London frontwork***. It's just plain ***frontwork***. You can see that it's symmetrical and looks quite easy, but you need to learn it very carefully as it contains a major elephant pit to trap the unwary – more of which in a moment.

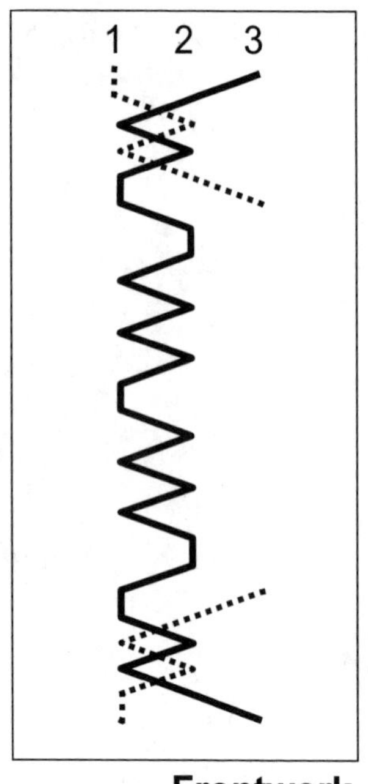

Frontwork

When Ringing Norwich

And when it comes to ringing it, there are four mistakes that are very common, and although thinking about them in advance won't necessarily *stop* you making them, it might at least help you make them less often.

First, it's very easy to miss the seconds near the end of the frontwork and so go up to fourths too early. You can avoid this by concentrating hard on ensuring that you never leave the frontwork until you've dodged 1-2 up with the treble.

Second, because Cambridge is rung so much more often than Norwich, people often put a 3-4 dodge on the beginning or end of their places. Mostly they put a dodge *on the end of the places up*. There's no easy way of avoiding this mistake. You just have to concentrate hard on not making it.

Third, many ringers confuse their ***lead and double dodge*** with their ***double dodge and lead***. Often they get themselves right again with little difficulty but by then the person doing the frontwork is well and truly scuppered. This normally results from not learning the method carefully enough, and going back to the drawing board should cure it.

Fourth, by nodding off during the backwork you can forget exactly where you are in all that 5-6 dodging. If that happens to you, get yourself right again by remembering the three rules.

> You always do three dodges in 5-6 – both up and down – unless you meet the treble there. If you *do* meet the treble there, you only do *one* dodge.
>
> Your backwork finishes shortly after dodging 5-6 up with the treble.
>
> If you've come down from the back and are making thirds but don't know where you are,
>
> > You must do places down ***if and only if*** your first blow in thirds is over the treble.
>
> Otherwise,
>
> > You must go out to the back again for more backwork.

Of course, you not only need to avoid making these mistakes yourself, you also need to stay right when others make them. I was recently involved in a ringing course in which I gave a short talk on Norwich. In the practical session afterwards, in a totally unscripted and thoroughly appropriate demonstration, two of the helpers missed the final seconds of their frontwork, and dodged at the end of their places up.

That, of course, is how the real world often is, and I couldn't have provided better practice for managing in the great outside.

Bobs

And now for the bobs. But before we look at them in detail, we need to go into a little bit of theory.

At the lead end in Norwich when the treble leads full, one bell makes sixths and the bells in 2-3 and 4-5 cross over. And because of this, we say that Norwich is a ***sixths place method***. At the lead end in Cambridge, on the other hand, one bell makes seconds and the bells in 3-4 and 5-6 dodge. So we say that Cambridge is a ***seconds place method***.

The bobs in a sixths place method always affect the bells in 4-5-6 and not those in 2-3, whereas the bobs in a seconds place method always affect the bells in 2-3-4 and not those in 5-6. This means that you have to learn some rather different rules for Norwich bobs than you learnt for Cambridge, Beverley and Surfleet bobs.

Fortunately, though, Norwich bobs are rather similar to Kent bobs. So if when a bob is called you're momentarily confused about what to do, you can proceed in a *Kentish* sort of way until you sort yourself out. Best of all, though, learn the following rules very carefully.

> If you are about to ***begin*** or ***end*** your ***frontwork***, you are ***not*** affected.
>
> If you are just ***finishing*** your ***places up***, you must make ***fourths*** and do your ***places down***.

> If you are ***dodging*** in ***5-6 up*** or ***5-6 down***, you must do ***four*** more dodges where you are – that's ***seven*** dodges in all – and then carry on with an extra piece of backwork.

If you're unable to work out exactly where you are after being affected in 5-6, then the rules on pages 329 should help. If you're unable to count up to seven – and, believe me, that is genuinely very difficult indeed – don't leave the back until the treble forces you to go down.

And Singles

Fortunately no one as yet calls singles in Norwich. Or, at least, no one *I* know does. That not only makes touches very much easier to ring, but it also makes this chapter a good deal shorter. If I'm now inundated by forward-thinking conductors sending me touches with singles in, you'll just have to make an amendment in the margin.

A Useful Tip

And lastly, a useful tip.

When you make fourths in Cambridge places, you always do it over two different bells. By the time you start ringing Norwich you'll probably have rung so much Cambridge that you'll look for two bells automatically.

But when you make fourths in Norwich, you sometimes do it over two different bells and you sometimes do it over the ***same*** bell, and this can be exceedingly disconcerting until you get the hang of what's happening. In your early attempts it's very, very easy to drift up to *sixths* place by insisting on ringing over a different bell for the second blow in fourths, and so latching on to the bell in fifths. If your places always seem to be going wrong, you've probably got this problem.

And if you feel at the end of all that, that Norwich shouldn't really be classed as *light relief* at all, then you're probably right. But if you found it *really* hard, then I recommend some very deep breathing over the next two weeks. Because in Chapter 38 we're moving on to London. And that certainly won't be light relief from anything.

In the event, no one did write in with touches of Norwich with singles in, but to some extent that sort of touch is a matter of fashion. Singles in Surprise aren't quite as common now as they were seven or eight years ago, and I believe they're getting less common. But if you keep this book for ten years or more, they may be all the rage again, and you'll just have to write about them in the margin or on one of the blank endpapers at the back.

And if you're a bit reticent about writing in a **proper** *book like this one, please don't be. I can assure you that I shan't mind a bit. After all, it's yours now. And any way, I only wrote it to help people ring methods, so if writing in it helps you even more, go ahead and write in it. And jotting down a few notes is at least one way of delaying that awful moment when you at last have to confront* **London**.

38. London

"All roads," someone once said, "lead to London." And there – via Cambridge, Beverley, Surfleet and Norwich – is where we've arrived this week. Most ringers avoid learning London as much as they avoid going there, but just like the town, the method looks much worse from a distance than it does close to. Indeed, there are a number of people who are quite fond of both. The hurly-burly side of life has always had its adherents, and if you fancy testing out the hurly-burly side of Surprise Minor, you've turned to the right article. Just take a deep breath and read on.

Why Learn It

London is the most complex Minor method that's widely rung. You'll come across it throughout the country wherever there's a band strong enough to ring it. You won't come across it very often, because in many areas there simply aren't enough experienced ringers to attempt it, but where there are, they'll almost certainly want to have a go.

That is one of the main reasons for learning London. Your efforts will provide *other* ringers with an opportunity they wouldn't get otherwise. When you can ring London, you'll frequently find that you just make up the number for it to be attempted.

So give it a go. In learning it you will not only be taking

on a challenge, you'll be achieving the zenith of the social ringer's standard repertoire.

Why it's Difficult

There are several reasons why London is difficult. It's a substantially ***backward*** method, it doesn't divide up easily into chunks, and it ***feels*** very unnatural. Some people look at it and recoil in horror before they've even started to learn it, and others feel they ought to be able to learn it but can't seem to succeed. Others still, learn it alright but then have enormous difficulty ringing it.

The point is that all these reactions and problems are perfectly normal and reasonable. Wrapping the brain around London is very difficult; learning London is very difficult; and – even when you've learnt it – *ringing* London is very difficult. So don't be dismayed if you have difficulty. Everybody does.

The Pieces of Work

So now, down to the nitty-gritty. This is the moment to take a quick look at the next page and that awful blue line.

And now that you've done that, I hope you're still reading. I hope it wasn't so much of a shock that you just gave up and turned to the Quarter Peal pages instead.

If you *are* still reading, you'll be relieved to know that you needn't start learning the whole thing immediately. Instead, we're going to take a closer look at some of the new pieces of work first. There are several of them and they all have their own names.

The first is called ***long London*** and it occurs in 5-6. It can either be done with the dodge first – in which case it is known as ***long London beginning with a dodge*** – or with the dodge

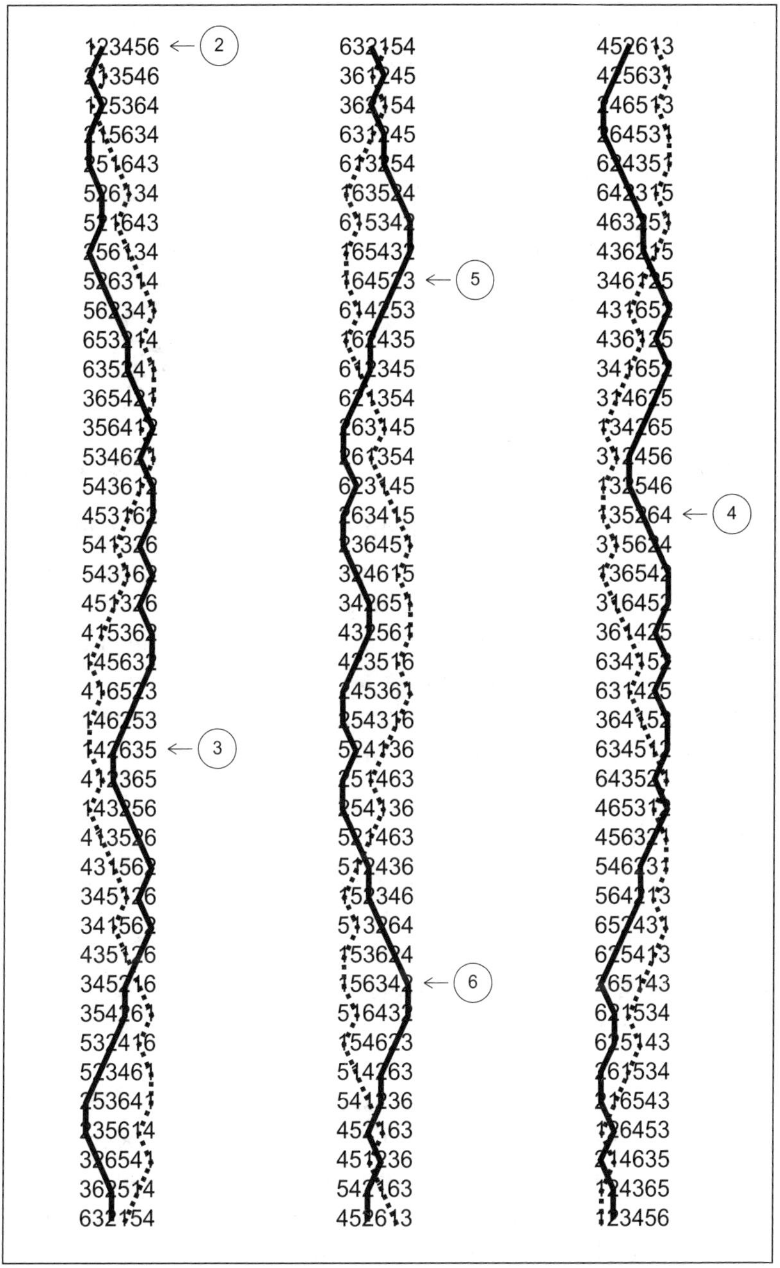

123456 ← (2)
213546
125364
215634
251643
526134
521643
256134
526314
562341
653214
635241
365421
356412
534621
543612
453162
541326
543162
451326
415362
145632
416523
146253
142635 ← (3)
412365
143256
413526
431562
345126
341562
435126
345216
354261
532416
523461
253641
235614
326541
362514
632154

632154
361245
362154
631245
613254
163524
615342
165432
164523 ← (5)
614253
162435
612345
621354
263145
261354
623145
263415
236451
324615
342651
432561
423516
245361
254316
524136
251463
254136
521463
512436
152346
513264
153624
156342 ← (6)
516432
154623
514263
541236
452163
451236
542163
452613

452613
425631
246513
264531
624351
642315
463251
436215
346125
431652
436125
341652
314625
134265
312456
132546
135264 ← (4)
315624
136542
316452
361425
634152
631425
364152
634512
643521
465312
456321
546231
564213
652431
625413
265143
621534
625143
261534
216543
126453
214635
124365
123456

London Surprise Minor

last – in which case it is known as ***long London ending with a dodge***. Here are the pictures.

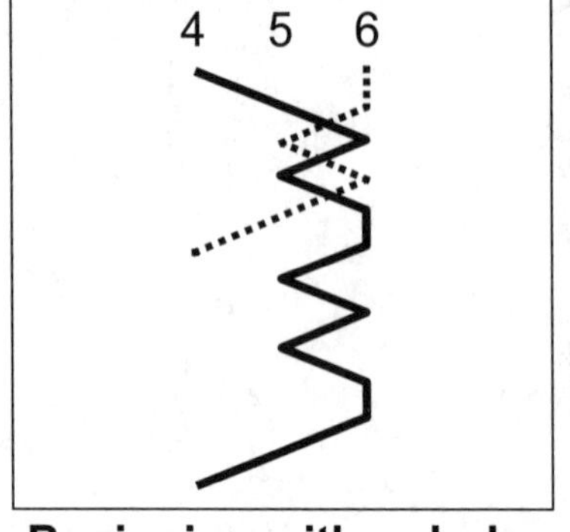

Beginning with a dodge

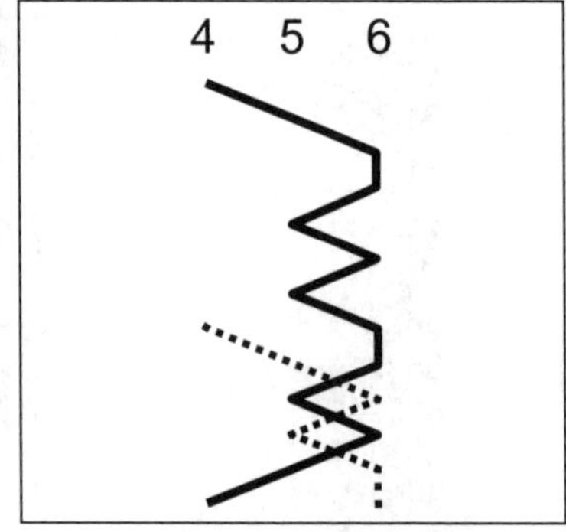

Ending with a dodge

Some people call it "single, lie, double, lie," and "lie, double, lie, single." ***Don't*** be beguiled into calling it that yourself. There is ***no*** double dodge in the middle – only two point-fifths. If you refer to these two point-fifths as a double dodge, you may end up ***doing*** a double dodge, and disaster will result. When ringing backward methods, it's essential to remember that a point blow is ***not*** a dodge.

Fish Tails

The next new work is a ***fish tail***, and it occurs in 5-6. You may also hear it referred to as ***two points up*** or ***rabbit's ears***. Increasingly, though, these colourful and descriptive terms are giving way to the more prosaic ***six-five-six*** particularly for Major and the higher numbers. It's been forcefully put to me that the expression ***six-five-six*** has definite advantages when ringing on eight or more, and I have to admit that it probably has. But London Minor is such a dry method, that a bit of life in the terminology must surely be a good thing.

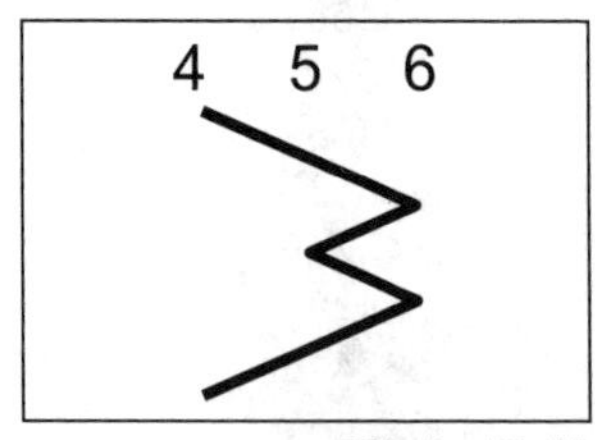

Fish Tail

You can see that I've only put in one picture of a fish tail because a fish tail looks like a fish tail no matter how you come upon it. Be warned, though, that the fish tail in one half of the method causes you to do the points at backstroke, but the fish tail in the other half causes you to do the points at handstroke. The two fish tails ***look*** exactly the same but they ***feel*** very different.

London Frontwork

London frontwork is something we came across in Beverley and Surfleet. I'm just including a picture here but you can read about it on page 320.

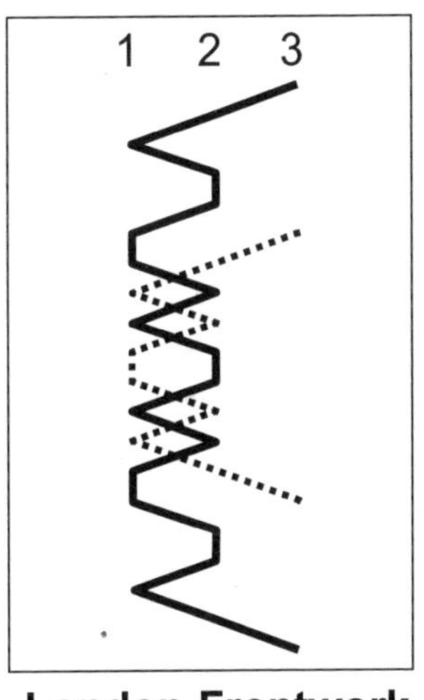

London Frontwork

Stedman

Stedman occurs on the front as well, and it's instantly recognisable as a Stedman whole turn. Rather oddly, though, it's generally referred to in London as just ***stedman*** as though that method consisted of whole turns and nothing else.

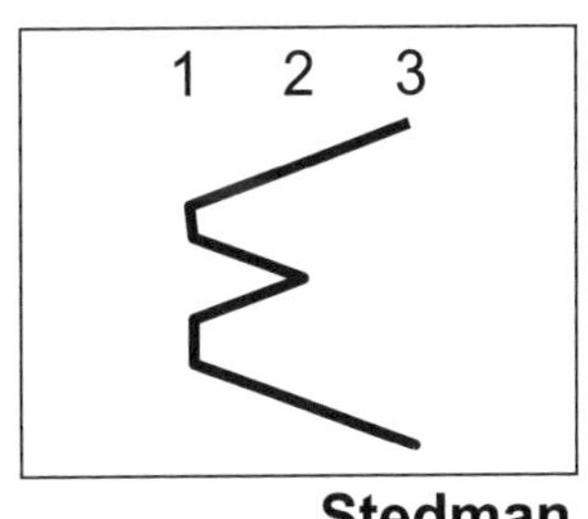

Stedman

There are two Stedman whole turns in a course of London, and just like in the real thing – one of them is ***lead right, point seconds, lead wrong***, and the other is ***lead wrong, point seconds, lead right***. But in London's generally perverse way, the whole turns come in the opposite order to Stedman. So when ringing London, remember Matthew, chapter 19, verse 30 and say, ***the last shall be first***.

Places

And lastly, ***the places***. They occur in 3-4, and in general they're not referred to by any particular name although some people occasionally call them ***London places***.

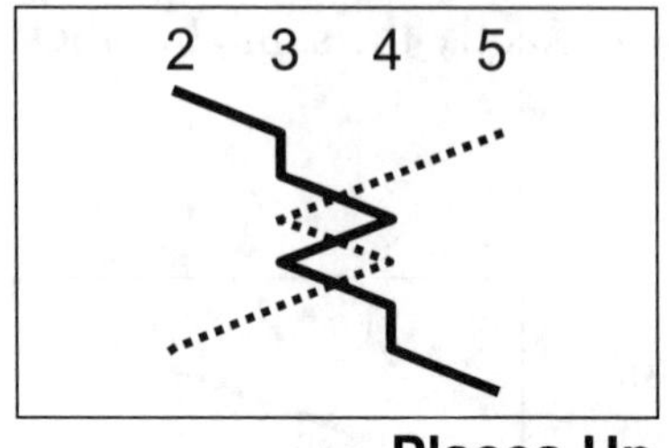

Places Up

Places Down

Learning It

And when you've learnt the named pieces of work, it's time to learn the order of the work. Starting on the Two it's

Second half of frontwork
fourths
long London starting with a dodge
thirds
fish tail
fourths, lead
places up
sixths
thirds, whole turn, thirds, whole turn, thirds
sixths
places down
lead, fourths
fish tail
thirds
long London ending with a dodge
fourths
first half of frontwork.

That's the biggest mouthful for an order of the work that we've come across so far, and it's a rather dry and unsatisfying one too. But there really is no option to learning it as thoroughly as you can. Unless you have a truly exceptional brain, you'll find it very difficult to ring no matter how well you've learnt it, but learning it is nonetheless an essential first step.

Putting it into Practice

And when you take hold of a rope for your first course of London, a war of attrition starts. It may be a long war and it may be a short war, but a war it certainly is. You'll keep on making mistakes, going back to the diagram, having another go, making more mistakes, going back to the diagram, and so on, each time overcoming a little more of the complexity of it all.

If you have a good band to ring with and an expert to tell you what your mistakes are, the time taken to master it will be very much shorter. But if you're not that lucky – and most people certainly aren't – you must be prepared for a very trying time.

The Tips

But even the most difficult task can be made easier with a few useful tips.

First, the biggest single problem in ringing London is that the point blows are not always done at the same stroke. The two points in the fish tail, for example, are sometimes done at hand and sometimes done at back. It's very easy – and totally devastating – to *force* yourself to do something at the wrong stroke because you have a sort of a feeling that that is that stroke it ought to be done at.

Needless to say, London is much too complicated for you

to learn what strokes you do what at before you start. But you can write little "H"s and "B"s on your diagram – as we did for Beverley and Surfleet – and then add in that knowledge as you get to know the method better. You can also learn when to lead right and when to lead wrong.

The second problem is that from time to time you have to make a place in the middle of a piece of hunting. Sometimes it will be thirds and sometimes fourths. It's very easy to miss these out and arrive at the back or front too early. Remember, though, that you are ten times more likely to arrive at the front too soon than too late. So if you start to lead and find someone else is also leading, wait ***one blow*** – not one whole pull – and start leading again.

A more complex tip is that you must make thirds or fourths whenever you have just passed the treble or are just about to pass the treble. Some people find this very helpful and others don't. But even if you don't, it might help you to remember to make fourths after dodging 3-4 up with the treble. 90% of ringers miss this out during their first few attempts.

The third problem arises when you come down from the back and make thirds. Is it thirds and back, or is it thirds and carry on down? There's no easy tip for this, but the commonest mistake by far, is carrying on down when you shouldn't. So if when making thirds you're in the slightest doubt, go back up again.

And lastly, bear in mind that the bells will come at you from unexpected directions. Long experience of forward methods may result in you always looking the wrong way at the wrong moment. So if there is one bit that you can never seem to get right, check which bells you should be ringing over. Your problems may then melt away as if by magic.

Touches

Not many people ring touches of London. A plain course is such an achievement that bobs are normally considered an unpardonable piece of over-egging. So don't worry about learning them until you know the method really well.

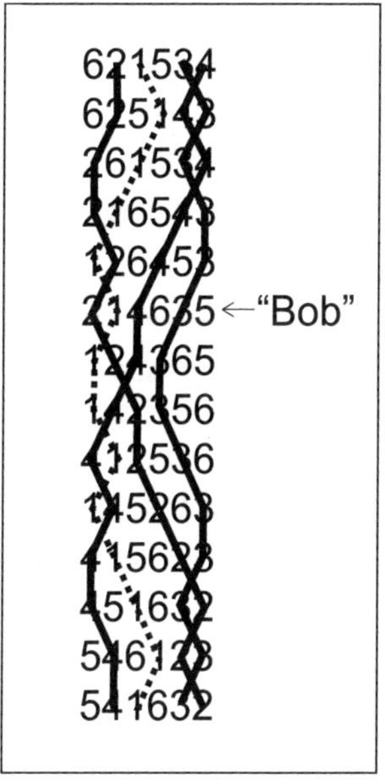

London Minor

But even when you *do* know the method well, you'll probably still find that the bobs – like everything else in London – are extremely difficult to get right. Learning them is difficult enough, but ringing them is very, very difficult.

As you can see, the bells on the back are unaffected – although it can be difficult to be sure that you *are* on the back – and the rules for the other three are.

> If you're in ***the middle of the frontwork*** and about to make seconds over the treble, ***run out***, ***make thirds*** and go on up to do a ***fish tail***.
>
> If you're ***making thirds*** having just done a fish tail, ***run in*** and do ***the second half of the frontwork***.

And,

> If you've just done ***long London*** beginning with a dodge, ***make fourths*** and do ***long London*** ending with a dodge.

Most people find that running in is the least hard way of being affected, but they're all difficult. Thorough learning beforehand is essential.

A Tip for the Coarse Ringer

And there's one last thing to mention. The tip for the ***coarse ringer***. Naturally you're not a coarse ringer yourself, but the tip may help you identify coarse ringers when you come across them.

The point is that London Minor is quite different from London Major, and London Major is quite different from London Royal. So the standard coarse ringer's response to being caught out going wrong in London Minor is to say with supreme and gushing confidence,

"I'm ***so*** sorry. I was trying to ring London ***Royal***."

I got a lot of letters after London appeared in The Ringing World, *all telling me of the considerable affection in which the writers held the method. For many it was like an old and close friend whom they only saw infrequently, or a favourite but expensive restaurant that they could only afford to eat in on special occasions. Indeed, a lot of them found it so special that they could remember in detail the times they had rung successful courses of it. They could remember the towers, the dates and the other people ringing, and they could even remember what the weather was like and what they'd done during the rest of the day.*

I felt privileged to share in these reminiscences, especially as they contained so much interesting detail about other ringing matters as well. The message that came over loud and clear was that all the time and effort spent learning

London is well worth it, even for those oh-so-rare opportunities to put it into practice. Indeed, the message came over so loud and clear that I wondered if I should have ended the series on that ultimate note.

But by then I'd already written the next chapter and the Editor had already had it typeset. And anyway, even if you are the most dedicated London-phile, you might nonetheless occasionally like to try **Rearranging your Repertoire**.

39. Rearranging your Repertoire

So here we are at the last chapter. I dare say you're a bit surprised to find it here at all, as you probably thought we'd finished last time. But it seemed a pity to end a series with something as difficult as London – particularly as you might have skipped it – and in any case, I never have liked stories that end in a great clash of excitement without letting you know what happens next.

So what does happen next? What happens once you're a thorough-going expert at the five methods we've looked at so far?

Not a lot, perhaps, if you don't want it to. Or quite a lot, if you want to spend week after week learning methods which you'll almost never get a chance to ring. But there's a middle way. A way of taking the Surprise methods you already know, and then rearranging them into a whole heap more. It can be a very big reward for relatively little effort, and *that* is what we're looking at this time.

Above and Below

So let's begin by recapping on something we looked at three chapters ago. When we were studying Beverley and Surfleet we noticed that they had long sections in them which were identical to Cambridge. In particular, whenever you passed the treble on the way up to the back, you started to ring exactly the same work as you would have done in Cambridge. And you carried on ringing that work until you passed the treble on your way back down to the front again.

Because of that, we said that Beverley and Surfleet were ***Cambridge above the treble***, and as long as we knew what to do above the treble in Cambridge, we also knew what to do above the treble in Beverley and Surfleet.

As you've probably guessed, all methods can be divided up into the work you do *above* the treble and the work you do *below* the treble. So if you know your methods well enough, you can rearrange all the *aboves* and all the *belows* and get a lot of new methods.

It's rather like that children's game where you stick a giraffe's head and neck on an elephant's body, and then giggle about it for minutes on end. Indeed, you may find yourself laughing about some of these methods too.

Some Possible Combinations

In the chart overleaf are four new methods which are combinations of methods you already know, and since you can combine any two methods in this fashion, it's a very good way of developing your skill at knowing your own position relative to the treble. It also produces a rather breath-taking excitement because you're ringing a method with no real idea as to what's going to happen next. But if you're going to try combining aboves and belows with complete abandon, you need to watch out for three things.

First, some of the "methods" produced will have less than five leads, and often only one lead. Second, they may have ***irregular*** lead ends – that is to say, different lead ends from

Aboves and Belows		
Above	**Below**	**Method**
Cambridge	London	York
Norwich	London	Rossendale
Kent	Cambridge	Oswald Delight
Oxford	Cambridge	Boat Race (although pedants call it Morning Exercise)

those occurring in Plain Bob. And third, if you're going to ring one of these methods for anything other than practice, it really is a good idea to learn the blue line very thoroughly.

Varying the Lead End

So far so good, but mixing up your aboves and belows is not the only way of rearranging your repertoire. For more variety still, you can vary the lead ends as well.

Recapping on something else for the moment, at the end of a lead of Cambridge when the treble leads full, one bell makes seconds and the bells in 3-4 and 5-6 cross over. So we say that Cambridge has a ***seconds place lead end*** and is a ***seconds place method***. London is also a ***seconds place method***. But at the lead end in Norwich, one bell makes sixths and the bells in 2-3 and 4-5 cross over. So we say that Norwich has a ***sixths place lead end*** and is a ***sixths place method***.

By ringing the methods you know, but changing the lead ends from seconds place to sixths place or vice versa, you can get yet another batch of new methods.

Here are four examples, one of which – Primrose Surprise Minor – is rung sufficiently often that it only just misses being included in the standard social repertoire in its own right.

Varying Lead End		
Base	**Lead End**	**Method**
Cambridge	Sixths	Primrose
Beverley	Sixths	Berwick
Surfleet	Sixths	Hexham
Rossendale	Seconds	Lightfoot

Once again, it can be very good practice to attempt these new methods by ringing the method you know but varying your work when the treble leads. It's particularly useful if you're trying to acquire the skill of ringing by ***place bells***. Don't forget, though, that if you do it totally at random, you may get some one-lead methods, and you may even have to make four blows in sixths at the lead ends.

Varying the Half-Lead

And lastly, if you thirst for yet more variety, you can obtain even more methods by changing the half-lead from fifths place to firsts place – or thirds place – and vice versa, and in the chart on the next page are four examples.

If you're exceptionally skilled, you may be able to ring a method you know, and then change the half-lead by first principles as you get to it. But it isn't easy, and even those who can do it, tend to make a few mistakes now and then. You either have to know the method so well that you know

Varying Half-Lead		
Base	**Half-Lead**	**Method**
Cambridge	Firsts	Ipswich
Cambridge	Thirds	King Edward
Primrose	Firsts	Norfolk
Primrose	Thirds	Queen Mary

exactly where the half-lead is – ***and*** what to do after it – or more satisfactorily, you need to be able to follow the treble's path by ear.

If you're already that skilled, you probably aren't reading this book anyway, and if you *aren't* that skilled, don't worry. Quite likely you will be some day, and in the mean time you can still manage to ring these variations with just a little extra learning.

One Last Word

And that, after seven chapters, is that. When you've got this far, you'll be able to attend any six-bell practice with complete confidence.

Well, *fairly* complete confidence.

And thereafter, it's on to the social ringer's Surprise ***Major*** repertoire. But *that*, you will be relieved to hear, must wait for another time.

I never did write a Surprise Major series for The Ringing World *as I wasn't really sure how many* Ringing World *readers would be at the right stage to be interested in it. I did, though, write a booklet called* ***The Occasional Surprise Major Package*** *which I gave as a handout when I did Surprise Major courses, and that package comes up later in Chapters 42 to 44.*

But even before I wrote it, lots of people had written to me about Surprise Minor. They had written about their own particular problems and they had asked about particular methods. But they had also wanted to know about **spliced**. *They didn't regard themselves as high-brow ringers but they nonetheless wanted to have a go. So for all those people, I wrote* ***The Novice's Guide to Ringing Spliced Surprise****, and* that *is what we are going on to next.*

The Other Surprise

40. Splicing Surprise

Getting Started

Time was, when I was inordinately impressed by spliced Surprise ringers. They seemed a race apart from other ringers. They were cool and confident, and they rang with a style and elegance of inherent superiority. They even seemed better dressed than the rest of us. On one occasion, as I sat rapt in admiration during a touch of ***eight-spliced***, an elderly man sitting next to me whispered in my ear.

"I taught that girl on the Three, you know," he said. "Of course, she's been to university since then. Only university people can ring that stuff." I nodded in agreement.

Fortunately, experience has taught me that all those preconceptions shared by the elderly man and myself were quite wrong. Spliced Surprise ringers are no different from anyone else. They are seldom cool, almost never confident, and they certainly don't think of themselves as superior.

Or, at least, *most* of them don't.

Going to university has got absolutely nothing to do with it either – except, perhaps, that it provides ringing opportunities not available at home – and the serene and elegant look on Spliced ringers faces is a mark of extreme concentration and worry rather than confidence. It's that special expression which I always think of as ***the look of Surprise***.

So this series is for all those who have always wanted to ring spliced Surprise but have never known how. And it's for all those others who believe it to be completely beyond them. To read it, no previous experience is necessary. It is genuinely ***the Novice's Guide to Ringing Spliced Surprise***.

Beginning at the Beginning

There are two places to start spliced Surprise ringing – the beginning and the end. Both are equally good, but for fitting in with the prevailing local ringing, the beginning is probably best. And you can't find a better beginning than a plain course of Cambridge Minor.

The very first Surprise method you learn must of necessity be Cambridge – not because it's the easiest method, nor yet because it's the most musical method, nor even because it will fit best into spliced, but because it is by far and away the Surprise method most commonly rung.

How to Learn Cambridge

But if you are ultimately going to ring spliced, you must learn Cambridge differently to the way you normally learn methods. Rather than learning it as a long continuous blue line, you must learn it instead as five pieces of blue line, each one lead long.

You start, for example, by learning the piece which takes the Two from the beginning of the course to its 5-6 down dodge when the treble next leads full. You then, quite separately, learn the piece which goes from that 5-6 down dodge to the 3-4 up dodge at the end of the 3-4 Cambridge places up. And so on. You aren't learning anything different, you're just dividing the blue line into pieces.

If you've already learnt Cambridge Minor as one long line, you may well feel disinclined to learn it again as five pieces, especially as those pieces seem rather arbitrary and irregular. But I must stress that in order to ring spliced, it is absolutely essential that you do. You won't find it difficult, and in the course of time you'll find it gives you substantial other benefits as well.

If you *haven't* already learnt the Cambridge Minor line, you may actually find it much *easier* to learn as five pieces. Not only can you take your time, thoroughly learning each piece before proceeding to the next, but you'll find that two of the pieces are the exact reverses of two of the others.

The Pieces of Cambridge

The five *pieces* of Cambridge Minor are below. But we don't call them *pieces*, we call them ***place bells***.

Place bells isn't really a very good term for pieces of work, but it's the universal and popularly accepted one, and in quite a short time you'll feel it to be perfectly reasonable. Pedants may point out that ***place bells*** strictly means something rather different, but common usage has now changed its meaning to *pieces of work*.

We'll start with ***seconds place bell***. It's called ***seconds place bell*** because it's the work you do if you find yourself in seconds place when the treble leads at backstroke at the lead end. Similarly ***thirds place bell*** is the work you do if you find yourself in thirds place at the lead end. And so on.

This is how you might say it.

> "***Seconds place bell*:** **Frontwork, two and one on the back, and become *sixths place bell*.**"

Or perhaps you might prefer a longer form.

“***Seconds place bell*: Dodge, lead, seconds, dodge, lead, dodge, two dodges 5-6 up, dodge 5-6 down, and become *sixths place bell*.**”

To begin with you may find the longer form best, but in time you’ll certainly find it easier to remember the blocks of work by their names, as explained in Chapter 33.

Whichever way you learn it, though, there are two absolute musts. First, you must always say to yourself, “***Seconds place bell***,” at the beginning. And second, you must always say to yourself, “***and become sixths place bell***,” at the end. That is what cements it in your mind, gives you the boundaries of the work, and points the way ahead.

Here are the other place bells.

> ***Sixths place bell*: Lead and dodge, 3-4 Cambridge places up, and become *thirds place bell*.**
>
> ***Thirds place bell*: Backwork, dodge 3-4 down, and become *fourths place bell*.**
>
> ***Fourths place bell*: Finish 3-4 Cambridge places down, dodge and lead, dodge 5-6 up, and become *fifths place bell*.**
>
> ***Fifths place bell*: Lie behind, double dodge 5-6 down, frontwork, seconds over the treble, and become *seconds place bell*.**

Ringing by Place Bells

Are you still reading? If so, if you’ve got past the last paragraph without saying, “I can’t be bothered with all that,” and turning to the notices page, then you’re definitely a spliced ringer in the making. Without doubt it's a wrench to start learning by place bells, but for spliced ringing it's absolutely essential.

When you next ring a plain course of Cambridge Minor, you must ring it by thinking of the place bells as you go along. You must ring seconds place bell until you get to the end of it, and then you must ring sixths place bell until you get to the end of that, and so on.

Looking Ahead

And that brings us to the end of the first chapter. We haven't got past a plain course of Cambridge Minor yet, so I hope you aren't disappointed. But like all ringing, spliced takes time. In the next chapter we really will be **Putting Methods Together**.

During the period that I was writing regularly for The Ringing World, *Chico Kidd was regularly drawing her ringing cartoons. They were beautifully drawn, with a warm and gentle humour, and they were invariably the first thing I turned to every week. Best of all was when the Editor fitted an appropriate one into the text of one of my articles. This happened quite often, and I'm sure that Chico's drawings added to my readership no end.*

In one of her cartoons, a fraught and perspiring ringer with his tail-end held the wrong way round, is frantically turning over blue lines with his toes while the conductor urbanely calls, "Bob. Beverley."

"Hold on. Hold on," the ringer replies.

If that's how ***you*** *think spliced ringing must be, read on.*

41. Splicing Surprise

Putting Methods Together

For those of you who didn't read the last chapter – and for those who read it but forgot it – I should explain that this series is a starting-from-scratch guide to ringing spliced Surprise. ***Scratch***, in this case, is being able to ring, say, Stedman Doubles or Kent Minor. If you can ring either of those, there is no reason at all why you shouldn't learn to ring spliced Surprise, and this series is designed to help you do it.

Getting the Practice

In the last chapter, I explained that an essential step towards ringing spliced is being able to ring Cambridge Minor by ***place bells***. Quite likely, though, you have little or no opportunity to ring Cambridge Minor by any system. So if your local band – like the great majority of local bands – is not strong enough to ring Cambridge Minor, you'll have to seek your practice elsewhere.

First off, try a neighbouring practice night or a District meeting. If you've done your homework thoroughly, the tower captain or District master will be very happy to ring Cambridge for you if he can. Just explain that that's what you'd like to ring if at all possible. The trouble is, though, that in many areas it *won't* be possible. There may not be a strong enough band present even at a District meeting, and in that case you'll either have to travel further afield still, or arrange a band yourself.

Self Help

Arranging a band yourself is nowhere near as difficult as it might seem. There may be a number of like-minded enthusiastic ringers in your own tower, or there may be a number in surrounding towers. Sound out their willingness for a special practice, then approach the nicest person you know who can call a plain course of Cambridge, and ask him or her to help you all get started. They will almost certainly be extremely pleased to oblige, and in no time at all you'll be off the ground. What's more, you'll have established a nucleus of ringers for progressing to spliced.

If you can't find an experienced Cambridge ringer, then you'll just have to do the calling yourself, or get another of your group to do it. Many top conductors started their conducting careers in exactly that way, so don't worry about your lack of experience. Your enthusiasm will more than make up for it.

Throughout the country there are numerous examples of small groups making enormous progress completely unaided, and some of the most complex ringing has been done by groups who first got together while still very inexperienced indeed. There is no reason at all why you shouldn't be the same.

Learning a Second Method

As regards the next method to learn, there is only one Surprise method which is rung everywhere, and that's Cambridge. London is probably the next most widely rung but, being more complex, it's rung much less frequently. Norwich, Beverley and Surfleet are rung fairly frequently in many areas but not at all in others; and thereafter, Surprise Minor methods are very much a matter of local taste and tradition.

If you are ringing with an established Surprise ringing band, you would do best to learn another method from their standard repertoire. But if you're going along the self-help route, I recommend Beverley because it splices well with Cambridge. When you learn it, you must learn it by its ***place bells*** as you did Cambridge, and when you do, you'll find that thirds place bell in Beverley – which is invariably shortened to ***thirds place bell***, ***Beverley*** – is exactly the same as thirds place bell, Cambridge.

Spend a while practising plain courses of Beverley. Then, armed with your knowledge of two methods, you're ready to splice them together.

Putting the Methods Together

The crucial factor in ringing spliced is that the change of method occurs when the treble leads at backstroke during its lead full. This means that you can only ever change method when you get to the end of a place bell. Each place bell is always rung in its entirety. If you start it, you must finish it.

For example, suppose you have the Two and the conductor calls, "Go Cambridge." Naturally, you begin by ringing seconds place bell, Cambridge. When you get to the end of it you become sixths place bell. If the conductor doesn't change the method, you must carry on and ring sixths place bell, Cambridge. But if he changes the method to Beverley, you must ring sixths place bell, Beverley instead.

At the end of sixths place bell you become thirds place bell. Whichever method is rung then makes no difference to you, because thirds place bell, Cambridge and thirds place bell, Beverley are the same. But at the end of thirds place bell you must ring either fourths place bell, Beverley or fourths place bell, Cambridge according to what method is being rung then. And so on.

How It's Called

The change of method is normally called during the treble's handstroke lead immediately before the backstroke when the new method starts. But there's a wide disparity between different towers and different areas. Sometimes you'll hear it called much earlier, and sometimes you won't hear it called until the backstroke itself. But wherever it's called, you must finish the place bell you are ringing before changing into the new method for the next place bell.

Note well, though, that the method is only called if it's being changed. If there's no change, nothing is said, and you can ring several consecutive place bells in complete silence. This can catch you out if you forget what method you're ringing thirds place bell to, since thirds place bell, Beverley and thirds place bell, Cambridge are the same. You're then in severe difficulty if you start fourths place bell with no change of method. So make sure you always remember what method is being rung.

The Order of the Place Bells

In Cambridge Minor the place bells come in the order 2,6,3,4,5. They come in that order in Beverley Minor as well, and it's a useful thing to remember because if you get lost you can concentrate on getting right at the next lead end. You can watch the treble, and when it leads full you can start the next place bell. If you are well and truly lost, the conductor may tell you, for example, "You're sixths place bell," and even if you can't get yourself right until the next lead end, you should at least be able to then.

Not all methods have the order 2,6,3,4,5, but the most common either have that order or the order 2,3,5,6,4. It's always best to know the orders of the methods you're ringing.

Bobs

You may feel that we've come a long way with no mention of bobs, but if you ring by place bells, bobs will be little problem to you. For example, if you're just finishing fifths place bell, Cambridge, you would normally become seconds place bell. If, however, a bob is called, you must run out, and having run out, you arrive in thirds place and so must ring thirds place bell instead.

The other affected bells can be dealt with similarly. You can either ring each bob by first principles and then work out which place bell you've become, or you can learn – as part of each place bell – which new place bell you will become if a bob is called at the end of it.

More Methods Still

And when all that's clear, all that's left is to learn more methods. But although I say, "all that's left," in reality it will be a long and difficult, though interesting and enjoyable, process. The extra methods I recommend are Surfleet, Norwich and London in that order. I recommend them because they're widely rung, and because they're in Chapters 36 to 38. What's more, they are good grounding for Spliced Surprise Major, which is something you can read about on page 390.

Starting and Stopping

But it's not so much learning the methods that makes ringing spliced Surprise so very difficult, it's remembering each method fast enough when it comes along. It's rather like someone creeping up on you and suddenly bellowing,

"Who's the Chancellor of the Exchequer?" You're certain you know the answer, but panic seems to prevent you thinking clearly. Time and practice help to overcome this, but in the meanwhile it can be very helpful to pause between leads. The system works likes this.

Suppose you're ringing the three lead touch with no bobs in, ***London***, ***Cambridge***, ***Norwich***. The conductor starts by calling, "Go London," in the usual way. Then, at the end of the first lead, just before the treble leads at backstroke, he calls, "Pause," and the band do exactly that, pausing in their lead end positions and ringing 142635 over and over again as though they were ringing call changes.

During this pause the conductor announces that the next method will be Cambridge. When the band have all prepared themselves for the new method, he calls, "Carry on, Cambridge," at a handstroke, and everyone sets off again into the touch at the next handstroke. At the end of that lead he again calls, "Pause," announces that Norwich will follow, calls, "Carry on, Norwich," and so on.

This is certainly an unorthodox procedure, but for some it will be an essential interim step to normal spliced. Pausing between leads can also be a very good way of practising the most difficult methods, like London.

A Last Word

And when you've made it. When you're one of those smooth and elegant ringers who so impressed the earlier me in Chapter 40. Spare a thought for those who are sitting in awe on the bench behind you. It's probably only lack of opportunity that prevents them from ringing beside you. And *that* is something you might just be able to do something about.

Although this isn't really a conducting book, I thought you'd like a few spliced touches to get you going. The simplest is to ring a plain course of Cambridge Minor and substitute in some leads of Beverley and/or Surfleet. Cambridge, Beverley, Cambridge, Surfleet, Cambridge, for example. Fortunately, you can put them in wherever you like, and it will still come round as normal. You can do the same with a touch of Cambridge too, but although it will come round alright, it may be false.

Another possibility is the London, Cambridge, Norwich that I just mentioned – and London, Cambridge, Beverley, Surfleet, is a good one too. For that matter, you can also ring Norwich, Cambridge, Beverley, Surfleet. None of these have any bobs in, but once you can manage them, you'll be pretty much an expert, and you can probably work out some others for yourself. Alternatively, you can find another couple of people and make a start on **Surprise Major**.

42. Cambridge Major

Somehow, before you've had a go at it, Cambridge Major seems like ***playing with the big boys***. It's as though it requires a quantum leap of ability that normal progress cannot match. But, I guarantee that it really isn't like that. If you can ring Cambridge Minor, and Kent or Plain Bob Major, Cambridge Major is a far smaller step than many you've already taken. So cast aside your preconceptions and give it a go.

The *Minor* Similarities

But before you start learning it, take a glance at the blue line on the next page and get a general idea of it. You'll notice a number of similarities with Minor.

> ***Cambridge places*** occur in 5-6 as well as in 3-4, but they're ***identical*** to Cambridge places in Minor.
>
> The ***frontwork*** is ***identical*** to the frontwork in Minor.
>
> The ***backwork*** is ***identical*** to the backwork in Minor, ***except*** that there is an extra dodge in 5-6 up on the way up to it, and an extra dodge in 5-6 down on the way down from it. In Major, most people think of those 5-6 dodges as being ***part*** of the backwork.

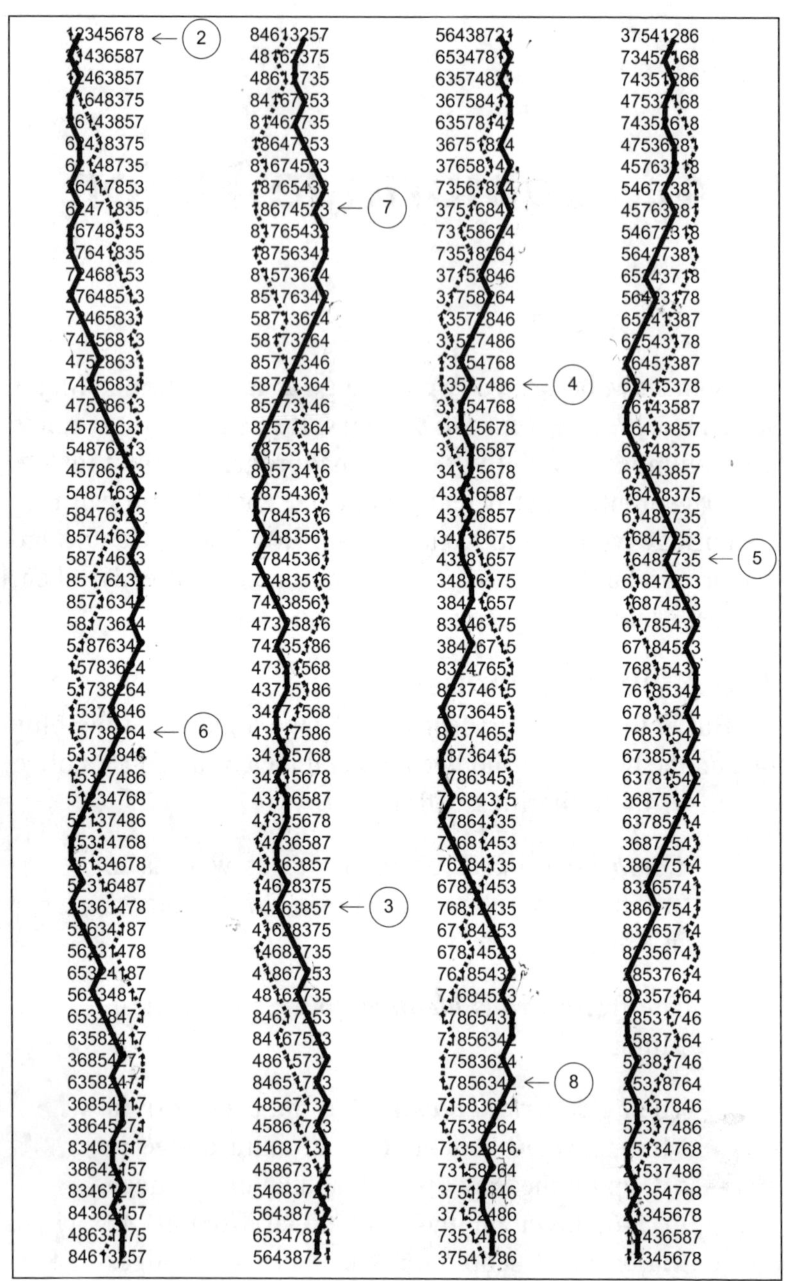

Cambridge Surprise Major

The differences are very few. Just a handful of extra dodges and a little extra hunting to join together the bits you already know. ***But*** it's the little extras that cause most people most trouble.

The Order of the Work

Now for the order of the work starting on the Two. Since it's the odd dodges that are most difficult, I'm putting them in soft italic type to make them stand out.

Second half of the frontwork
dodge 3-4
Two and One on the back
dodge 5-6
Lead and dodge
dodge 3-4
5-6 Cambridge places up
treble bob on the back
treble bob on the front
3-4 Cambridge places up
Backwork

and then reverse.

Learning the Odd Dodges

If you go through that again but leave out the odd dodges and the 5-6 places, you'll find that you have the order of the work for Cambridge Minor. So, if you have trouble remembering where the odd dodges come, the following tip may help.

In the first half of the method on the way ***to*** the backwork, ***after*** each piece of Cambridge Minor work, you do an odd dodge in the ***next*** dodging position. And ***between*** your 5-6 places and your 3-4 places, you treble bob on the back and treble bob on the front.

Similarly, in the second half of the method on the way ***from*** the backwork, ***before*** each piece of Cambridge Minor work, you do an odd dodge in the ***previous*** dodging position. And ***between*** your 3-4 places and your 5-6 places, you treble bob on the front and treble bob on the back.

A Half Course

Most times that you ring Cambridge Major, you'll probably only ring ***half a course***. That's because a plain course goes on too long to be fitted in to most practices. When the treble dodges 1-2 up after the fourth lead end, the conductor calls, "***Make this all at the snap***," or "***Make this all***," and the Three leaps a position to end up in rounds, like this.

13254768
13527486
31254768 ← "Make this all at the snap"
12345678

The snap is the expression used for the treble's dodge in 1-2 up. But another way to bring the bells round after four leads, is for the conductor to call, "***Plain hunt***," or "***Hunt through the lead end***," when the treble is in 1-2 *down*. Then, instead of dodging at the lead end, the bells run round like this.

13572846
31527486 ← "Plain hunt"
13254768
12345678

The Ropesight

But even though learning Cambridge Major is unlikely to be too much of a problem to you, what *will* be difficult will be the ropesight. Unlike in the easier Major methods, the additional bells come at you from unexpected directions. So,

> ***Keep an open mind about who you might be ringing over,***

And,

> ***Learn where you should be dodging with and/or passing the treble.***

In addition, you'll probably find that by far the most difficult part of ringing Cambridge Major is the 5-6 places. You're a long way from the front, still not on the back, and the other bells keep moving about. So if *you* have a problem,

First, keep cool and don't let your rhythm desert you. If you can stay in approximately the right place, you're half-way there.

Second, make sure you take the treble correctly in the middle of the places. This helps you get the second half right. Learn also, where you ring over the treble in *fifths* place.

Third, always count your place, even when you've lost the other bells completely. You'll then be able to lie or lead at the right moment.

And last, keep a look out for people nodding and winking at you, but *don't* dodge when you shouldn't, even if someone wants to dodge with *you*.

Course Bells and After Bells

And if you still have trouble, course bells and after bells will help your ropesight immeasurably. A lot of Cambridge Major ringers are very keen on them. They remember that,

> You ***always*** dodge ***7-8 up*** with your ***course bell*** and ***7-8 down*** with your ***after bell*** **except** when you are dodging with the treble.

When you are making the *first* set of contiguous places in your *places down*, your ***after bell*** passes through.

When you are making the *second* set of contiguous places in your *places up* your ***course bell*** passes through.

And the *last* dodge of your *5-6 places down* is with your ***course bell***, whilst the *first* dodge of your *5-6 places up* is with your ***after bell***.

But if you're not keen on course and after bells, you need take no notice of this whatsoever.

Two More Tips

And if you still have trouble, try two more tips. First, don't forget that Cambridge places – and particularly Cambridge places down – seem to go on for a very long time. Don't try to go down to the front too early.

And second, for preference, start on the Five. That will give you a very long time before you do any places, and a lot of it will be spent on the front. Suddenly, Cambridge will all seem very much easier.

The Bobs

And now for the bobs. Most Cambridge Major ringers never ring a bob from one year's end to the next because they only ever ring plain courses and half courses. But even if you never envisage ringing one, you might just as well know what to do. They won't take you long to learn, and what you learn for Cambridge will apply to a great many other Surprise methods as well.

In fact, the bob is just like the Cambridge Minor bob that we looked at on page 304. ***Don't***, though, just learn that you

run in, ***run out*** and ***make the bob***. It's essential that you're absolutely certain what to do next. In 5-6 and 7-8 you are unaffected, but as regards the other positions,

> If you're dodging 1-2 up with the treble in the middle of the ***frontwork***, you ***run out*** and do ***the whole of the backwork***, including the 5-6 dodge but not including the 3-4 dodge.
>
> If you're just finishing the ***backwork***, you ***run in*** and do ***the second half of the frontwork***.
>
> And if you're doing ***3-4 places up***, you ***miss off*** the last dodge, ***make fourths*** instead and do ***3-4 places down*** omitting the first dodge.

Singles

And since, nowadays, singles in Surprise Major are not uncommon, you might just as well learn those too, particularly as some conductors won't warn you about them in advance. They are exactly the same as Cambridge Minor singles and you can read about them on page 306.

A Tip for Touches

And, if you haven't rung many touches of Surprise, here's yet another tip. Be prepared for long periods of being unaffected. Don't force yourself to do something different at a bob when it doesn't affect you, but be prepared to be affected when the time comes.

Mind you, there's no need to rush into touches. Take four or five years just ringing half courses if you want to. After all, that's an achievement in itself. Certainly, when you've rung four leads of Cambridge Major at a District meeting, you can sit down to tea afterwards with that comfortable and satisfying feeling of being well pleased with yourself.

Shortly after I wrote the last chapter as one of a number of hand-outs for a ringing course, I visited a District practice in the Home Counties. The practice ended with a touch of Surprise Major, and the conductor got out his filofax *and looked up a composition with half lead singles. Shortly after the first one, it fired out.*

I wondered afterwards whether half lead singles, like filofaxes, were the coming thing, or whether they were simply a local initiative. I'm still not sure, but that was some years ago now and I haven't heard one called at a District practice since. So until you know that you're definitely going to ring half lead calls, I wouldn't bother with them. Much better, instead, to go straight on and learn the plain course of **Yorkshire**.

43. Yorkshire, etc.

Sometime after the Second World War, the very expert bands then ringing peals of spliced Surprise Major, started talking about ***the Standard Eight***. The expression caught on. The standard eight were the eight Surprise Major methods, Cambridge, Yorkshire, Superlative, Lincolnshire, Rutland, Pudsey, Bristol and London, and because they were ***called*** the standard eight, they ***became*** the standard eight. They are as standard now as they were then, and although there are literally thousands of Surprise Major methods, apart from the standard eight, very few are rung regularly anywhere.

Not all of the standard eight, though, are equally popular. Cambridge is the most popular, and Yorkshire comes second. Bristol and London are widely rung, but since they're very difficult, they're not rung anything like as frequently. Superlative, Lincolnshire and Rutland are all rung regularly somewhere, whilst Pudsey is the method that even the most experienced ringers go wrong in because they ring it so infrequently. We're starting with Yorkshire.

Yorkshire

Yorkshire is by far and away the second most popular Surprise Major method, and once you've learnt it, it's easier to ring than Cambridge because the ropesight is easier. It's also good grounding for Yorkshire Royal which is, in turn, easier to ring than Cambridge Royal.

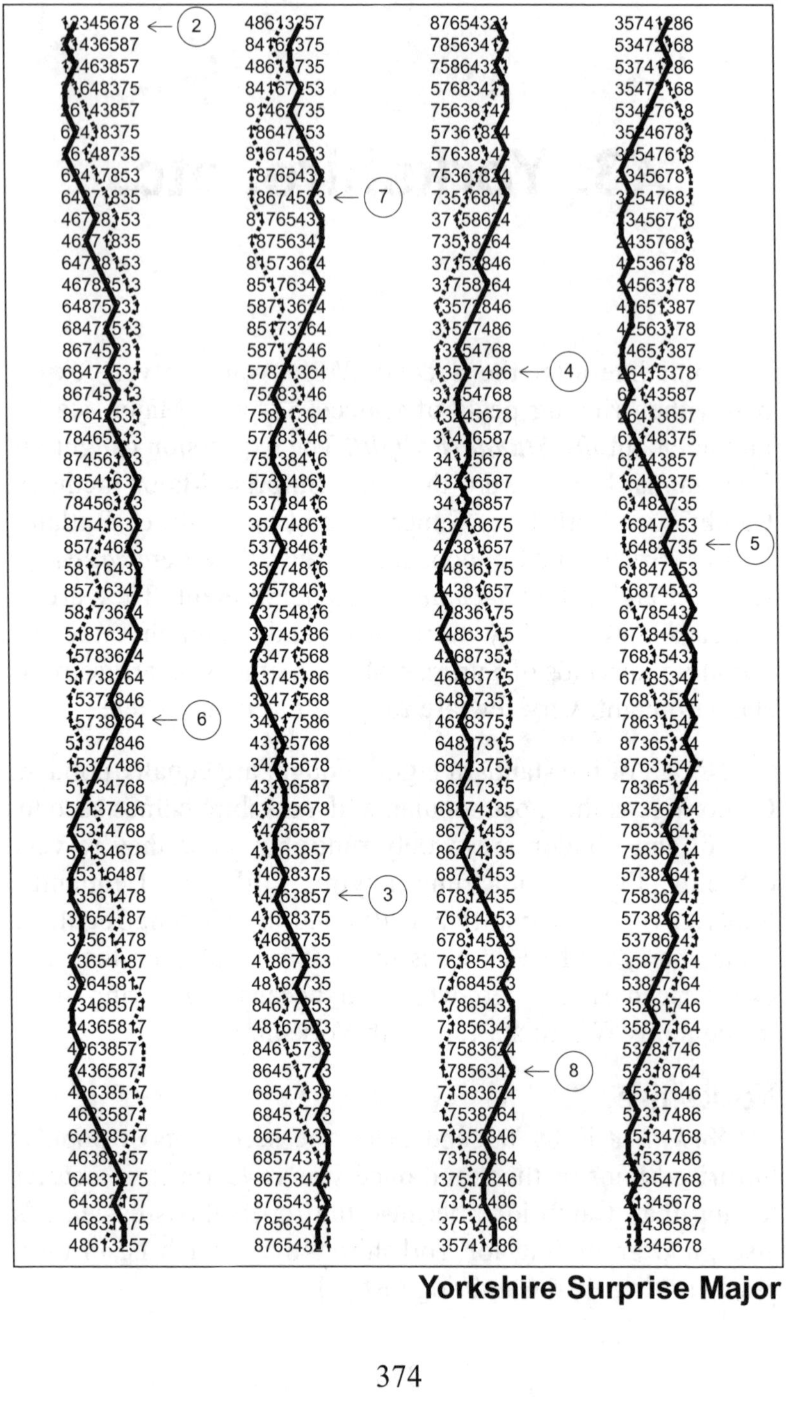

12345678 ← (2)
21436587
12463857
21648375
26143857
62418375
26148735
62417853
64271835
46728153
46271835
64728153
46782513
64875231
68472513
86745231
68472531
86745213
87642531
78465213
87456123
78541632
78456123
87541632
85714623
58176432
85716342
58173624
51876342
15783624
51738264
15372846
15738264 ← (6)
51372846
15327486
51234768
52137486
25314768
52134678
25316487
23561478
32654187
32561478
23654187
32645817
23468571
24365817
42638571
24365871
42638517
46235871
64328517
46382157
64831275
64382157
46831275
48613257

48613257
84162375
48612735
84167253
81462735
18647253
81674523
18765432
18674523 ← (7)
81765432
18756342
81573624
85176342
58713624
85173264
58712346
57821364
75283146
75821364
57283146
75238416
57324861
53728416
35274861
53728461
35274816
32578461
23754816
32745186
23471568
23745186
32471568
34217586
43125768
34215678
43126587
41325678
14236587
41263857
14628375
14263857 ← (3)
41628375
14682735
41867253
48162735
84617253
48167523
84615732
86451723
68547132
68451723
86547132
68574312
86753421
87654312
78563421
87654321

87654321
78563412
75864321
57683412
75638142
57361824
57638142
75361824
73516842
37158624
73518264
37152846
31758264
13572846
31527486
13254768
13527486 ← (4)
31254768
13245678
31426587
34125678
43216587
34126857
43218675
42381657
24836175
24381657
42836175
24863715
42687351
46283715
64827351
46283751
64823715
68427351
86247315
68274135
86721453
86274135
68721453
67812435
76184253
67814523
76185432
71684523
17865432
71856342
17583624
17856342 ← (8)
71583624
17538264
71352846
73158264
37512846
73152486
37514268
35741286

35741286
53472168
53741286
35472168
53427618
35246781
32547618
23456781
32547681
23456718
24357681
42536718
24563178
42651387
42563178
24651387
26415378
62143587
26413857
62148375
61243857
16428375
61482735
16847253
16482735 ← (5)
61847253
16874523
61785432
67184523
76815432
67185342
76813524
78631542
87365124
87631542
78365124
87356214
78532641
75836214
57382641
75836241
57382614
53786241
35872614
53827164
35281746
35827164
53281746
52318764
25137846
52317486
25134768
21537486
12354768
21345678
12436587
12345678

Yorkshire Surprise Major

The only really new bits in Yorkshire are ***Yorkshire places***. These are *half* Cambridge places, so 3-4 Yorkshire places up are ***dodge 3-4 up, fourths, thirds, dodge 3-4 up***.

Some people call them ***short places*** and we'll come across them in other methods as well. Cambridge places are then called ***long places***.

Yorkshire is ***Cambridge above the treble***, and I explained what this means on page 316. The two main results are that the backwork is identical to Cambridge, and so are the bobs and singles. It might also help you if you get lost near the back.

Essentially, Yorkshire is Cambridge chopped up and rearranged in a different order, but although you get the chance to ring both halves of the Cambridge frontwork, you have to do them separately and away from the lead end. A further tip is that you ***never*** dodge 3-4 ***before*** or ***after*** the ***Cambridge frontwork*** but you ***always*** dodge 3-4 ***otherwise***.

And if you're a *course bell* and *after bell* person, this tip is gold-dust.

> You ***never*** dodge in 3-4 or 5-6 with your course bell or after bell, but
>
> You ***always*** dodge in 3-4 and 5-6 otherwise.

Superlative

Superlative is the classic Surprise Major method par excellence. It is the earliest to have been invented, and the most pleasant to listen to; and even today, it is so popular in a few places that it's rung more often than Yorkshire. What's more, it's a ***double*** method, so as explained on page 92, if you're very brainy, you need only learn a quarter of the blue line. It is ***the*** method if you can find a band to ring it with.

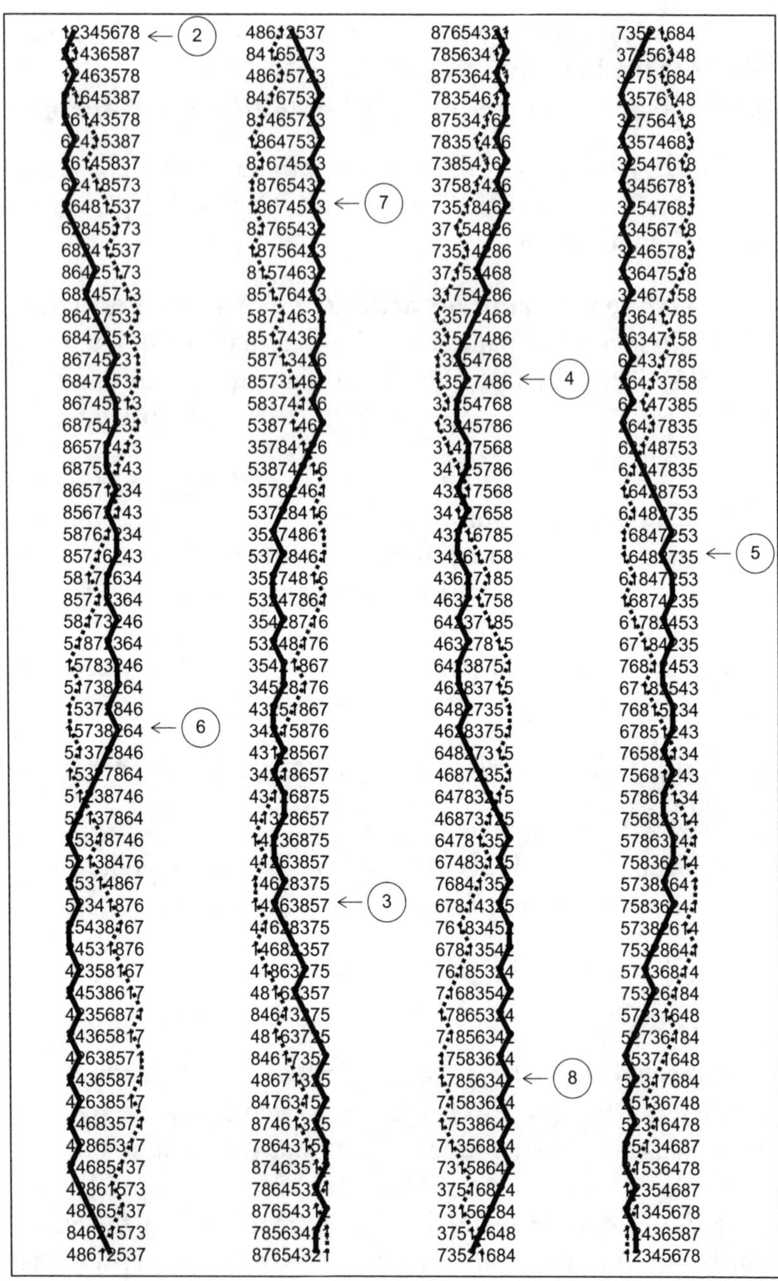

Superlative Surprise Major

As you can see, all the places in Superlative are Cambridge places ***except*** that they have an extra place and dodge – or dodge and place – on one end of them. That's what makes Superlative difficult. It is all too easy to try and ring the place and dodge at the wrong end of the places. And unlike Cambridge and Yorkshire, after each batch of Superlative places, you always end up going back the way you came. Worse still, many people find it overwhelmingly difficult to stop making places once they've started.

The other problems with Superlative are counting up to five for the long dodges, and making sixths at the start of fifths place bell. The good thing, though, is that the bobs and singles are the same as Cambridge.

Lincolnshire

Lincolnshire is a method which is rung from time to time in places where Surprise Major is rung regularly. Its great merit is that it's fairly easy to learn after Cambridge, and it's popular for that reason. It's a *we-haven't-rung-that-for-a-while-so-let's-ring-it-now* sort of method.

Take note that it is Cambridge above the treble and has Cambridge bobs and singles. It also has a backwork identical to Cambridge, and both Cambridge and Yorkshire places. It also has a kind of ***offset*** Cambridge frontwork.

In Chapter 40 we looked in detail at ringing Surprise Minor by place bells, and place bells are even more useful when ringing Surprise Major. They are particularly good for Lincolnshire because it divides neatly at the lead ends, and you already know great chunks of it.

Thirds place bell is identical to thirds place bell, Cambridge, and eighths place bell is ***almost*** identical to eighths place bell, Cambridge. The difference is that you lead

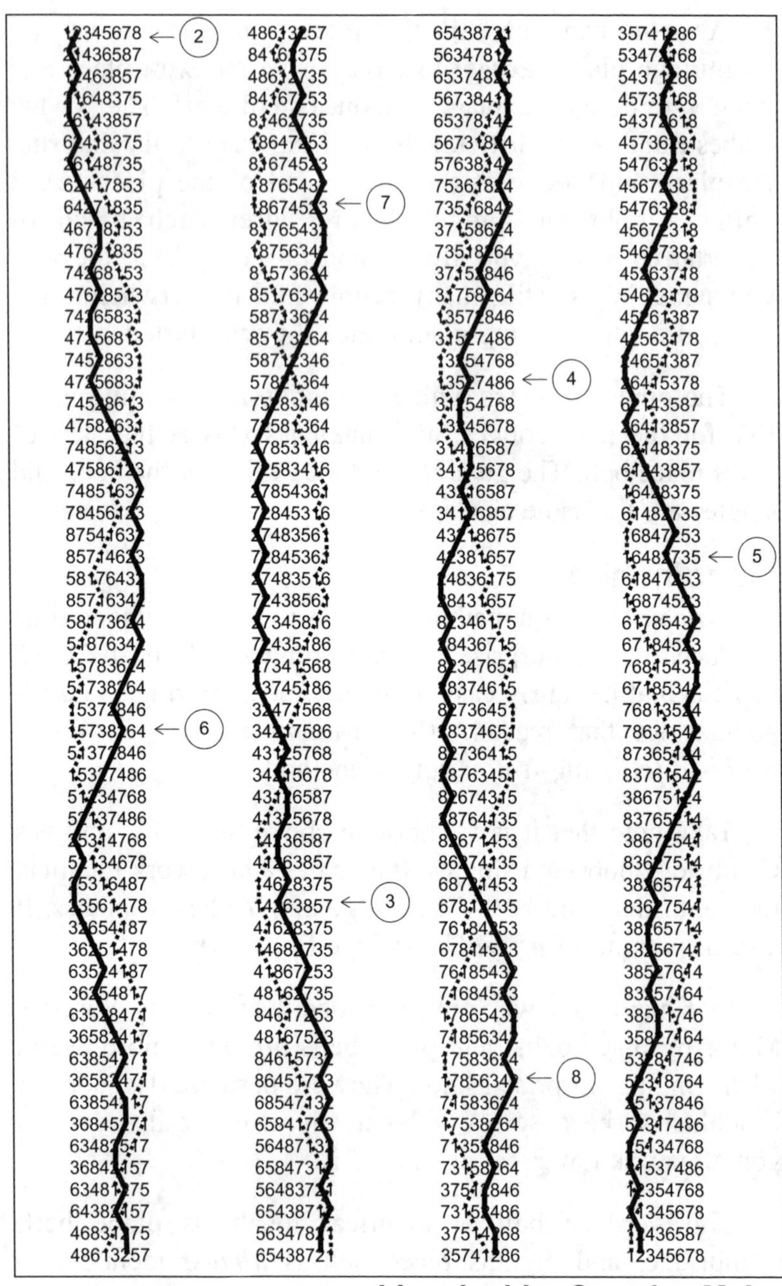

Lincolnshire Surprise Major

and dodge instead of dodge and lead. Sixths place bell is eighths place bell backwards.

Seconds place bell is identical to seconds place bell, Cambridge ***except*** that you offset your frontwork by doing treble bob on the front, and then doing ***fourths***, ***dodge***, ***thirds***, ***dodge***. Fifths place bell is seconds place bell backwards.

So the only really new learning is sevenths place bell and fourths place bell, which are the reverses of each other. Beware, though, of the five dodges, and count them exceedingly carefully. Even if *you* don't make a mistake, the person dodging with you probably will. Beware also of doing lead and five dodges when you should be doing five dodges and lead.

In addition, seconds place bell and fifths place bell can also catch you out. Make sure you do fourths nearest to the treble bob rather than putting in a 3-4 dodge there. And lastly, remember that the 5-6 places are always ***Cambridge*** places but the 3-4 places are always ***Yorkshire*** places.

Rutland

As you'll see when you turn the page, the place bells in ***Rutland*** come in a different order to the other methods we've looked at, so many bands find it useful in spliced. And since it gets rung in spliced, it also gets rung by itself as well, and in some areas it's very popular.

Once again, it's Cambridge above the treble – with Cambridge bobs and singles – and it has Yorkshire places in both 5-6 and 3-4. But because it's so different *below* the treble, it *feels* very different from the rest. It doesn't have Cambridge backwork, Cambridge frontwork or Cambridge places, and you need to learn it as something completely new.

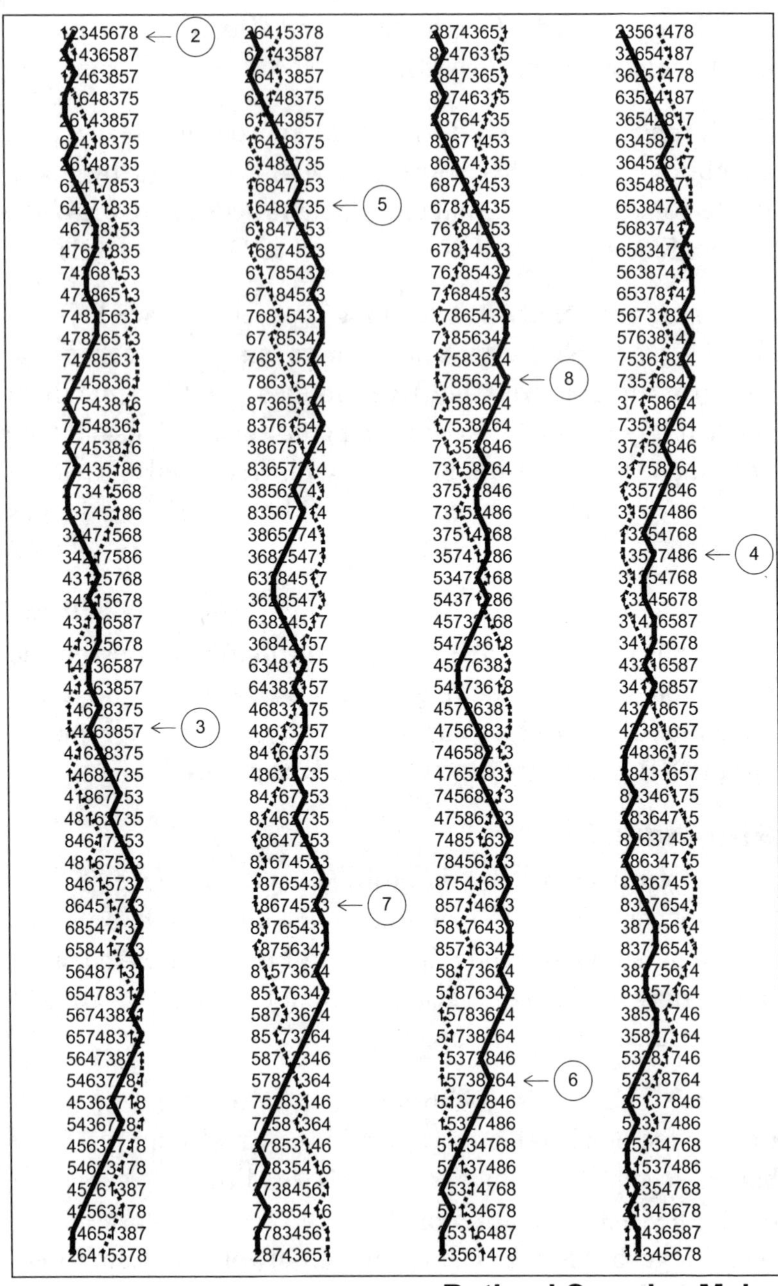

Rutland Surprise Major

Even with all your experience of Cambridge, Yorkshire, and the like, there's still a rag-bag of details to think about. In particular, ***always*** dodge in 5-6 ***except*** when you're sevenths place bell; ***beware*** of the strong but fatal temptation to make sevenths under the treble when you're thirds place bell; and when you're making your ***fourths***, ***thirds***, ***fourths***, remember that one lot of fourths is over the ***same*** bell and one lot isn't.

And lastly, you can't ring half-courses of Rutland like you can the previous four. So if you're going to catch hold, be prepared to go the whole way.

Pudsey

Pudsey is the rogue method of the ***standard eight***. Few ringers know it properly, most people go wrong in it, and many Surprise ringers hate it. But it's rung regularly in spliced, and it's also rung on its own from time to time. So if you get the opportunity, you might as well have a go at it.

Pudsey is Cambridge ***below*** the treble, but that isn't likely to help you very much. It does have Yorkshire places – but in rather odd positions – and thirds place bell is hazardously similar, but distinctly different, to thirds place bell, Cambridge.

Pudsey is full of elephant pits to entrap the unwary. Rather than remember the Do's, it's easier to remember the Don'ts.

> ***Don't*** start each place bell like Cambridge while wondering what to do next.
>
> ***Don't*** miss the 3-4 dodge at the start of thirds place bell.
>
> ***Don't*** miss the fifths at the start of sixths place bell.

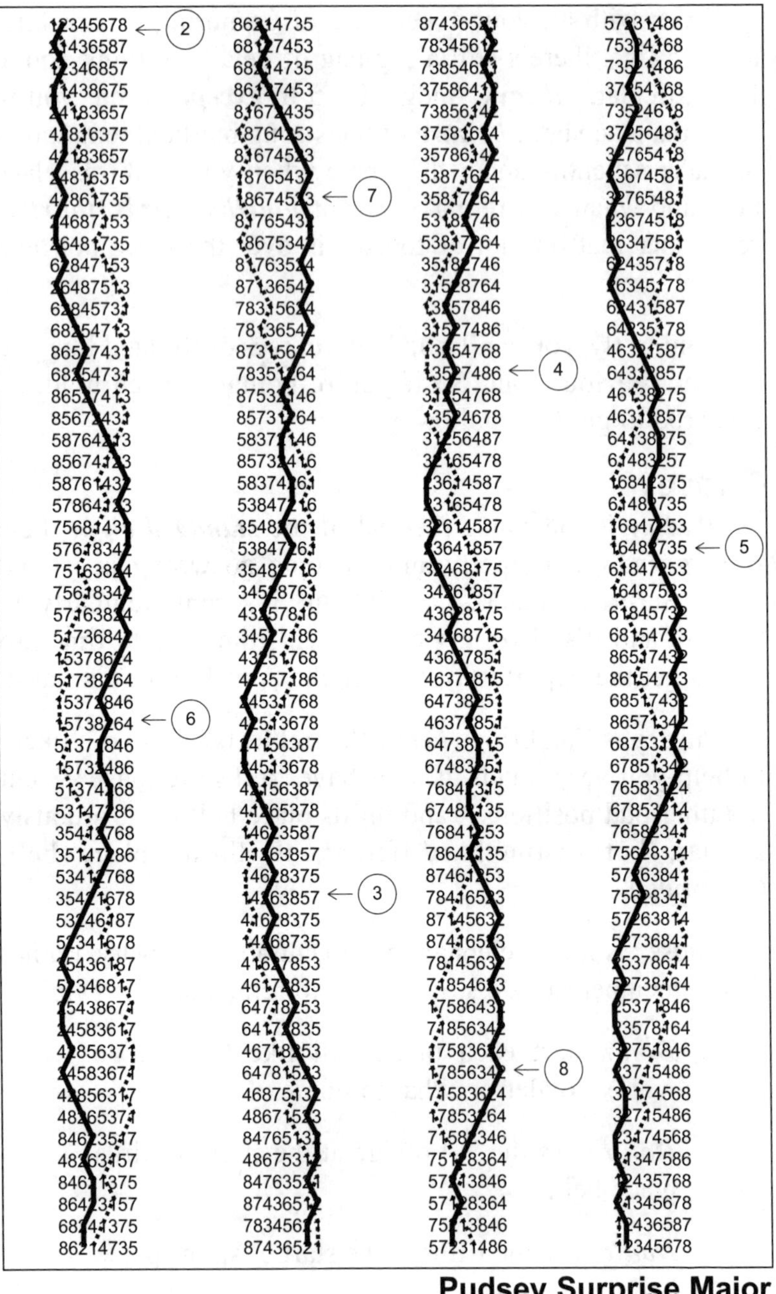

12345678 ← 2	86214735	87436521	57231486
21436587	68127453	78345612	75324168
12346857	68214735	73854621	73521486
21438675	86127453	37586412	37254168
24183657	81672435	73856142	73524618
42816375	18764253	37581624	37256481
42183657	81674523	35786142	32765418
24816375	18765432	53871624	23674581
42861735	18674523 ← 7	35817264	32765481
24687153	81765432	53182746	23674518
26481735	18675342	53817264	26347581
62847153	81763524	35182746	62435718
26487513	87136542	31528764	26345178
62845731	78315624	13257846	62431587
68254713	78136542	31527486	64235178
86527431	87315624	13254768	46321587
68254731	78351264	13527486 ← 4	64312857
86527413	87532146	31254768	46138275
85672431	85731264	13524678	46312857
58764213	58372146	31256487	64138275
85674123	85732416	32165478	61483257
58761432	58374261	23614587	16842375
57864123	53847216	23165478	61482735
75681432	35482761	32614587	16847253
57618342	53847261	23641857	16482735 ← 5
75163824	35482716	32468175	61847253
75618342	34528761	34261857	16487523
57163824	43257816	43628175	61845732
51736842	34527186	34268715	68154723
15378624	43251768	43627851	86517432
51738264	42357186	46372815	86154723
15372846	24531768	64738251	68517432
15738264 ← 6	42513678	46372851	86571342
51372846	24156387	64738215	68753124
15732486	24513678	67483251	67851342
51374268	42156387	76842315	76583124
53147286	41265378	67482135	67853214
35412768	14623587	76841253	76582341
35147286	41263857	78642135	75628314
53412768	14628375	87461253	57263841
35421678	14263857 ← 3	78416523	75628341
53246187	41628375	87145632	57263814
52341678	14268735	87416523	52736841
25436187	41627853	78145632	25378614
52346817	46172835	71854623	52738164
25438671	64718253	17586432	25371846
24583617	64172835	71856342	23578164
42856371	46718253	17583624	32751846
24583671	64781523	17856342 ← 8	23715486
42856317	46875132	71583624	32174568
48265371	48671523	17853264	32715486
84623517	84765132	71582346	23174568
48263157	48675312	75128364	21347586
84621375	84763521	57213846	12435768
86423157	87436512	57128364	21345678
68241375	78345621	75213846	12436587
86214735	87436521	57231486	12345678

Pudsey Surprise Major

Don't do 5-6 places down when you're eighths place bell.

Don't do 3-4 places down when you're fourths place bell.

Don't trust to luck if you've forgotten the method. Always have a quick burst of revision before you ring it.

And lastly, even the bobs and singles can catch you out. You run in, run out and make the bob as normal, but if you ***run out*** at a bob – or you ***make the bob*** – you must ***dodge 3-4*** immediately afterwards.

Surprisingly, since it's rung so infrequently, I get a lot of requests for help with Pudsey. Many people apparently feel that if they can't ring it properly they aren't really **complete** *ringers. On the other hand, not being able to ring Pudsey is, in some circles, almost a mark of achievement. If you say brusquely and crossly, "**I can't ring Pudsey**," many people will assume you can ring everything else, which is a very useful way to impress if you're a Bob Doubles ringer. Unfortunately, though, it's not the quite same when you have to admit that you can't ring* **Bristol and London**.

44. Bristol and London

Surprise Major methods fall into three groups. The difficult, the extremely difficult, and the almost impossibly difficult. The six in the last two chapters fall in the first category, and two methods which are given an occasional airing in some areas – ***Glasgow*** and ***Belfast*** – fall in the third. ***Bristol*** and ***London*** fall in the second.

Bristol

Bristol, like Superlative, is a ***classic*** method. One of the oldest of the Surprise Major, it is extremely musical and a real pleasure to ring. And although backward, it is nowhere near as difficult as it looks. It bears no resemblance to any of the methods we've looked at so far, but, like Superlative, it is a ***double*** method, and many people rely on that when ringing it.

Most of Bristol is new, but only some of the new bits have their own names. The Stedman whole turns are simply called ***stedman*** no matter where they occur, so *fourths, point thirds, fourths* is called ***stedman fourths***, and *fifths, point sixths, fifths* is called ***stedman fifths***. The fish tails are not normally called fish tails at all but are referred to by their position. So the fish tail on the back is called ***eight-seven-eight***, and the one on the front is called ***one-two-one***. Sometimes they're also known as ***points***. ***Single*** point blows, though, for reasons

12345678 ← 2	24618735	87654321	53781642
21436587	42168375	78563412	57386124
12346857	24613857	75864321	75831642
21438675	42163587	57683412	78536124
24136857	41265378	75863142	87356214
42316587	14623587	78561324	78532641
24135678	41263857	87653142	75836214
42315768	14628375	86751324	57382641
24351786	16482735 ← 5	68715342	53728461
23457168	61847253	86175432	35274816
32541786	16487523	68714523	32578461
35247168	61845732	86174253	23754816
53427618	68147523	81672435	32574186
35246781	86417253	18764253	35271468
32547618	68142735	81674523	53724186
23456781	86412375	18765432	57321468
24365871	68421357	17856342 ← 8	75312486
42638517	64823175	71583624	57132846
46235871	46281357	17853264	75318264
64328517	42683175	71582346	57138624
46238157	24863715	75183264	51736842
42631875	42687351	57813624	15378624
24368157	46283715	75186342	51738264
23461875	64827351	57816432	15372846
32416857	68472531	75861423	13527486 ← 4
23146587	86745213	78564132	31254768
32415678	87642531	87651423	13524678
23145768	78465213	86754132	31256487
21347586	87645123	68574312	32154678
12435768	86741532	86753421	23514768
21345678	68475123	87654312	32157486
12436587	64871532	78563421	23517846
14263857 ← 3	46817523	75836243	32571864
41628375	64187253	57382614	35278146
14268735	46812735	53786241	53721864
41627853	64182375	35872614	57328146
46128735	61483257	53782164	75238416
64218375	16842375	57381246	57324861
46123857	61482735	75832164	53728416
64213587	16847253	78531246	35274861
46231578	18674523 ← 7	87513264	32547681
42635187	81765432	78153624	23456718
24361578	18675342	87516342	24357681
23465187	81763524	78156432	42536718
32645817	87165342	71854623	24356178
23468571	78615432	17586432	23451687
24365817	87164523	71856342	32546178
42638571	78614253	17583624	35241687
46283751	87641235	15738264 ← 6	53214678
64827315	86742153	51372846	35124768
68423751	68471235	15732486	53217486
86247315	64872153	51374268	35127846
68427135	46782513	53172486	31528764
64821753	64875231	35718246	13257846
46287135	68472513	53178264	31527486
42681753	86745231	35718624	13254768
24618735	87654321	53781642	12345678

Bristol Surprise Major

lost in the depths of time are often known as ***spikes*** – ***spike lead*** or ***spike fifths***, for example.

The jagged bit that's the first part of fifths place bell is sometimes called ***lightning work***, and you can see that it really does look like a piece of lightning. The reverse, though, is also known as ***lightning*** and not ***reverse lightning***. Bristol is like that. Due to its long history there is no standard terminology, and you'll often find people using different terms interchangeably.

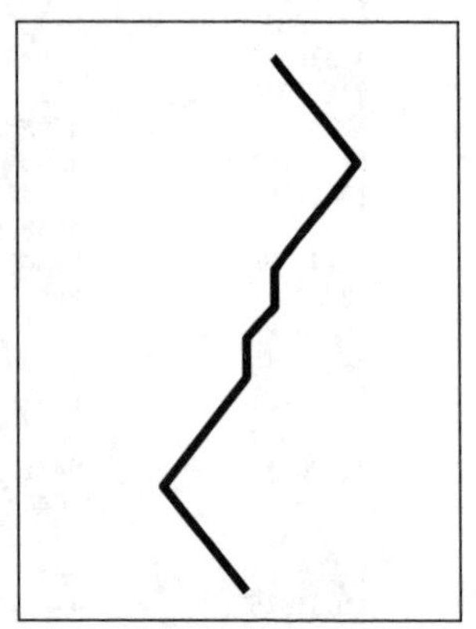

Lightning Work

There is only one way to learn Bristol, and that's a bit at a time. Take particular note that seconds, thirds, and fourths place bells never get above fourths place, whilst sevenths and eighths place bells never get below fifths place. Learn also which places are made *right* and which are made *wrong*, and get a general idea of where the work on the back is the upside down of what you know better on the front.

Learning where you pass the treble, helps too. And if you're a course bell person, you'll wish to know that you ***never*** meet anyone on the front ***or*** back that isn't your course bell, your after bell or the treble. And in addition, ***whenever*** you do stedman or a spike, it's your course bell or after bell that's with you.

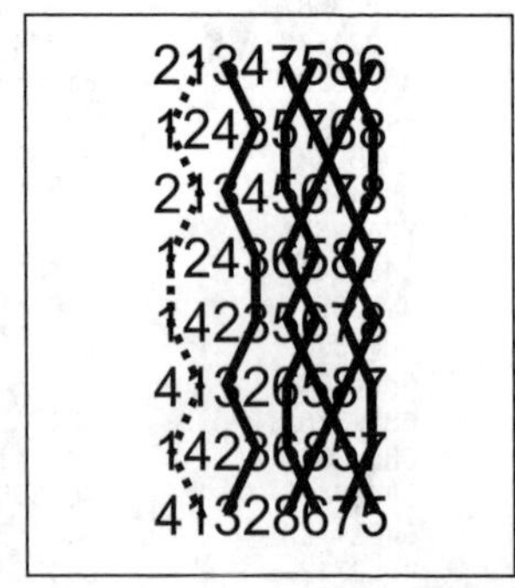

The Bob

Bobs – and there are no singles – are rather like Kent

bobs, so by far and away the most popular touch is ***three leads*** with a bob every lead. ***Three leads of Bristol***, like ***three leads of Kent***, is rung many times more often than all the plain courses and other touches put together. It's also the best possible way to ease yourself gently into the method as you only have to learn a bit at a time.

And lastly, Bristol is one of those methods which some people ring by a mnemonic. I don't recommend it myself, but if someone says to you, "**dosspl, lpssod**," you'll know – more or less – what they're talking about.

London

London is the absolute zenith of the standard Surprise Major repertoire. Like climbing Mount Everest, you learn London because it's there. When you can ring it, you'll have nothing left to conquer but the rarefied heights of the very occasionally rung, super-complex methods.

London scarcely seems to have a structure, and that's what makes it difficult. It's not double, it's nothing like the rest of the standard eight, and it's not much like London Minor either. Turn forward and take a glance at the horrendous complexity of it, and then read on.

Although it's not much like London Minor, it does have bits in common. There are fish tails, London frontwork, stedman whole turns, long London and London places. But despite these familiar aspects, there are very few ringers who *don't* ring London Major by place bells, and you'd do best not to join them.

Oddly, though, learning London is less work than learning Bristol because each place bell has a limited number of things going on in it. But you need to learn it very thoroughly indeed because it's so difficult to ring. Pay

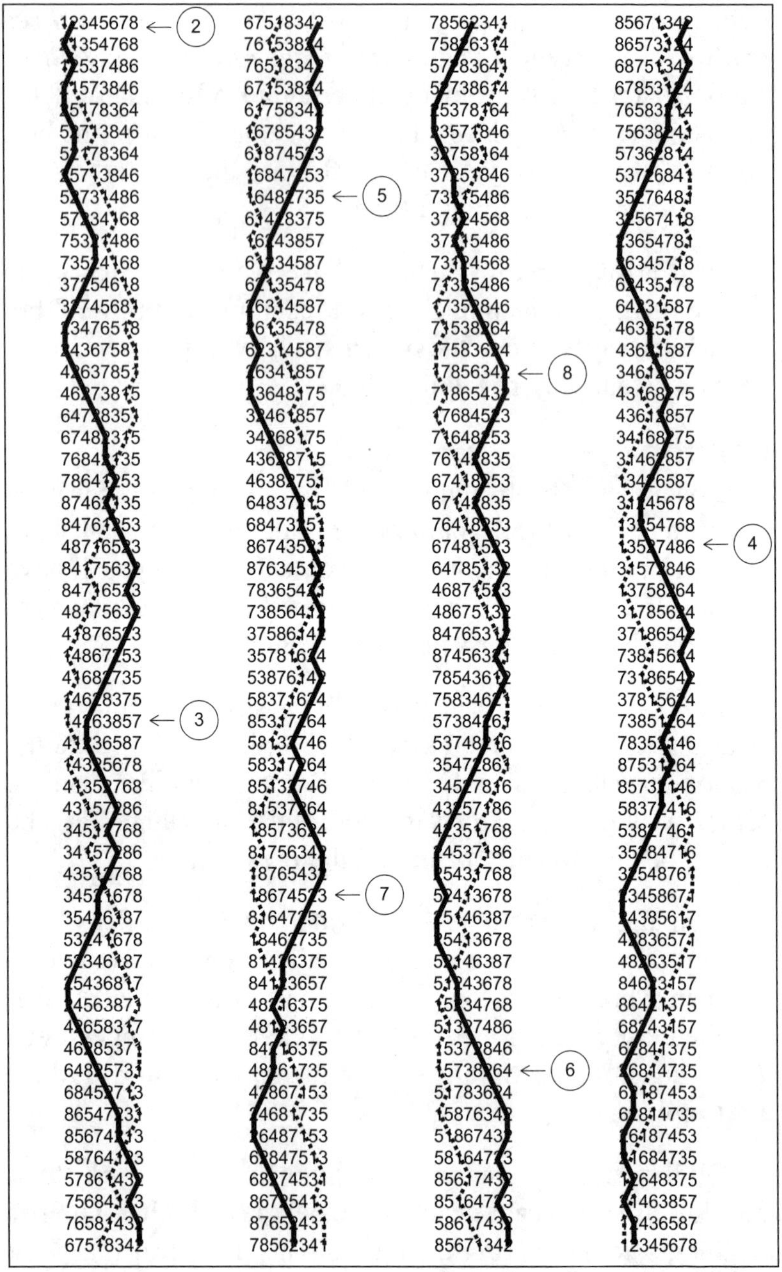

12345678 ← 2	67518342	78562341	85671342
21354768	76153824	75826314	86573124
12537486	76513842	57283641	68751342
21573846	67158324	52738614	67853124
25178364	61758342	25378164	76583214
52713846	16785432	23571846	75638241
52178364	61874523	32758164	57362814
25713846	16847253	37251846	53726841
52731486	16482735 ← 5	73215486	35276481
57234168	61428375	37124568	32567418
75321486	16243857	37215486	23654781
73524168	61234587	73124568	26345718
37254618	62135478	71325486	62435178
32745681	26314587	17352846	64231587
23476518	26135478	71538264	46325178
24367581	62314587	17583624	43621587
42637851	26341857	17856342 ← 8	34612857
46273815	23648175	71865432	43168275
64728351	32461857	17684523	43612857
67482315	34268175	71648253	34168275
76842135	43628715	76142835	31462857
78641253	46382751	67418253	13426587
87462135	64837215	67142835	31245678
84761253	68473251	76418253	13254768
48716523	86743521	67481523	13527486 ← 4
84175632	87634512	64785132	31572846
84716523	78365421	46871523	13758264
48175632	73856412	48675132	31785624
41876523	37586142	84765312	37186542
14867253	35781624	87456321	73815624
41682735	53876142	78543612	73186542
14628375	58371624	75834621	37815624
14263857 ← 3	85317264	57384261	73851264
41236587	58132746	53748216	78352146
14325678	58317264	35472861	87531264
41352768	85132746	34527816	85732146
43157286	81537264	43257186	58372416
34512768	18573624	42351768	53827461
34157286	81756342	24537186	35284716
43512768	18765432	25431768	32548761
34521678	18674523 ← 7	52413678	23458671
35426187	81647253	25146387	24385617
53241678	18462735	25413678	42836571
52346187	81426375	52146387	48263517
25436817	84123657	51243678	84623157
24563871	48216375	15234768	86421375
42658317	48123657	51327486	68243157
46285371	84216375	15372846	62841375
64825731	48261735	15738264 ← 6	26814735
68452713	42867153	51783624	62187453
86547231	24681735	15876342	62814735
85674213	26487153	51867432	26187453
58764123	62847513	58164723	21684735
57861432	68274531	85617432	12648375
75684123	86725413	85164723	21463857
76581432	87652431	58617432	12436587
67518342	78562341	85671342	12345678

London Surprise Major

particular attention to the odd places which occur in the middle of plain hunting, and take careful note that all leads ***except those near the lead ends***, are ***wrong***.

Bobs are like London Minor bobs, but the bell that makes the bob, comes down from eight-seven-eight, makes fourths, and goes back to eight-seven-eight again.

The main things that make London so horrendously difficult to ring, are that it's largely backward and many bits of it are hazardously similar to each other but distinctly different. In addition, the ***other*** ringers keep going wrong, so ***never*** give way to someone just because they're ringing in your place. Stick to your position as though bonded to it by super-glue and you'll be doing everyone a favour.

And if you find yourself leading right when you should be leading wrong, ***wait one blow*** and then lead again. You are ten times more likely to get to the front too soon than too late.

Regrettably, there aren't many other tips for ringing London, and most of them aren't very useful. But the best one is that, whenever you pass the treble, you must do something to put you ***wrong***. You must either make a place or you must do a fish tail. And if that isn't much of a tip, at least it's something.

And lastly, when all else fails, the ***coarse ringer's*** excuse may come in just as handy in Major as it does in Minor. "I'm ***so*** sorry. I was trying to ring London ***Royal***."

After I had sent the last chapter to someone who had written to me about London, he very reasonably wrote back and asked about the methods that were even more complex yet nonetheless rung. Well, there are two.

***Glasgow** is an excessively difficult method, although quite an old one. It's rung very widely – but very infrequently – at Association meetings, and if you can't persuade your own Association to try it, you could look out for it being rung as a special method elsewhere. Think nothing of travelling 100 miles for a plain course, but if you ever get the chance of a touch or a quarter peal, check carefully what bobs are being used. Some compositions have fourths place bobs, and others have sixths place bobs.*

***Belfast** is the very topmost top of the rung methods. It has **bird's beaks** and **cat's ears** and prodigious quantities of spiky blue line. It's so rare that you could spend a whole lifetime ringing and never see a course of it being rung. If you crave for a go, you'd do best to ask around to find out where you might stand a chance.*

And the other thing I'm often asked about is spliced. Chapters 40 and 41 apply as much to Major as they do to Minor, but naturally, Major is more difficult. There is, though, some terminology to be learnt.

*When someone says they're going to ring **eight-spliced** they mean that they're going to ring all the **standard eight** spliced together. If you're asked, "Can you ring eight-spliced," you're being asked if you can ring all those eight methods. If you're asked, "Can you ring nine-spliced?" you would reply, "Which is the ninth?" If you're asked, "Can you ring seven-spliced?" you would reply, "Which one are you leaving out?" and so on. Normally, the one being left out is Pudsey. In five-spliced and less, there's usually no London or Bristol either.*

And if you long to progress to Glasgow, Belfast or Spliced but can't find a band that rings them, don't despair. You are now a leading ringer, so train a band of your own to the level you want. It may take you years – indeed, you may never make it – but the effort will nonetheless prove best for everyone in the end. And when the pressure and strain of all that exotic ringing gets too much, take a break from it. Refresh yourself with **Something Different**.

Something Different

45. Original

What is *Original*? The ringers from Yagton were talking about it over tea at the meeting on Saturday, but when they realised I was listening, there was so much joking and giggling that I decided I must have caught them out in something smutty.

M.P.
Suffolk

Original, you will be relieved to hear, is nothing more than the posh name for plain hunt. So ***Original Doubles*** is quite simply plain hunt on five. In some towers plain hunt is *always* called Original – which impresses visitors – but in most places, plain hunt is only called Original when it has bobs in it. So this chapter is about putting bobs into plain hunt.

If you've never rung it before, you may wonder why anyone bothers. After all, if you can ring bobs in Original, you can ring methods as well. But there's a zip and pep to Original that even the most complex methods can't match, yet at the same time it's within the grasp of anyone who can ring a plain course of Grandsire Doubles. It's just the method for enlivening a flagging practice night.

How it Works

So let's look at how to ring it on five. Since you can

already ring plain hunt, I'm starting with a picture of a bob.

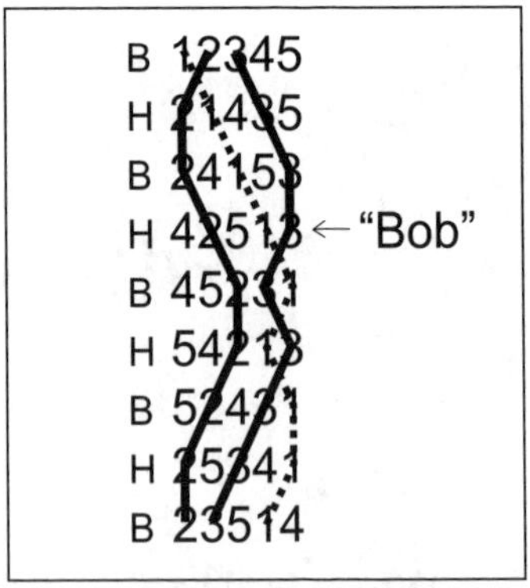

You will see in this particular example that the treble is affected, and since bobs can be called at ***any*** handstroke, ***all*** the bells can be affected. And the rules for ringing a bob are,

B 12345
H 21435
B 24153
H 42513 ← "Bob"
B 45231
H 54213
B 52431
H 25341
B 23514

Original Bob

> If you're in ***first*** or ***thirds*** place when the bob is called – i.e. you are leading or about to lead – you are ***not affected***.
>
> If you're in ***seconds*** place when the bob is called, you ***make thirds*** – from backstroke to handstroke – and go back to lead again – just like making thirds in Grandsire.

And,

> If you're in ***fourths*** or ***fifths*** place when the bob is called, you do ***one dodge*** in 4-5 of the kind that comes most natural. So if you're in fourths place, you dodge 4-5 up, and if you're in fifths place you dodge 4-5 down.

And after that, you just carry on plain hunting until the next call.

I've put "H"s and "B"s up above to show which are handstrokes and which are backstrokes. The bob is called at one handstroke and it takes effect at the following handstroke. So the dodges are back-hand dodges, as they are in Grandsire, rather than hand-back dodges, as they are in Plain Bob.

Twin Bobs

So far so good, but here's what makes Original so exciting. Since bobs can be called at ***any*** handstroke, they can be called at ***consecutive*** handstrokes. And that means that you can still be ringing one bob while the next is being called. So you have to be constantly on your toes, listening carefully and concentrating like crazy. This is what consecutive bobs look like.

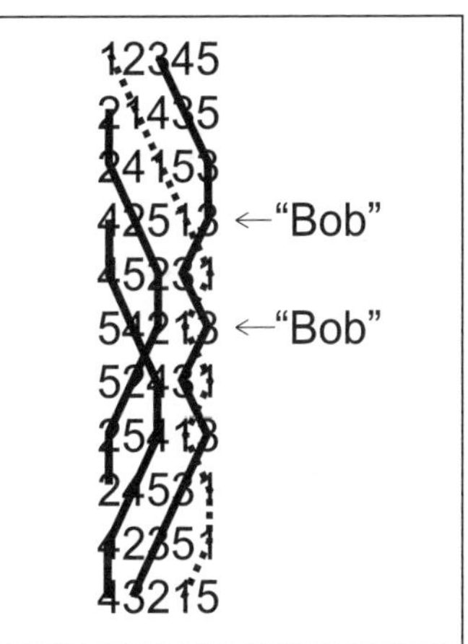

Consecutive Bobs

At first sight that doesn't look easy – and of course, it isn't – but don't try learning it as a block. Just note where you are when each bob is called, and act accordingly. Each bob must be handled separately and independently. So concentration is more important than expertise. Enthusiastic learners often ring Original far better than experts.

And Singles

And to make it even more exciting, there are singles too. Not all conductors call them, but this is what a single looks like. You can see that this one has been called in the same place as the bob on the opposite page. The first two bob rules apply equally to singles. But in addition,

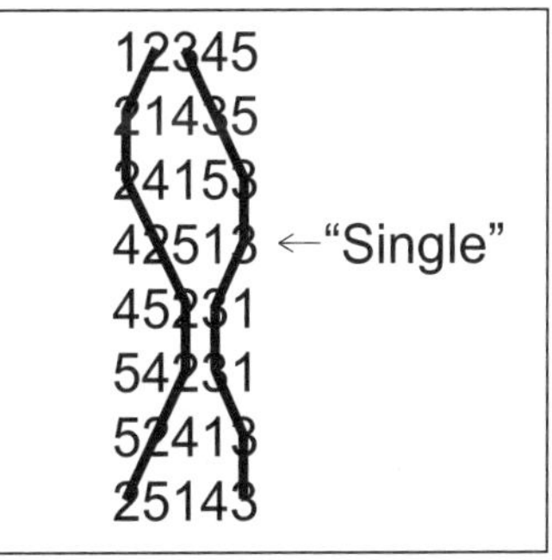

Original Single

If you are in ***fourths*** place when the single is called, you must ***make fifths unaffected***.

And,

> If you are in ***fifths*** place when it's called, you must ***make fourths*** from backstroke to handstroke and then lie behind again.

Making fourths is the most difficult way of being affected, and it's especially difficult because both blows are over ***the same bell***. Similarly, when you make fifths at a single, both blows are over the same bell. Be very careful about this.

A Useful Tip

And now for a stunningly useful tip. By far the commonest mistake in Original is making thirds when ***no bob has been called***. You hear a bob while you're leading – which doesn't affect you – and you then make thirds when you get there. Somehow, your Grandsire habits overcome you, and you make thirds even though you shouldn't.

This is usually a completely unconscious mistake, and many ringers protest vigorously that they haven't made it when they have. So the moral is, whenever a bob is called while you're leading, repeat to yourself three times, "I am not affected, I am not affected, I am not affected," until the danger time has passed.

Starting with a Bob

And for those who want more excitement still, Original Doubles can ***start*** with a bob. A bob can actually be in the process of being rung at the very moment you begin.

Most conductors will warn you in advance if they're going to start this way, and when it comes to it, they'll either say, "Go-Original-Bob," in one slurred mouthful as fast as they possibly can, or, "Bob. Go Original."

If they choose the former, someone will quite likely miss the bob completely, so I normally recommend the latter. Besides, it's clearer, safer and – I have to admit – a good deal more fun. Considerate conductors always say, "Bob," loudly and clearly so that no one is in any doubt about what's going on.

And just in case ***you*** are in doubt, here are the first few changes with two rows of rounds in front to show how far in advance the bob is called. Quite simply, you start as though you were ringing a plain course of Grandsire.

12345 ← "Bob. Go Original"
12345
21354
23145
32415

The Bob Start

It's also possible for the conductor to call, "Single. Go Original." And although I'm sure you'd have no trouble working that out for yourself, here's the picture.

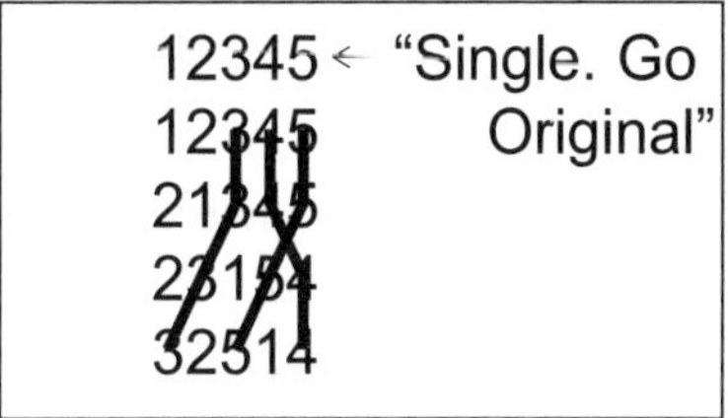

The Single Start

And Upwards

Normally, Original is rung far more on five than on any other number, but you can ring it on six and upwards if you want to. On six the bob is a ***fourths place bob*** like this.

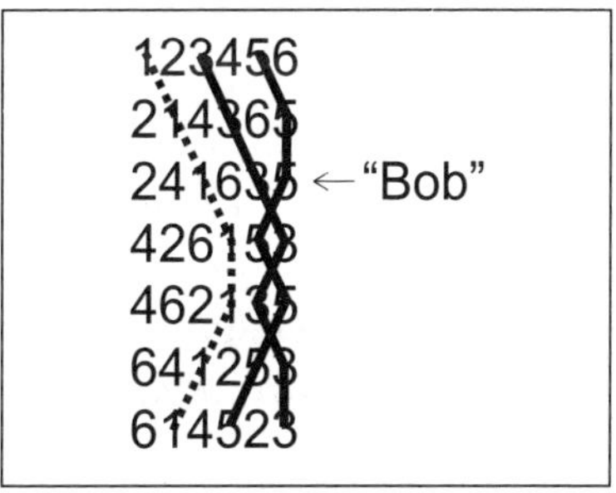

Original Minor Bob

It's called at any ***backstroke*** – not at handstroke as in Doubles – and it takes effect from hand to back. As you can see, three bells are unaffected, one makes fourths, and the other two dodge.

On Triples there is a fifths place bob, on Major a sixths place bob, and so on up to a tenths place bob in Maximus. You probably don't need to know that, though. No one ever seems to ring Original at the big twelve bell towers.

Now, I wonder why that should be.

I get a good few enquiries about Original Doubles, mainly asking how to call touches. So although this isn't really a conducting book, I'm sneaking in a few touches just in case you need them

For a 30, *call any bell three times at lead.*

For a 60, *call any bell to make thirds and double dodge 4-5 up – all repeated twice. That's three times in all.*

For a 120, *call the sixty but, replace one of the bobs at thirds with a single, and then repeat.*

Beware, though, that depending on which bell you're calling from, you may have to start with a bob, or the first one may be very soon afterwards.

In all these touches there's one bell that rings plain hunt throughout – although it's not normally the treble – and that's excellent ropesight practice for someone who can already plain hunt to Bob Doubles and is looking for an extra challenge. So Original is a good learner's method as well as being a good ***fun*** *method.*

And while we're on the subject of ***fun methods*** *...*

46. The Fun Methods

Now and again the old tried and true methods that I enjoy so much, turn to dust and ashes in my mouth. "Boring old Bob," I think, "Groany old Grandsire," and "Stodgy old Stedman," and I long to ring something startling, way out and entertaining to shake me out of my blues. What is there?

M.R.
Somerset

A change, they say, is as good as a rest, and a change of changes is just as good as a change of anything else. No matter how much you enjoy the old standards, you might just as well ... *ring the changes* as it were. So when the blues come, you could simply try ringing something new. That might do the trick. And if you want even more excitement, there are lots of other methods that might fit the bill too – such as Original, the Doubles variations and, if your band can manage them, the treble dodging possibilities in Chapter 39. You could even have a crack at the options in *A Walk on the Wild Side*. But when you and your band are ***really*** low, that's the time for the ***fun*** methods.

Fun methods are methods to dust off just now and again. They need zing and freshness, and the ability to make people who haven't rung them before say, "Good Heavens, how extraordinary!" They must be good for learners too.

Slough Big Bob

Slough Big Bob is a method which few ringers have heard of and which the *Central Council* doesn't recognise. It's a mixture of Doubles and Minor and it's not rung by the top bands. You won't hear a well-struck course of it at St Paul's Cathedral but it's been around since the 1950s and has all the hallmarks of a fun method.

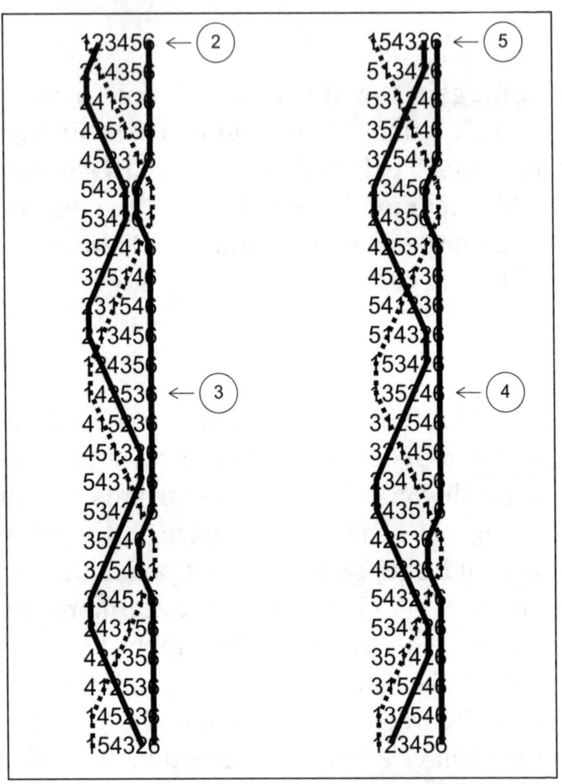

Slough Big Bob

As you can see, there is no dodging in it at all. The Two, Three, Four and Five hunt up and down between lead and fifths place ***except*** when they take the treble from lead. Then, they only hunt up to fourths place. The treble, on the other hand, hunts to sixths place and back, and the tenor rings behind except for the two blows when the treble is in sixths place. Then, it makes fifths.

If you think this looks easy because it's just plain hunt, try it and you'll find it's far from easy. The treble hunts down over the bells in a different order to hunting up, and the inside bells have to notice when they're taking the treble off.

The tenor has to pay very close attention, and handle his bell with precision accuracy as well. Few bands can get it right first time, yet it's an excellent method for plain hunting learners to develop their ropesight and bell awareness skills.

It extends naturally to all numbers. So on eight the inside bells hunt up to sevenths except when they've taken the treble off, when they hunt up to sixths. The treble goes all the way to eighths.

Bastow

Bastow Little Court is one of the few methods to be named after a person rather than a place. It was first rung on 6th October 1934 in a peal at Lamberhurst in Kent to celebrate the marriage of Miss G.L. Bastow of Kensington to Mr J.C. Morland of Court Lodge. For good measure the band also rang ***Morland Special Alliance*** but we're not concerned with that here.

Whether or not Mrs Morland enjoyed a long and happy marriage, I do not know. But her maiden name lives on in a method

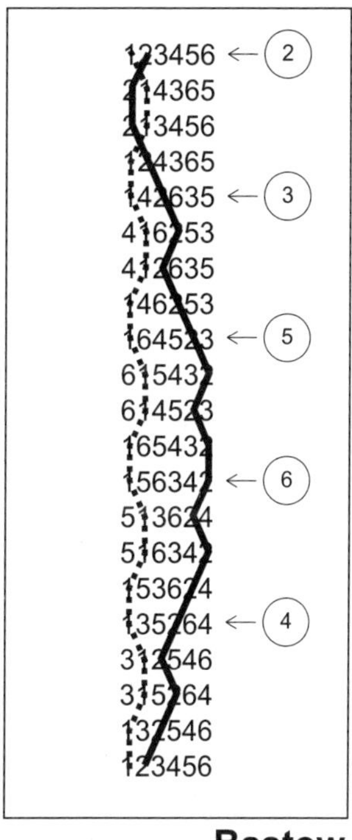

Bastow

which has enjoyed a consistent, if limited, popularity ever since. Pronounced to rhyme with hoe rather than with cow, it is an extremely useful method for providing the struggling band with a step between Plain Bob and Kent.

As you can see, the treble never gets above seconds place. It just leads and makes seconds, providing very useful experience for a learner just starting to acquire ropesight. The other bells treble bob everywhere except in 1-2. It's just like ringing an inside bell to a lead of Kent except that there are no places or slow work.

As each lead of the method is only four changes long, bobs can occur frequently. The bob is a fourths place bob and looks like this.

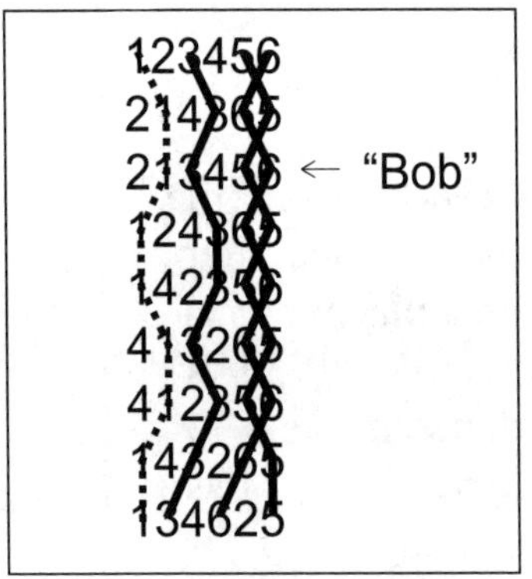

Bastow Bob

The bells running in and out are unaffected, whilst the bells in 5-6 do two extra dodges, making three in all. The bell dodging 3-4 up when the bob is called, makes fourths and dodges 3-4 down.

To make it even more fun, there can be bobs at consecutive treble leads, so the bells in 5-6 have to do two extra dodges for each one. That can mean five dodges in all – the first one plus two extra lots of two.

And if you're going to conduct it, call the same touches as for Kent, although they'll turn out very much shorter.

Kent Little Court

Kent Little Court is just like Bastow Little Court except that you always make Kent places in 3-4 – both up and down – instead of dodging. It's just as good as Bastow for the treble ringer but better Kent practice for everyone else.

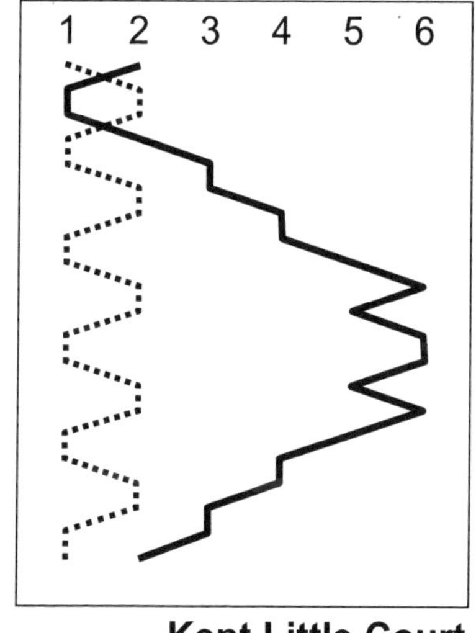

Kent Little Court

1234567 ← 2
2143657
2416375
4213657
4126375
1462735
1426375 ← 3
4162735
4617253
6412735
6147253
1674523
1647253 ← 5
6174523
6715432
7614523
7165432
1756342
1765432 ← 7
7156342
7513624
5716342
5173624
1537264
1573624 ← 6
5137264
5312746
3517264
3152746
1325476
1352746 ← 4
3125476
3214567
2315476
2134567
1243657
1234567

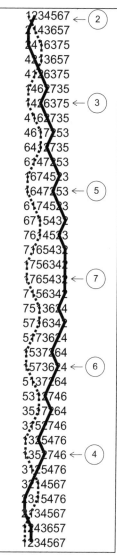

Ashford Triples

Ashford

In ***Ashford Little Court*** – now sometimes known as Ashford Little Bob – the treble only goes to thirds place and back. The result is that the other bells spend their time dodging in so many positions that treble bob looks pale by comparison. In treble bob you dodge everywhere, but in Ashford you dodge ***absolutely everywhere***.

The picture here is Ashford Triples. Having lead, you dodge 3-4 up, 4-5 up, 5-6 up, and 6-7 up. You then do long sevenths, and dodge 6-7 down, 5-6 down, 4-5 down, and 3-4 down. You also make seconds over the treble.

Believe me, dodging in all the odd positions as well as all the even ones is devastatingly difficult, and remembering to dodge 6-7 down after making long sevenths, is a nightmare. Yet when you get it right, Ashford is extremely pretty to listen to and hugely entertaining.

On numbers other than seven, you dodge absolutely everywhere in the same way, and you make four blows behind between your highest ***up*** and your highest ***down*** dodges. This applies whether you're ringing on an odd or even number.

Bobs are just like Plain Bob bobs. You run in, run out and make the bob, and are unaffected above fourths place. If you run out, though, you run all the way to 4-5 up. Singles are just like Plain Bob singles.

Cloister

Cloister Doubles – also known as ***St Helen's*** – is a method in the great tradition of Bastow Little Court and Slough Big Bob. It only hovers on the fringes of orthodox respectability, but it's nonetheless much enjoyed by a fair smattering of towers up and down the country. Its popularity rests on its being short, pleasant to listen to and, above all, easy for the struggling band to ring.

As you can see on the next page, it has two bells hunting to thirds place and back. These can either be the treble and

Two – as in the top picture – or the Two and Three as in the bottom one. The other three bells hunt out, double dodge 4-5 up, double dodge 4-5 down, and hunt back in again.

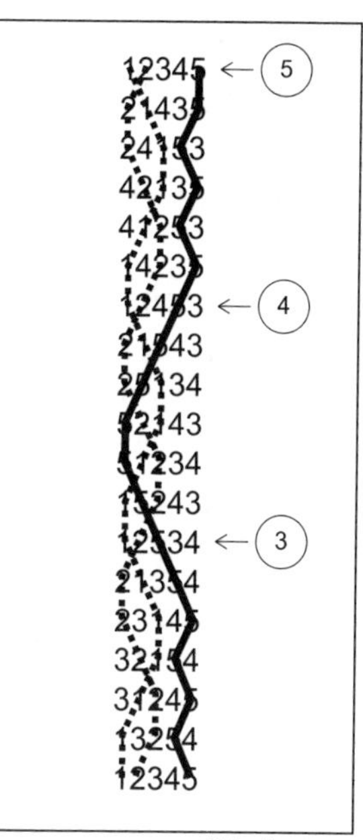

Cloister

It's excellent first stage ropesight and plain hunt practice for the hunting bells as they only have to find ***one*** new bell every six changes, and it's excellent dodging practice for the others. It also enables a band with only three experienced ringers, one tenor behind ringer, and two shaky plain hunters, to ring a musical method.

There's a picture of Cloister Triples on Page 194, and inveterate Cloister ringers ring it with Stedman Triples calls – as explained on pages 194 and 197.

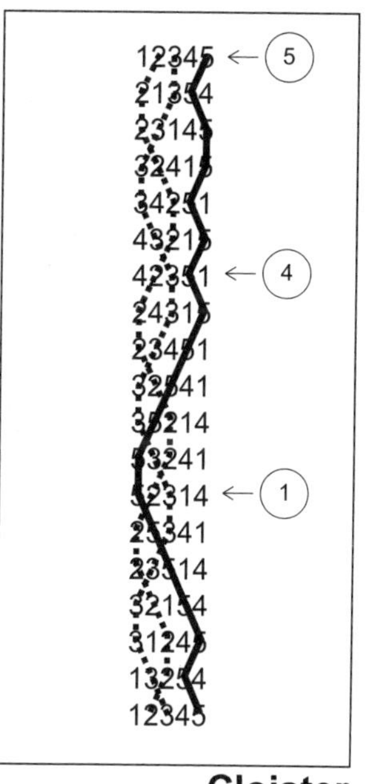

Cloister

Incidentally, it *is* possible to ring Cloister with a different and rather complicated bob which causes the Two to become a working bell. Modernised and regularised in this way, it's apparently more satisfying to the purists and still quite interesting to ring. Somewhat oddly, it's even called ***Bastow***. But then the magic is gone, and it's not really Cloister any more.

Bala Bob

And now for something more advanced – ***Bala Bob***. Or to be more exact, a touch of Bala Bob with silent bobs at every lead. Towards the end of the nineteenth century and well into the twentieth, people rang this touch as a method in its own right under the far more sensible name of ***Double Stedman's Slow Course***. Indeed, in 1881 Jasper Snowdon included it under that name in his book *Standard Methods*.

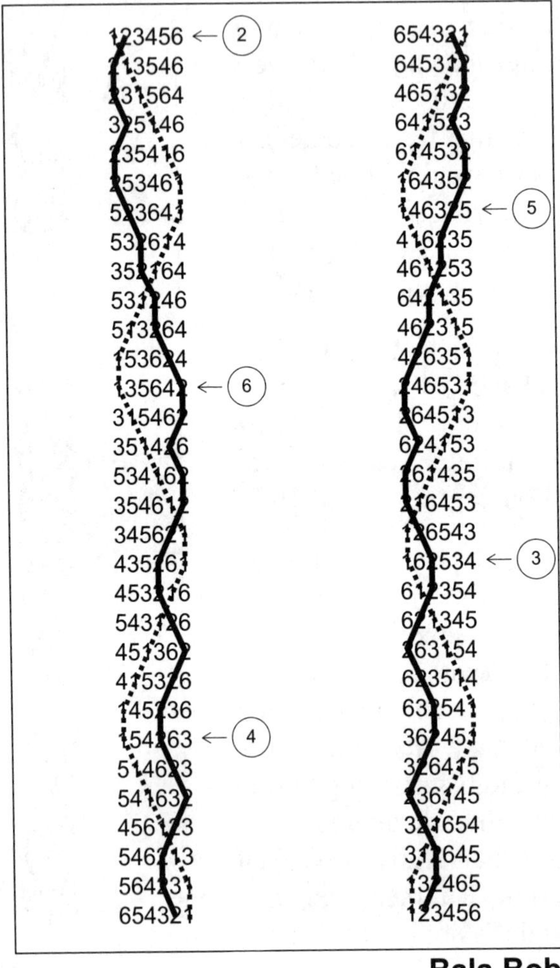

Bala Bob

As you can see, the treble plain hunts, but the other bells all ring Stedman slow work. They ring Stedman slow work in the normal way on the front, and they ring Stedman slow work ***upside down*** on the back. It's singularly entertaining and a definite challenge.

If you're going to try ringing it – and I recommend that you do – make sure you know everybody's starts ***before*** you suggest catching hold. The idea may be simple, but working out the starts of the back bells, is a real puzzle.

Incidentally, the technically minded will note that the treble is really ringing the quick work on the front and the quick work *upside down* on the back. But it's much easier to think of it as plain hunt.

Orpheus

Orpheus Doubles is another Stedman variation – although this one was invented by Fabian Stedman himself. As explained in Chapter 27, seventeenth century ringers went in for a lot of odd method names, and this is one of them. The essence of it is that everyone simply rings Stedman Doubles ***except*** that every blow

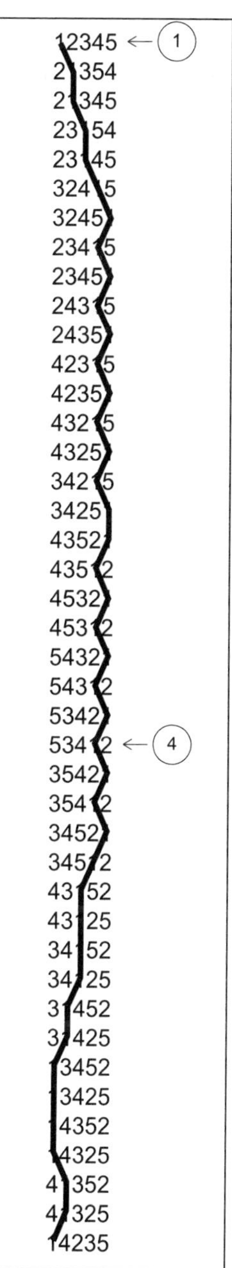

Orpheus (part of)

below fourths place is doubled, and there are ***five*** dodges in 4-5 up and 4-5 down to compensate.

As a result of all this doubling, your slow work becomes very laboured indeed. It starts,

Four blows in thirds
two blows in seconds
four blows lead
two blows in seconds
four blows lead
two blows in seconds
and so on.

And since the quick work is doubled too, forcing yourself to lead for four blows in the middle of it, can be a real problem.

As long as you don't ring it *too* often, Orpheus is definitely a fun method. There are no calls as a plain course is 120 changes long.

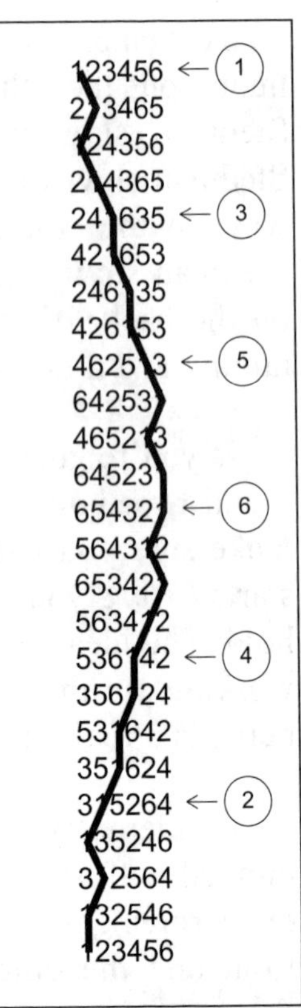

Forward

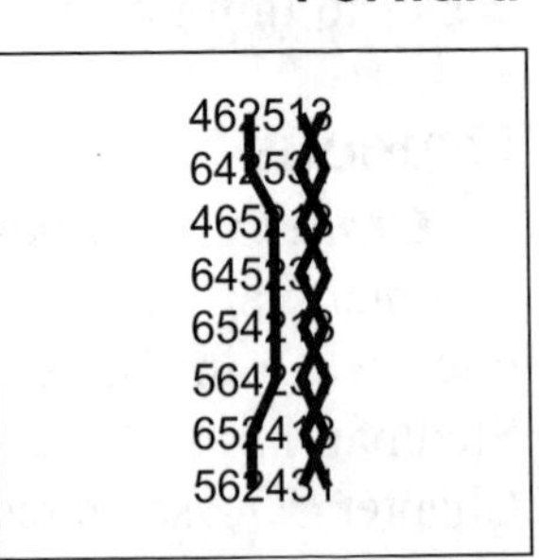

Forward Bob

Forward

Forward Minor is another ***principle*** – i.e. everyone, including the treble, does the same thing – and it's another treble bob variation. You treble bob everywhere, including 1-2, but you ***always*** make Kent places in 3-4, both up and down. The plain course is only 24 changes long and doesn't take too long to master, but the bobs are a real entertainment. They can be called any time anyone dodges in 1-2, so consecutive bobs can be as close as four changes apart. They affect you just like a Kent bob, but if you get caught in 5-6, you have to do two ***extra*** dodges for ***each*** bob. So three bobs in a row can keep you there for ages.

Coal

Coal Minor – now officially known as Kidderminster – was named as someone's idea of a joke. It's in the great tradition of such names as ***Tennis Court***, ***Turkish Delight***, ***Nice Surprise***, and – although in poor taste – ***Titanic Cinques***. It's another principle, and the structure of each section is the

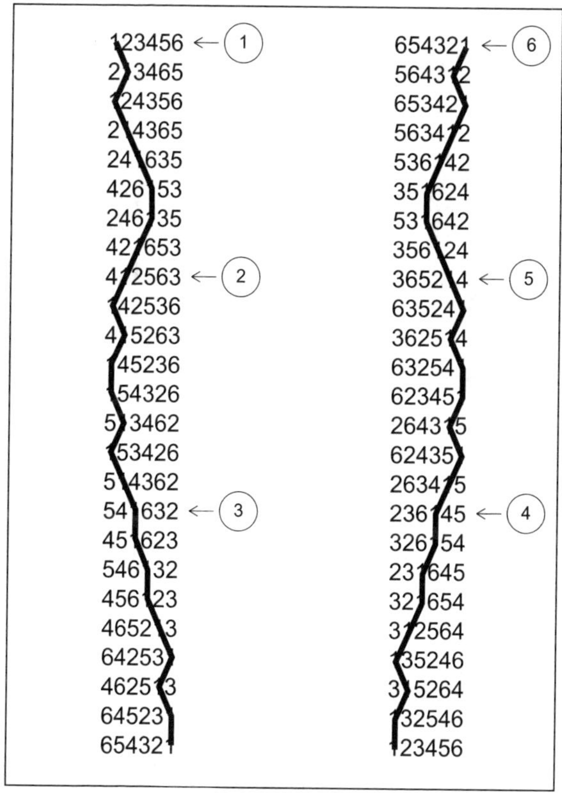

Coal Minor

first four changes of a lead of Kent followed by the first four changes of a lead of Oxford. So you treble bob in 1-2 and 5-6, and in 3-4 you either do Kent places or Oxford places.

Now, that doesn't sound easy, and in fact it isn't, particularly if you ring it from first principles rather than by learning the blue line. Worse still, bobs can either be at the end of a Kent section or at the end of an Oxford section. The bells in 5-6 ring a ***Forward*** bob in either case, but the bell making the bob has to do ***three*** blows in fourths. After that it either does thirds and out if it's a Kent to Oxford bob, or thirds and in if it's an Oxford to Kent bob. Tricky!

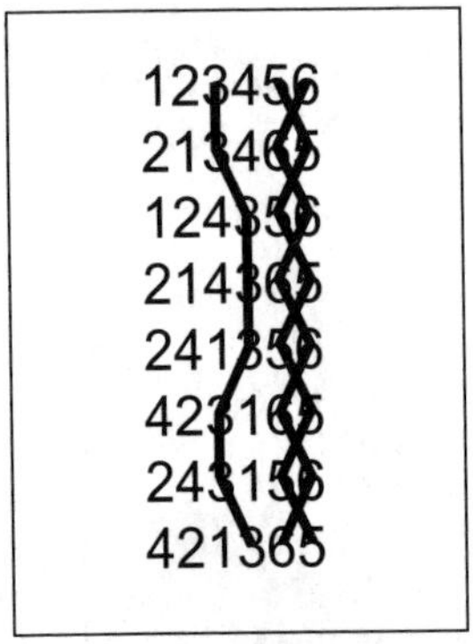

123456
213465
124356
214365
241356
423165
243156
421365

Kent to Oxford Bob

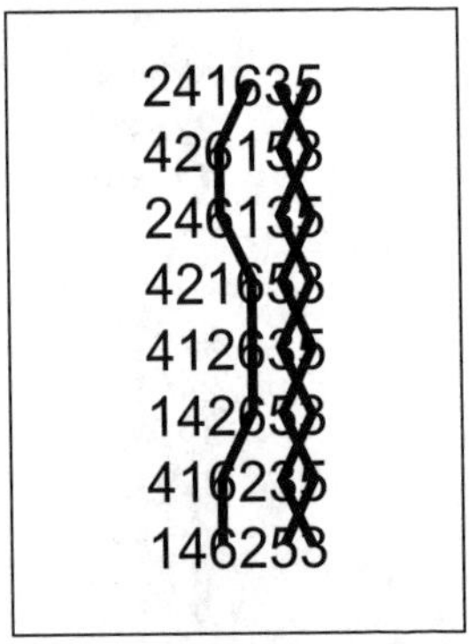

241635
426153
246135
421653
412635
142653
416235
146253

Oxford to Kent Bob

And even worse is that you might get an Oxford to Kent bob immediately following a Kent to Oxford bob. One bell then does ***two*** lots of three blows in fourths, and that really is a problem.

Boat Race

And lastly, ***Boat Race***. As explained in Chapter 39, Boat Race is Oxford treble Bob *above* the treble, and Cambridge Surprise *below* the treble. That's why it's called Boat Race. If you ring it by the blue line, it's just another treble dodging method and not much fun at all, so I'm not including a picture. Instead, while you're above the treble, ring Oxford, and when you pass the treble on the way down, change to Cambridge. Then when you pass the treble on the way up again, change to Oxford again, and so on.

Simple isn't it?

Well, no, it isn't at all simple. But it will give you a lot of excitement as well as valuable insight into the structure of Oxford and Cambridge.

Pedants, of course, call Boat Race by its official name of ***Morning Exercise Delight***. But then, unlike you and me, I don't suppose pedants much enjoy ringing ***fun*** methods anyway.

Not long after my article on Bastow appeared in The Ringing World, *I rang at Lamberhurst in Kent on a ringing course. An extremely kind gentleman let us in, and I mentioned to him that it was good to visit the tower where* ***the*** *peal had been rung. Perfectly reasonably, he misunderstood me and showed me the peal board of a record breaking multi-method peal rung by the same band.*

Of course, the Lamberhurst band of the period was indeed one of the very best in the country, and they achieved all sorts of remarkable performances. Yet like the Leeds band of the late eighteenth century, their legacy to us was not their peals, but a popular and valuable method that hardly anyone associates with them at all.

Similarly with Slough Big Bob. Peter Lawrence wrote to say that a number of ***big*** *methods were invented by a group of young ringers in the Windsor/Slough/Staines area in the*

1950s. They were obviously looking for a bit of fun, and the original Slough Big Bob was Plain Bob Doubles above the treble and Reverse Bob Minor below. Bobs could be called either at the lead end or at the half lead, so the tenor could get to do all the work. Now, that **is** *a method to conjure with.*

Later on, though, the inventors had a renaming session, and the method in this chapter became Slough Big, *although with scrupulous correctness they omitted the word "Bob" as there was no dodging. So the originators didn't call it* Slough Big Bob *at all, although everyone else seems to call it that nowadays.*

But as is the way of the world, in due course the young men in question all turned into distinguished and senior ringing figures, albeit still retaining their sense of fun. One of them, for example, was for many years a member of the Central Council Education Committee, *and Frank Blagrove was not only a long serving member of the* Methods Committee *but also the regular conductor at the Curfew Tower in Windsor Castle –* ***Conductor by Appointment****, as it were.*

And while on the subject, I once filled in at the Curfew Tower for some special ringing when a regular member of the band was absent. The fee was to be £3 and I anticipated immediate payment in sovereigns by a bewigged ***Lord High Chamberlain of the Queen's Belfry*** *or some such person. In the event, though, payment came in a cheque the following January – some eight months after the event.*

Ah well!

All part of ringing's rich tapestry, though, and I wouldn't have missed it for anything. The sort of occasion, indeed, that our next correspondent would most definitely be dreaming about ...

47. A Walk on the Wild Side

I have fantasies. Ringing fantasies. I sit and dream of astounding everybody with a sudden revelation of my true ringing ability. It's like *Sparky's Magic Piano*. To begin with I dreamt of ringing a faultless course of Bob Doubles, and later on it was Stedman. But somehow, the reality, nice as it was, never measured up to the dream. So now I'm fantasising about something totally unachievable. I'm passing by St Paul's Cathedral one Saturday afternoon when the tower captain rushes out and grabs my arm.

"Are you a ringer?" he asks breathlessly.

"Yes," I reply.

"Thank God," he shouts, "we are one short for a special royal wedding peal. Can you spare four hours and join in?"

"Of course," I declare robustly, and he hurries me up the stairs.

"By the way," he adds on the way up, "we are breaking entirely new ground here today. This method is so hard that only a few people in the whole world can manage it. We are going to ring ... ..."

Well ... what? Here my fantasy fails me. What

methods are on the very borders of the possible? Tell me what I can choose from to make my fantasy complete.

Definitely Anon

What fun day dreaming is. Certainly, most ringers do it – often while they're ringing – and whilst for some it's towers grabbed or peals rung, for others it's a quarter of Bob Doubles or a touch of Stedman. And for yet others it's the chance to ring the most complex methods that exist.

Double Darrowby

Let's start with ***Double Darrowby Surprise Major***. Double Darrowby was invented by Tony Smith – the current chairman of the *Central Council Methods Committee* – in 1980. He was looking for something really different and he certainly found it. New Surprise methods are invented in vast numbers nowadays, but unlike Double Darrowby they don't have 1344 changes in a plain course.

1344 changes in the plain course?

Yes indeed. That's so many that it would take 45 pages of this book to write them all out in a column, and many weeks – if not months – to learn the blue line. One plain course is long enough for a quarter peal – which would take about 45 minutes to ring – and that means that you wouldn't need to worry about the bobs until you wanted to ring a peal.

Astoundingly, a peal of it has actually been rung, and although Tony Smith – who rang in it – hoped that it would be the first of many, all these years later the second is still awaited.

Since it's a double method, you only need the place notation for a quarter of a lead to work out the entire course. So here's a quarter-lead's worth in case you want to write the whole thing out for yourself. You can read about converting place notations into blue lines in Chapter 26.

↓	↓	↓	↓
x	x	x	x
36	36	58	58
x	x	x	x
34	56	58	56
x	x	x	x
36	36	58	58
x	x	x	x
56	34	56	58
x	x	x	x
36	36	58	58
x	x	x	x
34↑	14↑	58↑	

Quarter lead 36
Half lead 78
Lead end 12

Double Darrowby
Place Notation

Essentially, it gets to be so long because the treble does eleven dodges in each position. The other bells either do dozens of dodges or they ring parts of Bob Minimus, Double Bob Minimus or Reverse Bob Minimus in varying places. Structurally it's a bit like a vastly extended Double Oxford.

To give you the flavour, here's a small section of the order of the work starting on the Seven.

12 Dodges 7-8 up and lie
fifths, sixths, fifths
lie and dodge 7-8 down
fifths
12 dodges 7-8 up

11 dodges 7-8 down
sevenths
11 dodges 7-8 up
12 dodges 7-8 down
fifths
dodge 7-8 up and lie
fifths, sixths, fifths
lie and 25 dodges 7-8 down
and so on.

If you're going to try ringing Double Darrowby and you don't think you can count 25 dodges reliably, try watching the non-dodging bells doing *their* work. When they change, it's either halftime in your dodges or it's the end of them – or the other bells have gone wrong before you have.

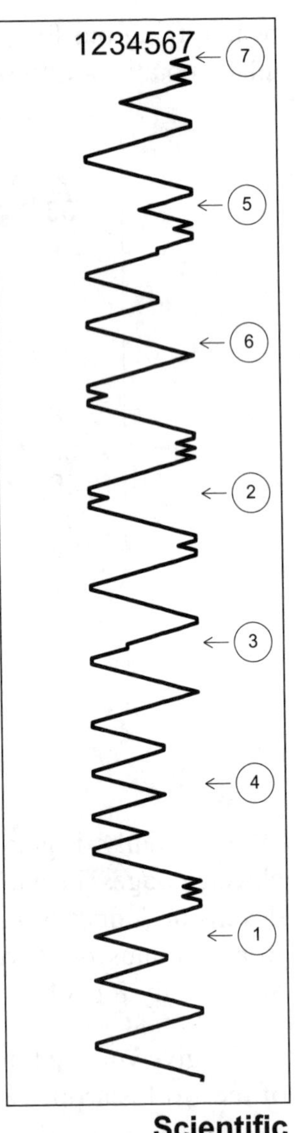

Scientific

Scientific

And now for ***Scientific Triples***. ***Scientific*** is an asymmetric principle, and that means that the treble does the same as everyone else and you can't just learn half and then ring it backwards. It's dry, uninteresting and totally characterless, and it's full of odd places and points stuck together with plain hunting. Its lack of any rhyme or reason makes it fiendishly difficult to remember and even more difficult to stay right in. Worse still, it's normally rung with bobs in three different places. The compressed blue line shows how really awful it is.

Carter

John Carter was one of the great ringers of the late nineteenth and early twentieth centuries. He was a gunsmith by trade, lived in Birmingham, and was famous for all sorts of ringing exploits. He composed a peal of Stedman Triples, known as ***Carter's Odd Bob***, which is still rung today, and in 1912 he built a most remarkable machine – known as ***The Carter Ringing Machine*** – capable of generating and playing changes up to Surprise Maximus. This is now owned by the *Central Council* and is on permanent exhibition in the *John Taylor Bell Foundry Museum* in *Loughborough*. You can attend a demonstration if you get in contact with the Machine's trustees or the Museum Curator.

But in addition to ringing and composing peals and making the Ringing Machine, John Carter also invented principles. Scientific was one of his, but in a saner moment he also invented a five bell principle called ***Carter Doubles***. Its plain course is 60 changes long and looks like this.

12345 ← (1)	53412 ← (4)	24153 ← (3)	31524 ← (2)	45231 ← (5)
21354	35421	42135	13542	54213
12534	53241	24315	31452	45123
15243	52314	23451	34125	41532
51234	25341	32415	43152	14523
15324	52431	23145	34512	41253
51342	25413	32154	43521	14235
15432	52143	23514	34251	41325
51423	25134	32541	43215	14352
54132	21543	35214	42351	13425
45312	12453	53124	24531	31245
54321	21435	35142	42513	13254
53412	24153	31524	45231	12345

Carter Doubles

But as you can see, challenging though it is – and the single is on the next page – it scarcely qualifies to be included in our *Walk on the Wild Side.* The trouble comes, though, when it's extended to Triples. In 1984 John McDonald conducted the first ever peal of Triples, and he thought it so complex that he offered £50 to the next person to do the same. Chris Rogers, later to be secretary of the Central Council, took up the challenge, and in due course he called it twice – although he only got one lot of £50 which he gave to a belfry repair fund. Repeating his performance would undoubtedly class as a solid achievement even though the £50 is no longer on offer. The place notation is 1.3.7.1.3.5.3.5.3.1.7.3, and the bob is a 5 instead of the first 7. The single is a 567 in the same place.

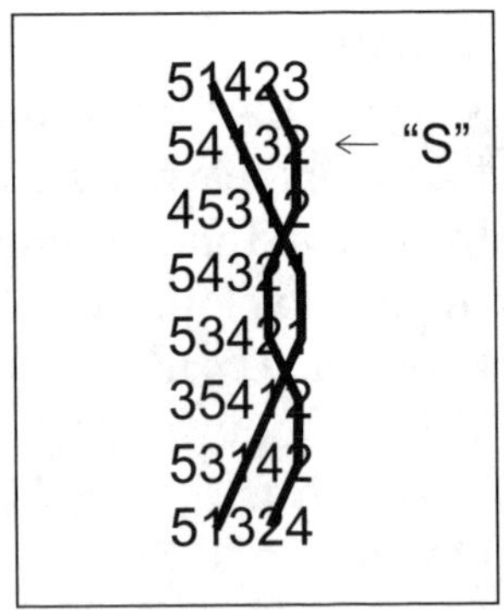

Carter Single

Call Changes

But it's not just complex methods that make for breath-taking achievements. In 1990 at Buckland in the Moor in Devon, seven local ringers and one extra, became the first band ever to ring the extent of Triples in call changes.

This was undoubtedly one of the greatest ringing feats of modern times, and it took 6 hours and 36 minutes. Three of the band conducted it, and the changes were called either every handstroke or every other handstroke. Of course, the striking was of the highest class.

Ringing call changes accurately for nearly seven hours is itself truly astonishing, but keeping track of and calling a sequence of 5,040 different calls is positively mind blowing. If you want a taste of what it must have been like, try ringing and/or calling the extent on five in call changes – that's 120 calls. The extent on seven must be hundreds of times harder.

Original

And also in the amazingly simple but fiendishly difficult line, why not test the limits of plain hunt. You'll find Original Doubles – that's plain hunt with bobs and singles in – in Chapter 45. Extents of Original Doubles are hard to call at the best of times, but the more the calls, the harder they are, and the maximum number of calls you can have in a single extent is an amazing ***forty six***.

That really is a hard extent to call. But if you called forty two different extents, all with 46 calls in, you would ring a peal of 5,040 changes with 1932 calls altogether. That's an average of one call every 2·6 changes, and quite apart from the conductor's problems, the concentration needed by the ringers would be phenomenal.

As far as is known, no one has done this yet, so the field is open to you. Although now I've written this, I expect someone will have a go.

The Big One

But getting back to St Paul's, I asked Jim Phillips, the secretary of St Paul's Cathedral, what his band would *really* ring for a Royal Wedding peal.

"Stedman Cinques," he replied. "The band can ring Orion Surprise Maximus and such, but for a Royal Wedding it would probably be Stedman."

Nothing on the wild side at all then, but a beautiful and traditional method that has fully stood the test of time. "Like Bach," as Jim put it. The ringing would, though, be of the very best, and the striking would be of the highest class.

So go back to your fantasy, ring Stedman Cinques, get to the end of your peal, and have the eleven other ringers turn to you and say, “Thanks for filling in, you rang really well.”

Now, there ***is*** something to fantasize about.

And on that pleasantly whimsical note we've reached the end of the book. I hope you enjoyed reading it as much as I enjoyed writing it, and I hope it has helped you with your method ringing too.

Of course, I don't mind in the least if you keep turning back to the tricky bits and going over them again with me. But in addition, you may also think it's time to start calling some plain courses and touches and things. I certainly hope so, because as soon as I've had a cup of tea, I'll be starting a book on that **very** *subject.*

Index

Method names are in italics.
Chapter titles are in bold.
Blue lines are marked *